WORKING MEMORY IN DEVELOPMENT

Working memory is the system responsible for the temporary maintenance and processing of information involved in most cognitive activities, and its study is essential to the understanding of cognitive development. *Working Memory in Development* provides an integrative and thorough account of how working memory develops and how this development underpins childhood cognitive development.

Tracing back theories of cognitive development from Piaget's most influential theory to neo-Piagetian approaches and theories pertaining to the information processing tradition, Camos and Barrouillet show in Part I how the conception of a working memory became critical to understanding cognitive development. Part II provides an overview of the main approaches to working memory and reviews how working memory itself develops across infancy and childhood. In the final part, the authors explain their own theory, the Time-Based Resource-Sharing (TBRS) model, and discuss how this accounts for the development of working memory as well providing an adequate frame to understanding the role of working memory in cognitive development.

Working Memory in Development effectively addresses central and debated questions related to working memory and is essential reading for students and researchers in developmental, cognitive, and educational psychology.

Valérie Camos is Professor of Developmental Psychology at the Université of Fribourg, Switzerland.

Pierre Barrouillet is Professor of Developmental Psychology at the University of Geneva, Switzerland, and Director of the Archives Jean Piaget.

ESSAYS IN COGNITIVE PSYCHOLOGY

Series Editors:

Henry L. Roediger, III, Washington University, USA
James R. Pomerantz, Rice University, USA
Alan Baddeley, The University of York, UK
Jonathan Grainger, Université de Provence, France
Daniel Baker, University of York, UK

Essays in Cognitive Psychology is designed to meet the need for rapid publication of brief volumes in cognitive psychology. Primary topics will include perception, movement and action, attention, memory, mental representation, language and problem solving. Furthermore, the series seeks to define cognitive psychology in its broadest sense, encompassing all topics either informed by, or informing, the study of mental processes. As such, it covers a wide range of subjects including computational approaches to cognition, cognitive neuroscience, social cognition, and cognitive development, as well as areas more traditionally defined as cognitive psychology. Each volume in the series will make a conceptual contribution to the topic by reviewing and synthesizing the existing research literature, by advancing theory in the area, or by some combination of these missions. The principal aim is that authors will provide an overview of their own highly successful research program in an area. It is also expected that volumes will, to some extent, include an assessment of current knowledge and identification of possible future trends in research. Each book will be a self-contained unit supplying the advanced reader with a well-structured review of the work described and evaluated.

PUBLISHED

Moulin: *The Cognitive Neuropsychology of Déjà Vu*

Barrouillet and Camos: *Working Memory in Development*

Schmidt: *Extraordinary Memories of Exceptional Events*

Lampinen, Neuschatz & Cling: *Psychology of Eyewitness Identification*

Brown: *The Tip of the Tongue State*

Worthen & Hunt: *Mnemonology: Mnemonics for the 21st Century*

Surprenant & Neath: *Principles of Memory*

Kensinger: *Emotional Memory Across the Lifespan*

Millar: *Space and Sense*

Evans: *Hypothetical Thinking*

Gallo: *Associative Iliusions of Memory*

For updated information about published and forthcoming titles in the *Essays in Cognitive Psychology* series, please visit: www.routledge.com/Essays-in-Cognitive-Psychology/book-series/SE0548

WORKING MEMORY IN DEVELOPMENT

Valérie Camos and Pierre Barrouillet

First published 2018
by Routledge
2 Park Square, Milton Park, Abingdon, Oxon OX14 4RN

and by Routledge
711 Third Avenue, New York, NY 10017

Routledge is an imprint of the Taylor & Francis Group, an informa business

© 2018 Valérie Camos and Pierre Barrouillet

The right of Valérie Camos and Pierre Barrouillet to be identified as authors
of this work has been asserted by them in accordance with sections 77 and
78 of the Copyright, Designs and Patents Act 1988.

All rights reserved. No part of this book may be reprinted or reproduced or
utilized in any form or by any electronic, mechanical, or other means, now
known or hereafter invented, including photocopying and recording, or in
any information storage or retrieval system, without permission in writing
from the publishers.

Trademark notice: Product or corporate names may be trademarks or
registered trademarks, and are used only for identification and explanation
without intent to infringe.

British Library Cataloguing in Publication Data
A catalogue record for this book is available from the British Library

Library of Congress Cataloging in Publication Data
A catalog record for this book has been requested

ISBN: 978-1-138-95905-7 (hbk)
ISBN: 978-1-138-95906-4 (pbk)
ISBN: 978-1-315-66085-1 (ebk)

Typeset in Bembo
by Wearset Ltd, Boldon, Tyne and Wear

CONTENTS

List of illustrations	*vii*
Preface	*ix*

PART I
The role of working memory in development   **1**

1	The emergence of working memory in developmental psychology: from constructivism to cognitivism	3
2	Working memory in neo-Piagetian theories	22
3	Working memory in domain-specific developmental theories	43

PART II
The development of working memory   **63**

4	The evolving concept of working memory	65
5	Age-related increases in short-term maintenance	76
6	The development of the executive control	95
7	The sources of working memory development	115

vi Contents

PART III
Development in the Time-Based Resource-Sharing model   127

8   Sources of development in the TBRS model   129

9   How a developing TBRS working memory can frame our
    understanding of cognitive development   150

    Epilogue: searching for working memory in cognitive
    development   169

References   *172*
Index   *209*

ILLUSTRATIONS

Figures

1.1	Illustration of the mechanisms of majoring equilibration in Piaget's theory of cognitive development	5
1.2	Successive elaborations of the Subject's cognitive structures and Object coordination of features in Piaget's theory	6
2.1	Apparatus used by Case for studying the balance beam problem and illustration of the successive executive control structures constructed by children at the four substages of the dimensional developmental stage for this problem in Case's theory	25
2.2	Schematic illustration of two hypotheses about the mechanism governing the developmental increase in short-term storage space (STSS) according to Pascual-Leone (1970) and Case (1985)	30
2.3	Relationship between repetition latencies and word span in children aged 3 to 6 and between counting speed and counting span in children aged 6 to 12	32
2.4	Illustration of three trials of the Latin square task	39
3.1	Percentage of retrieval uses by 9-year-old children to solve additions as a function of the size of the minimum addend and working memory capacity	58
5.1	Relationship between number of words recalled and articulation rate in different age groups with linear regression line	84
6.1	Hierarchical tree structure depicting formal relations among rules (A–E)	103
6.2	Unintegrated rule systems, in the absence of a high order rule, for the DCCS task	103

viii Illustrations

8.1	Mean working memory span as a function of the cognitive load in adults when the processing component was either parity or location judgement task in the study by Barrouillet et al. (2007)	132
8.2	The working memory architecture according to the TBRS model	134
8.3	Evolution of the mean working memory spans in 9- and 12-year-old children	143

Table

| 2.1 | Hypothesized short-term storage space (STSS) and mean spans in STSS measures reported by Case (1985) for the relational, dimension, and vectorial stages | 29 |

PREFACE

Human cognitive development is at the same time a common phenomenon – one finds almost natural that our infants become progressively speaking beings, eventually able of abstract thinking – and probably the most amazing and complex transformation that one can witness in nature. Eighty years ago, Piaget suggested accounting for this phenomenon by considering thinking as the continuation of biological adaptation and operating through the same general mechanisms (Piaget, 1950). According to Piaget, cognitive development results, under environmental pressure, from the progressive differentiation and coordination of mental schemes into increasingly complex and powerful structures of thought. This conception that located the motor of development in the continuous interplay of general biological-like processes of assimilation and accommodation tending toward a permanently compromised equilibrium did not fit very well within the intellectual revolution in the middle of the previous century that arose from the idea that thinking could be assimilated with a calculation on symbols that machines could perform (Newell, Shaw, & Simon, 1958). The abandonment of a biological for a mechanical metaphor obliged a complete reconsideration of the causes of intellectual development. If our mind is a system for processing information through elementary computational steps (McCulloch, 1949; McCulloch & Pitts, 1943; Turing, 1950), the capacity of this system understood as a communication channel became a key question (Miller, 1956). As it rapidly appeared that this capacity was surprisingly limited, the immediate corollary of the information processing thesis was to imagine that the motor of cognitive development was to be found in an age-related increase in this capacity (Pascual-Leone, 1970) rather than in a quite mysterious process of equilibration of cognitive structures under adaptive pressure. But what is the part of the information processing system the capacity of which could be limited?

The machine imagined by Turing (1950) consisted of three parts: a store of information broken up into small packets or chunks that corresponds to human

x Preface

memory, an executive unit carrying out the operations contained in some 'book of rules', and a control verifying that the instructions have been correctly obeyed. Miller, Galanter, and Pribam (1960) went further and introduced the idea that the executive part of the machine has to maintain in an active state the rules (in their terms *plans*) to be applied in some memory that they called *working memory*. The intrinsic need for the information processing approach of a structure temporarily maintaining a small amount of information in a state appropriate for processing made a success of the concept of working memory, which became increasingly popular in cognitive psychology literature. Hence, several theories and models have been dedicated to the description of the structure and functioning of working memory, which is now recognized as the keystone of human cognitive architecture.

The aim of this book is to address the question of the complex relationships between working memory and cognitive development in childhood. The central role that cognitivism confers on working memory led developmental psychologists to consider it as a main driving force and explanatory factor of cognitive development, and to investigate how working memory itself develops. The originality of this book is thus to present the two faces of this relationship: how working memory drives development, and how development modifies working memory. Thus, the book is naturally organized in two parts, entitled 'The role of working memory in development' and 'The development of working memory'. A final part is dedicated to the presentation of our own view on these questions through the Time-Based Resource-Sharing (TBRS) model.

Part I traces the evolution of theories of development back to Piaget's conception of the forces that drive age-related changes in children's thinking and shows how the attempts to introduce information processing views within Piagetian constructivism led people to imagine that development was strongly related to the increase in some central mental capacity, an idea that prefigured modern conceptions of working memory and executive functions (Chapter 1). This part shows how notions like 'mental power' or 'mental capacity' for activating schemes have evolved into a notion of working memory capacity for storing and processing information in neo-Piagetian theories, and how the evolution of these concepts led to emphasizing the importance of a central system holding and integrating a strictly limited amount of information (Chapter 2). The complexity and diversity of the process of cognitive development led to a progressive abandonment of general theories that aimed at embracing in a single explanatory framework this abundance of dynamic phenomena to favour more specific models focused on particular domains and activities. Chapter 3 is devoted to the presentation and analysis of some domain-specific theories of cognitive development in which working memory has a prevalent role.

Part II offers an overview of the different approaches to working memory development. How does the system taken as responsible for developmental changes develop itself? This part begins with a short presentation of the leading models of working memory (Chapter 4). We argue that the evolution of the concept of working memory has led to a strict delimitation between storage and processing functions. The next chapters show how this delimitation has influenced further developmental studies, leading to a segregation between the study of short-term maintenance capacity on the one hand (Chapter 5), and the examination of age-related changes in executive functions on the other (Chapter 6). This part ends with a chapter reviewing the main hypotheses that have been put forward concerning the possible sources of working memory development (Chapter 7).

Part III proposes an integrated view of working memory development based on our own theory, the TBRS model. After a brief summary of the main tenets of our model, we present the factors that could account for working memory development within our model (Chapter 8). In a final chapter, we elaborate on how the cognitive architecture and functioning proposed by the TBRS model can provide a suitable framework to understand cognitive development (Chapter 9).

We would like to thank the people from Psychology Press for the trust they have placed in us and their support throughout this project, with a special thanks to Ceri Griffiths-McLardy and Lucy Kennedy. We are in debt to Bob Siegler for several ideas that helped us to frame this book, and we would like to warmly thank him for thoughtful discussions, valuable support and cherished friendship. We would also like to thank some of our colleagues for their inspiring work and ideas, and support in the course of this project. We are grateful to John R. Anderson, Alan Baddeley, Agnès Blaye, Jean-Michel Boucheix, Charles Brainerd, Marcel Brass, Andrew R. A. Conway, Nelson Cowan, Jason Doherty, Randall Engle, Graham Hitch, Violette Hoareau, Agnieszka Jaroslawska, Christopher Jarrold, Dylan Jones, Sid Kouider, Christian Lebière, Benoît Lemaire, Patrick Lemaire, Stephen Lewandowsky, Baptist Liefooghe, Xiadong Lin, Robert Logie, Bill Macken, Akira Miyake (who suggested to us the name of the TBRS model in June 2002), Moshe Naveh-Benjamin, Klaus Oberauer, Pierre Perruchet, Lynn Reder, Valérie Reyna, Stephen Rhodes, Satoru Saïto, Scott Saults, John Towse, André Tricot and André Vandierendonck, our past colleagues from the LEAD-CNRS at the Université de Bourgogne, as well as the Departments of Psychology at the University of Geneva and University of Fribourg. Moreover, our research work would not have been possible without the dedication and enthusiasm of young researchers who have worked with us through the years. We express our gratitude for their help to all of them, and more especially to Marlène Abadie, Clément Belletier, Sophie Bernardin, Raphaëlle Bertrand, Caroline Castel, Lina Chaabi, Lucie Corbin, Isabelle Dagry, Annick De Paepe, Sebastien De Schrijver, Nele Dewaele, Kevin Diependaele, Nicolas Dirix, Christophe Fitamen, Vinciane Gaillard, Nathalie Gavens, Alessandro Guida, Egbert Hartstra, Prune Lagner, Naomi Langerock, Raphaëlle Lépine, Vanessa Loaiza, Annalisa Lucidi, Stéphanie Mariz-Elsig, Gérome Mora, Anne-Laure Oftinger, Gaën Plancher, Benoît Perriard, Sophie Portrat, Kim Uittenhove, and Evie Vergauwe. Thank you to Juliette Danjon for helping us in compiling relevant literature to support the writing of this book. The work presented in this book also benefited from the support of grants mainly from the Agence Nationale de la Recherche, the Institut Universitaire de France, and the

Fonds National Suisse de la Recherche Scientifique. Finally, we warmly thank Jacqueline Thurillet-Camos for having once more opened the door of her home and supporting us during the many weeks we spent writing up this book in Burgundy.

Valérie Camos and Pierre Barrouillet
Jallanges
July 2015–August 2017

PART I

The role of working memory in development

As mentioned in the Preface, the concept of working memory was introduced by Miller et al. (1960) as a kind of mental space, located somewhere in the frontal lobes of the brain, corresponding to a quick-access memory able to hold temporary, transient plans for guiding behaviour, in the same way as programs govern the successive operations of a computer. This store, in which information could be represented and remembered while executing the operations of the selected plan in Miller et al.'s terms, has been more recently described as the hub of cognition (Haberlandt (1997), or 'perhaps the most significant achievement of human mental evolution' (Goldman-Rakic, 1992, p. 111). Indeed, its central role in selecting, temporarily holding, and processing information relevant for ongoing cognition makes it the keystone of cognitive architecture. Thus, it does not come as a surprise that many authors have viewed in working memory and its development one of the main, if not the main, factor of cognitive development.

However, the long-lasting immersion of cognitive psychology in the information processing approach should not lead us to forget that intellectual development was, for a long time, conceived and theorized without any recourse to the idea that the increase in capacity of some central system allowed for greater intellectual achievements with age. The most prominent example is provided by Piaget, who conceived development as resulting from a process of equilibration that allowed for the integration of more and more complex operational structures. Chapter 1 describes how, with the advent of the information processing approach, what was initially conceived as the result of an equilibration process was progressively envisioned as the consequence of an increase in mental capacity, called by Pascual-Leone (1970) the *central computing space M*. It could be considered as paradoxical that those theoreticians known as neo-Piagetian, who were the closest to the Piagetian approach, were at the same time those who have ascribed to working memory the most important role in cognitive development. However, this was rather natural

2 The role of working memory in development

for these authors who aimed at overcoming the limitations of Piaget's theory through its synthesis with the information processing approach. Piaget envisioned intellectual development as the assembly of increasingly complex structures through the coordination and integration of more basic elements like schemes. Thus, assuming that the integration of an increasing number of schemes was made possible by the increase in capacity of the working memory in which these schemes are assembled and coordinated was an ideal solution. Chapter 2 analyses two of the most remarkable attempts to integrate the concept of working memory within a Piaget-inspired structural framework, namely those of Case (1985, 1992) and Halford (1993). Although neo-Piagetian theories are probably those that have ascribed to working memory the most important role in cognitive development, several theories and models focusing on specific domains have also explained development in terms of an increase in working memory capacity. The presentation of some of these domain-specific models makes the subject of Chapter 3, in which is discussed the possibility of reducing cognitive development to the development of working memory.

1

THE EMERGENCE OF WORKING MEMORY IN DEVELOPMENTAL PSYCHOLOGY

From constructivism to cognitivism

The cognitivist revolution at the turn of the 1950s has had such an impact in our conception and understanding of cognition and its development that it is nowadays difficult, maybe impossible, to envision cognitive functioning without any recourse to notions such as cognitive resources and capacities. If thinking is a matter of selecting and encoding relevant items from the continuous flow of information in which we are immersed, and to process the resulting representations in a way appropriate to reach our current goals, the amount of information that can be processed and the efficiency of this processing, that is the capacity of the channel of information that human mind constitutes, becomes a key aspect of human cognition (Miller, 1956). Within this theoretical stance, individual and developmental differences are naturally seen as resulting from variations in some general capacity to temporarily store relevant information (Cowan, 2005), set aside intruding irrelevant aspects (Zacks & Hasher, 1994), lock the system on the pursuit of current goals (Engle, 2002), and efficiently (i.e. rapidly) process this information before its corruption and vanishing (Kail, 1991; Salthouse, 1996). Most of these limitations have been attributed to a central system of the cognitive architecture called working memory, in which representations would be temporarily stored in view of their processing (see Atkinson & Shiffrin, 1968; Baddeley & Hitch, 1974; and Miller, Galanter, & Pribam, 1960, for seminal illustrations of this concept). Exercise allied with maturation would progressively alleviate these constraints, making cognitive functioning more and more efficient. These ideas are so profoundly entrenched in contemporary psychology that it becomes increasingly difficult to imagine that, for decades, developmental psychologists have thought in a different way. This was nonetheless the case for Piaget's theory that dominated the field of developmental psychology during a large part of the twentieth century.

4 The role of working memory in development

Cognitive development without working memory: Piaget's theory

Although the notion of information was extraneous to his theorizing, the fact that young children are limited in their capacity to efficiently process information, that is to take into account and integrate all the relevant aspects of a situation, did not escape Piaget. In one of his first books (Piaget, 1923/1971), he noted the incapacity of young children to handle judgements of relations, as for that boy who explained that there were two brothers in his family and that, consequently, he had one brother, Paul, but denied that Paul himself had a brother. This incapacity to understand relative notions was attributed by Piaget to the egocentrism of child's thought, the tendency to take as absolute his or her own immediate perception, whereas relative judgements require consciousness of at least two objects, to take into account two different points of view at the same time. Piaget initially explained this phenomenon by the narrowness of the child's *field of attention*, which also explained limitations in transitive reasoning or part-whole comparisons (Piaget, 1921, 1923). In this initial view, egocentrism and narrowness of the field of attention both resulted from a certain number of habits or schemas of thought that were described as *realistic* in analogy to the illusions occurring in the history of science. Realism, the naive belief that our senses and perceptions provide us with a direct access to the world and its comprehension (e.g. the sun that seems to rotate around the earth), was conceived by Piaget as one of the main characteristics of intellectual egocentrism (e.g. 7-year-old children believing that the moon or the sun follow them in their walks). These primitive habits of thought lead children to see many things, often more than adults do as Piaget noted, but being unable to organize these observations, they cannot think of more than one thing at a time due to a synthetic incapacity.

These primary ideas were further developed during decades within the operational theory of intelligence and received their final formulation 50 years later in *The equilibration of cognitive structures* (Piaget, 1975/1985), which was considered by Piaget as the central problem of development. The main idea of this book was that the development of knowledge results not only from the experience with objects, nor from some innate and preformed programming within the subject, but from successive constructions. The mechanisms underpinning these constructions are regulations that compensate the disequilibrium that continuously occur in cognitive functioning and structures, due to the actions of the subject and their (never entirely anticipated) outcomes in the environment. A key point for Piaget was that these regulations do not lead to static forms of equilibrium, but to re-equilibrations improving the previous structures through a process known as *majoring equilibration*. A general model of the functional aspects of equilibration was proposed and formalized. We will present it in some detail for two reasons. First, its analysis questions the possibility of a continuity between Piaget's constructivism and information processing approaches that seem to be in a relation of incommensurability. Second, we will encounter later in this book some modern equivalent of this equilibration model in current attempts to account for the development of executive functions (see Chapter 6, and Zelazo, 2015).

The starting point of Piaget's analysis is a general model of the Subject–Object interactions. In this model, observables related to the objects (*Obs. O*) inform observables related to the subject's actions (*Obs. S*) through a process of awareness of these actions. Conversely, the coordination of the subject's actions (*Coord. S*, i.e. the coordination of schemes in pre-operations and operations) shapes the way in which observables related to the objects are coordinated (*Coord. O*), a coordination requiring to go above and beyond the mere observables to understand their relations (e.g. in a causal explanation, Figure 1.1; see Barrouillet & Camos, 2017). The symbol ◄──► in Figure 1.1 represents a global equilibrium that can be either momentary or lasting.

According to Piaget, two characteristics of these interactions lead to a recursive process of equilibration. The first is that observables do not correspond to a mere registration of pre-existing objects or properties that could be directly read out from reality, but depend on the degree of elaboration of the available schemes and their coordination at the previous developmental level,[1] leading to inaccurate or erroneous observations. The second is that, as long as the models constructed by the child are not sufficiently accurate, the existing coordinations would sooner or later produce the discovery of new observables. Thus, the initial states of interactions only reach unstable forms of equilibrium prone to perturbations and contradictions. Three successive developmental levels of compensation, noted α, β, and γ by Piaget, can intervene to re-establish the compromised equilibrium: the mere neglect of the perturbation leading to ignoring or minimizing the importance of the corresponding observable (level α), its integration in a modified system as a new but innocuous variable (level β), and finally its complete integration allowing for a genuine anticipation of its possible variations that means that the integrated element is no longer disruptive (level γ). Each developmental level n provides the observables that will be integrated at level $n + 1$ (Figure 1.2).

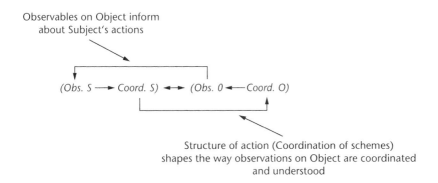

FIGURE 1.1 Illustration of the mechanisms of majoring equilibration in Piaget's theory of cognitive development

Source: J. Piaget (1975). L'équilibration des structures cognitives: problème central du développement [The equilibration of cognitive structures]. *Etudes d'épistémologie génétique*, 33, p. 59. Paris, France: Presses Universitaires de France, adapted with permission.

6 The role of working memory in development

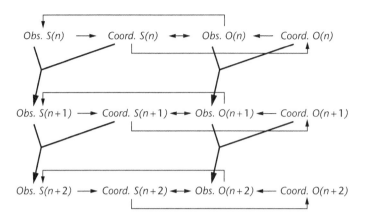

FIGURE 1.2 Successive elaborations of the Subject's cognitive structures and Object coordination of features in Piaget's theory

Source: J. Piaget (1975). L'équilibration des structures cognitives: problème central du développement [The equilibration of cognitive structures]. *Etudes d'épistémologie génétique*, 33, p. 62. Paris, France: Presses Universitaires de France, adapted with permission.

However, and more importantly for our purpose, these different levels in the majoring equilibration process do not reflect some widening of the field of attention, the narrowness of which would have explained the first and immature levels of interaction. For example, in the classical task of conservation of solid quantity, one of two identical balls of clay is stretched into a long oblong shape. The well-known young children's error is to assume that the modified ball contains more clay. Focusing only on the increased length resulting from the stretching transformation, children neglect the correlative reduction in thickness of the object that is now thinner. Piaget notes that we are here in a situation akin to the perceptual centration with its two main characteristics: on the one hand, the impossibility of embracing all the aspects at the same time and, on the other hand, a systematic distortion that overestimates the aspect on which attention focuses (the increased length) while depreciating peripheral features (the reduced thickness). However, the incapacity to take into account the two aspects of the transformation receives within the theory of equilibration a more elaborate explanation than the recourse to the 'habits of thought' that prevailed in the first formulation of the intellectual egocentrism. According to Piaget (1975), the unnoticed aspects of the situation are not simply neglected, and the correlative incomplete conceptualization does not result from some incapacity to grasp all the relevant aspects at the same time within the field of attention. The equilibration model provides us with a more precise reason. According to Piaget, the neglected aspect has been actually ruled out as it contradicted an usual conceptual schema which is that the action of stretching results in having 'more', more length, and consequently more matter. What could be seen as resulting from a narrow field of attention is the outcome of a regulation process aiming at preserving the coherence of children's conceptual system (level α

described above). The restricted thickness is perceived, and this observable constitutes a content that exerts a cognitive pressure on the conceptual form (*Coord. S*) that assimilates the stretching with an increased amount of matter (*Coord. O*). While this perturbation is the first time compensated by the mere deletion of the perturbing aspect (level α), the further regulations would tend to reduce the perturbation created by this deletion and lead to its compensation by reorganizing the initial concept. In other words, the regulations transform a latent observation into a conceptualized aspect of the situation that empirically covaries with the length of the object (level β), the reduced thickness being finally conceived as the inseparable corollary and predictable effect of the increase in length, opening the door to the understanding of their perfect compensation (level γ).

Beyond the fact that this development is not underpinned by some increase in the amount of information attended, it is doubtful that Piaget's theorizing can be reformulated within an information processing approach and its quantitative constructs. Indeed, the notion of information presupposes that some aspects of the environment are intrinsically informative for solving a class of problem in a given situation, and that integrating more of these aspects would lead to a better understanding of this situation and a higher level of adaptation. This conception seems to have inherited the empiricist assumption of a pre-structured reality with its subdivisions (the objects, their features, their relations) that have an a priori relevance preceding the acts of thought. However, for the constructivist approach favoured by Piaget, the information processed at each developmental level depends on a process of assimilation that conveys a meaning to the assimilated objects (e.g. applying sensorimotor schemas to an object does not provide the same type of information as conceptual schemas). Moreover, this process itself, allied with the necessary accommodations, modifies the assimilating schema through generalization and differentiation in such a way that the information provided by the assimilation process varies continuously over development, even for what can be considered as the same aspect of the environment. As Figure 1.2 makes clear, the observables on which thinking operates differ in nature from one developmental level to the other. Thus, despite frequent claims (e.g. Barrouillet & Gaillard, 2011; Pascual-Leone, 1970), it is probably incorrect to assume that Piaget's account of cognitive development could be reformulated in terms of an increase in the amount of information processed due to an expansion of the field of attention. Nonetheless, several attempts were made in this direction during the 1960s that opened the door to a conception of development in terms of a working memory capacity increase and that are reviewed in the remaining of this chapter.

From Piaget to Miller: toward the first accounts in terms of mental capacity

To the best of our knowledge, the first attempt to interpret Piaget's theory and its structures in information processing terms was put forward by Simon (1962). Although Simon's proposal is set out in a simple note reporting his intervention in

8 The role of working memory in development

a conference, it presents most of the main tenets on which modern approaches of cognitive development are based, and mainly those that give a central role to theoretical constructs such as attentional resources and working memory capacity. The first important point that departs from the Piagetian tradition is the emphasis put on memory. In line with the General Problem Solver (Newell et al., 1958), Simon assumed that thinking is governed by a program comprised of a system of processes and a memory storing symbols organized in lists and list structures (i.e. hierarchically organized lists of lists). Importantly, the processes are matched and implicitly adapted to memory organization. This differs from Piaget and Inhelder (1968/1973) who assumed that, instead of being matched to memory organization, cognitive operations determine the way knowledge is retained in, and retrieved from, memory (see Liben & Bowman, 2014, for a recent review of this approach). This explains why memory processes, which were assumed by Piaget to simply reflect the general organization of cognitive operations without any motor role in intellectual development, were neglected in his theorizing. The emphasis in mnemonic processes introduced by Simon will be retrieved in all the subsequent information processing accounts of cognitive development.

The second idea is that what evolves with development is the complexity of the processes that put symbols on lists, find these symbols in these lists and put them on immediate memory. For example, due to the ubiquity of the list structure in memory, a central process is Find Next (FN) that brings into immediate memory the next symbol in a list already held in immediate memory, a process involved, according to Simon, in the operation of seriation studied by Piaget (e.g. the next item after 6 is 7). Later, children could acquire the capacity to perform a more complex process such as Find Circular Next (FCN), which allows for a recursive use of FN and the production of cyclical repetitions of lists of the form ABCDAB-CDABCD .... An even more complex process called Find Circular Next with Carry (FCNC) would embed FCN into a loop holding in memory the position on several lists. For example, in writing numbers, the use of FCN produces 0, 1, 2, …, 7, 8, 9, 0, 1, 2, …, 7, 8, 9, 0, 1, 2, and so on by recursively producing the list of units. The transition from 9 to 10 can be produced by creating a new list for tens and increment it by 1 when FCN prompts the return to 0 of the units list, the same process creating hundreds when the tens list reaches 9 and returns to 0, and so on. Simon notes that the FCNC process can perform the combinatorial operations described by Piaget. This integrative succession of processes of increasing complexity echoes the succession of stages in Piagetian theory and will be retrieved in Case's theory for example (see Chapter 2). However, clear differences remain with a genuine constructivist approach. Indeed, each developmental level in Simon's idea is characterized by a process that is integrated, but remains absolutely unchanged, in the upper level (e.g. FN integrated in FCN, or FCN integrated in FCNC), whereas in Piaget's approach, the integrative process involves the reorganization and transformation of the elements of level n when integrated into structures of level $n + 1$. Moreover, the structures that define the different stages in Piaget theory do not necessarily differ in complexity. For example, contrary to processes in

Simon's model, the structure governing the sensorimotor intelligence, the *groupe pratique des déplacements*, is not less complex than the *groupements* governing the concrete operational stage. Nonetheless, we will see that this hypothesis of increased complexity of the successive cognitive structures over development is a constant of the neo-Piagetian theories.

A more direct reference to the impact of immediate memory capacity on cognitive development was introduced by McLaughlin (1963) who proposed a *psychologic* as an alternative to Piaget's formulation. He noted that Piaget's attempts to express the structures underpinning each developmental level (stage) in logical terms led to highly complex systems that were not free from confusions and hazardous proposals (e.g. the introduction of the new structure of *groupement*). Thus, McLaughlin suggested to simply define each developmental level by the number of different classes that are distinguished simultaneously, a number that can be directly identified with a measurable psychological characteristic, namely the memory span. Of course, this idea of the number of classes that can be distinguished follows Miller's (1956) proposal about the amount of information that the human cognitive system can process. Although McLaughlin does not present his idea in this direct way, his suggestion is that each developmental level can be defined by the number of bits of information that children can process, which directly determines the number of classes or concepts that can be distinguished and simultaneously held in mind. If N is the number of bits, the number of distinguishable classes is 2^N.

According to McLaughlin, the level 0 that corresponds to the stage of sensorimotor intelligence is assumed to require the capacity to process $2^0 = 1$ concept at a time, a level at which no inference is possible because an inference, by definition, involves relating two concepts. The level 1, which demands a capacity to retain $2^1 = 2$ concepts at a time, would characterize the stage of pre-operational intelligence. This limitation to two concepts or dimensions, that has often been advocated to account for children's failures in understanding transitivity or class inclusion, which requires the coordination of at least three elements, is also reminiscent of the reasoning by transduction (Stern, 1924) so frequent in 3- and 4-year-old children according to Piaget, or the *pensée par couple* (thinking by pairs) described by the French psychologist Henri Wallon (1945) as a primitive mode of thinking characterizing young children. The level 2, which corresponds to the capacity to process up to $2^2 = 4$ concepts, characterizes the stage of concrete operations and the access to all the conservations as well as the understanding of transitivity and class inclusion (e.g. understanding that there are more animals A than birds B requires understanding that animals are the reunion of birds and non-birds animals, $A = B + B'$, an addition requiring the consideration simultaneously of three different classes and their coordination). Finally, a level 3 corresponding to the ability to process up to 8 (i.e. 2^3) concepts simultaneously would correspond to the stage of formal operations.

Although this conception of cognitive development may seem rather simplistic, several of its main tenets can be retrieved in subsequent developmental theories. The idea that limitations of reasoning correspond to limitations of some mnemonic

10 The role of working memory in development

or attentional system, and that the capacity of this system, following Miller's (1956) seminal intuition, can be precisely measured is common to almost all the neo-Piagetian theories of development (Andrews & Halford, 2011; Case, 1985, 1992; Halford, 1993; Halford et al., 2014) and to theories of working memory (Cowan, 2005; Halford, Cowan, & Andrews, 2007). However, the most perfect illustration of the attempt to account for cognitive development and its successive levels by a precise quantification of a cognitive or mental capacity in terms of the number of chunks that can be simultaneously held in mind has been proposed by Pascual-Leone (1970; Pascual-Leone & Johnson, 2011) in his *Theory of Cognitive Operators*.

The central processor or computing space *M*, precursor of working memory

In keeping with the trend towards analysing cognition in terms of information processing during the 1960s, the main intuition of Pascual-Leone was that the successive developmental stages described by Piaget's theory could be ordered along a natural scale of informational complexity (considered from the subject's point of view) of the tasks that children can solve. Thus, any general stage could, in principle, be characterized by the number of separate chunks of information in Miller's (1956) terms that children are able to process, this number increasing with age. Within a Piagetian tradition of behaviour analysis, the chunks would correspond to the schemes simultaneously activated by the subject to solve a task, schemes that can be perceptual, conceptual, cognitive, behavioural, or motivational in nature. According to Pascual-Leone (1970), Piaget would have in some sense anticipated these views when introducing the notions of 'attention span' and 'field of centration', or even 'field of equilibrium' (Piaget, 1956) in which children would consider more elements as they get older. Pascual-Leone (1970) proposed formalizing these ideas within the concept of *central computing space M*, the size of which would increase in a lawful manner during normal development, this increase explaining cognitive growth. However, Pascual-Leone was fully aware of the limitations of the concepts of stage and structure in Piaget's theory, and of the numerous deviations from this normative framework that Piaget himself observed, such as the horizontal *decalages*[2] and the effects of familiarity. Thus, his theoretical proposal aimed at accounting for both the general structural characteristics of development as well as for the variability in performance across different contents and contexts.

The *M-operator* model

In Pascual-Leone's theory, a child's behaviour can be described as reflecting a psychological system made of three components. The first is the repertoire *H* of the available schemes conceived of as behavioural units. Within this repertoire *H*, a subset *H** corresponds to the schemes activated at any given moment. The second component is the operator *M*, that is a central computing space within which the information processed by the subset *H** of activated schemes is transformed or integrated into a novel behaviour. The third component consists of a number of organizational laws (e.g. Gestalt laws) that govern the way in which information is perceived and learned.

It is important for a complete understanding of Pascual-Leone's view to detail how the schemes work and why they require a central processor for their functioning. Among the several definitions proposed by Piaget for the notion of scheme, Pascual-Leone favours that of an 'organized set of reactions (i.e. a behavioural, perceptual or mental blueprint) susceptible to be transferred from one situation to another' (Piaget, 1966/1969). He suggests translating this definition into a structural language by defining any scheme as an ordered pair of responses, each response being itself a subscheme within a superscheme. The first of these responses corresponds to the perception and categorization of the cues constituting the input of the assimilation process. In other words, these cues are the elements that trigger the scheme and release the effecting response, as for example the perception of the object that will be the target of an attempt of assimilation by a scheme of prehension. The perception and categorization of these cues pertain to what Piaget called figurative schemes. The corresponding effecting responses (in our example, grasping the object) are called by Piaget operative schemes. Thus, the resulting compound superscheme requires the simultaneous or serial activation of figurative and operative subschemes. It is this activation that requires 'the executive service of a central processor or finite computing space M' (Pascual-Leone, 1970, p. 307).

Although this way of analysing cognitive processes can seem to be dated for modern psychologists, it has direct counterparts in more contemporary theoretical frameworks. The superschemes described by Pascual-Leone with their figurative and operative subshemes are no other than the production rules hypothesized by production systems like ACT-R (Anderson, 1993, 2007; Anderson & Lebière, 1998). Indeed, productions in ACT-R theory are 'If … then' rules with a set of conditions (the 'if' part) that triggers some action (the 'then' part) when these conditions match the current content of working memory and the current goal. The role of the actions in the production rule is to modify the content of working memory, which in turn triggers a new production rule, and so on. It is exactly in this way that Pascual-Leone (1970) describes the functioning of the psychological system. The cues hypothesized by Pascual-Leone, which are figurative schemes, correspond to the representations of declarative knowledge held in working memory in ACT-R. When these representations match the condition part of a production rule, they release the actions of this rule that transform the current content of working memory in the same way as the cues in Pascual-Leone's approach release the effecting response (the operative schemes). Indeed, Pascual-Leone explains that transforming information consists in processing activated figurative schemes z_i by operative superschemes[3] ϕ_{zi} to activate new figurative schemes z'_i. This is done by placing each different subscheme z_i in one of the channels, or 'centration places', of the central processor M along with schemas representing task situation (ψ_s) and instructions (ψ_I).[4] In this way, the schemes z_i along with ψ_s and ψ_I activate the corresponding schemes ϕ_{zi}. This clearly means that the central operator

12 The role of working memory in development

M hypothesized by Pascual-Leone plays exactly the same role as working memory in modern psychology.

The key assumption is that the maximum number of schemes (or discrete chunks of information) that the central operator M can attend to, or integrate, in a single act increases with age, each developmental stage being characterized by the measure of M. This measure is expressed by Pascual-Leone as

$$M = a + k \qquad (1.1)$$

in which a is 'an unknown but constant across-age quantity corresponding to the processing space taken by ψ_s and ψ_l' (Pascual-Leone, 1970, p. 308). We will turn back to this surprising claim that the representation of task setting and instructions requires the same processing space whatever the age. The variable k represents the number of schemes that can be activated for solving the task, evolving from two at the end of the pre-operational period (i.e. age of 5 or 6), to three at the beginning and four at the end of the concrete operational stage, at the age of 9 or 10. Note that these values correspond to those characterizing the levels 1 and 2 hypothesized by McLaughlin (1963). It is assumed that at the beginning of the formal stage, at the age of 11 or 12 when children understand the conservation of volume, this number would be five. The influence of Miller (1956) in this theorizing is made evident when Pascual-Leone assumes that a logical generalization of his model is to assume that the magical number seven represents the upper limit of the central computing space M reached at the end of adolescence. Consequently, the M-operator capacity was assumed to increase by one scheme every two years from age 3 ($M = a + 1$) to 15 ($M = a + 7$).

Measuring M

It should be remembered that, according to Pascual-Leone (1970), the schemes activated by the operator M are recruited from the repertoire H and depend on its content, which can vary independently of M capacity between and within individuals from one domain to another, depending on learning opportunities and personal inclinations. Thus, Pascual-Leone (1970) suggested that an accurate estimate of M capacity can only be achieved by testing the capacity of the subject to integrate recently acquired schemes from an artificial repertoire. For this purpose, he created the compound-stimuli visual information task (CSVI) in which individuals learn in the first place a set of stimulus-response units (S-R), and are then asked to produce the appropriate response to a maximum number of the corresponding cues nested in a compound stimulus. In the CSVI task, the S-R units forming the repertoire link up simple cues of a visual stimulus (its shape, colour, size, etc.) with motoric responses (raising or clapping hands, opening mouth, closing eyes, or nodding head). For example, a red square with a cross inside requires clapping hands, opening mouth, and nodding the head. To keep the difficulty of the task equivalent across ages, children aged 5, 7, 9, and 11 learned a number of S-R

Working memory in developmental psychology **13**

units equal to their hypothetical M capacity k plus three (i.e. five, six, seven, and eight S-R units, respectively) and were presented with figures involving a number of relevant cues varying from two to the maximum number of learnt units.

Predicting the probability of producing a given number of learnt responses R from the number of cues S'' present in the compound stimulus and the hypothetical size k of the M operator was rather complex. At first sight, it could be imagined that a capacity k allows for the sampling of k cues in the stimulus, releasing k responses, but the problem is more intricate. To make a long story short, Pascual-Leone drew the metaphor of k units of energy available to turn on or increase the luminosity of a panel of S'' light bulbs corresponding to the cues present in the stimulus to be processed. Each energy unit is applied to one of the bulbs independently from the other units, in such a way that a given bulb can receive more than one unit while other bulbs can remain out, even if their number does not exceed k (i.e. the patterns of resulting lights can range from one bulb receiving all the k units to k different bulbs receiving one energy unit each). To make things more complex, as children had free time for responding, this application of k units to S'' bulbs constitutes a single attending act, but after having produced a first burst of motoric responses, children are free to initiate a second (or more) attending act in order to discover still neglected remaining cues. In order to avoid an endless recursion of attending acts, Pascual-Leone was obliged to assume that the capacity k is reduced by one unit at each of these attending acts. This unit would be used to maintain active a scheme recoding the representation of the previous responding activities. Thus, the capacity k being reduced by one unit at each of these attending acts, their maximum number is k. Thus, Pascual-Leone reasoned that the probability of producing x responses with k energy units after k successive attending acts was the same as producing these x responses in a single attending act for which k^2 energy units would have been available.[5] Using the Bose-Einstein occupancy model, Pascual-Leone proposed that the probability, with a capacity of k, to have produced at the end of the process x responses (lighting x bulbs) when n cues were present in the stimulus (in a panel of n bulbs) was given by the following formula:

$$\Pr(x) = \left(\frac{n}{n-x}\right)\left(\frac{k^2-1}{x-1}\right) \div \left(\frac{n+k^2-1}{k^2}\right) \tag{1.2}$$

For example, with a capacity $k = 3$ and three cues in the stimulus, the probability of producing a motoric response for each of these three cues is only .509, and not 1 as one might have expected. We have detailed this reasoning and calculations only to illustrate the complexity of the approach and the difficulty inherent to the quantification of the size of a mental computing system, even in the simple task of producing discrete responses to a limited series of cues. As we will see below, both the method and the model used by Pascual-Leone to establish that the k value increases as his model predicted was subject to strong criticisms. Nonetheless, at each of the ages studied, observed probabilities in Pascual-Leone's (1970) study matched reasonably well the predictions of a model assuming a k value increasing from two to five between 5 and 11 years of age, with children producing an increasing

14 The role of working memory in development

number of responses with age that rarely exceeded the predicted size k of their M operator (i.e. two, three, four, and five for 5, 7, 9, and 11-year-olds respectively).

Variability in performance

By now, the operator M model could be seen as a mere translation of the stage theory, predicting an equivalent level of performance across tasks and domains due to the strict limitation in the number of schemes that can be simultaneously activated. However, several factors can influence performance that do not depend on the M capacity.

First, we have already mentioned that the schemes activated by the operator M depend on the content of children's repertoire that can vary independently of M capacity. Second, Pascual-Leone distinguished between a structural capacity M_s (the maximum capacity available for a given subject at a given age), and a functional capacity M_f, suggesting that some variables could act as moderators and lead a subject to frequently function with only a fraction of his or her structural capacity. Among these variables, the cognitive style of field dependence[6] as described by Witkin (Witkin, Dyk, Faterson, Goodenough, & Karp, 1962) was of major importance for Pascual-Leone. He noted that some cues (or figurative subschemes) have a greater probability to release their response, due to their salience, which in turn depends on learning or on the innate perceptual organization law, such as the laws of Gestalt. Thus, different schemes can have different probability weights in the subject's repertoire. This is, according to Pascual-Leone, what occurs in many Piagetian conservation tasks where children's responses are led by some salient perceptual characteristic that releases an irrelevant but irrepressible scheme, leading to what Pascual-Leone calls *misleading situations* (e.g. in the number conservation task, the length of the longest row releases a 'longer = more numerous' scheme that leads to the incorrect response). Field-dependent individuals would be more sensitive than others to field factors influencing their functional capacity M_f. Based on a master thesis dissertation by Eccles, Pascual-Leone (1970) reported that field-independent individuals perform better in the CSVI task than field-dependent individuals, the latter tending to be low information processors because they perform with a functional M size inferior to their structural capacity.

The theory of constructive operators

The intuitions that led to the M-operator model were subsequently extended within the theory of constructive operators (TCO; Pascual-Leone, 1995, 1996; Pascual-Leone & Johnson, 1999). Our aim here is not to describe this theory (see Morra, Gobbo, Marini, & Sheese, 2008, for an authoritative analysis of the TCO), but to identify the main theoretical proposals concerning the role of working memory in cognitive development as it is conceived by Pascual-Leone. In the more recent presentations of Pascual-Leone's approach (Pascual-Leone, 1988; Pascual-Leone & Johnson, 2011), the idea that the maturational growth of M capacity, called M power, enables the transition from one cognitive developmental stage to the next has always been reiterated. However, specifications have been introduced concerning the M capacity, and more generally working memory, that are of interest for analysing its relationships with cognitive development.

The first elaboration concerns the constant a in Equation 1.1, the space needed by the schemes representing task situation (ψ_s) and instructions (ψ_i), which is assumed to remain constant from 3 to 15 years of age. This constant is now expressed as e for executive, M capacity being expressed as $e + k$. In the TCO theory, e refers to the mental attention used to activate the relevant executive schemes. Executive schemes differ from ordinary schemes in that they are higher-level units that define tasks within situations, regulate the application of organismic resources to the action schemes, monitor and control the application of suitable action schemes for the task at hand, in other words plan and control cognitive activity (Pascual-Leone & Johnson, 2011). Whereas this conception remains akin to the role attributed to the central executive in Baddeley's theory (Baddeley, 1986; Baddeley & Logie, 1999) or more generally to the executive functions (see Chapter 6), it is less common to assume that the resources needed to activate these schemes remain constant from 3 years onwards. The explanation is that executive schemes would require a modest amount of energy for their activation which is approximately equivalent to the M capacity of a 2-year-old child (Pascual-Leone & Goodman, 1979). Thus, the M capacity corresponding to e is assumed to grow during the sensorimotor period by one unit per substage as defined in Piaget's theory, from 0 at substage 1 (from birth to 1 month) to 5 at substage 6 (from 18 to 24 months), reaching a value of 6 after 24 months and eventually 7 at 3 years.

Another interesting elaboration for our purpose is the conception of working memory the TCO theory proposes (see Pascual-Leone & Baillargeon, 1994; Pascual-Leone & Johnson, 2011). Working memory is conceived as the set of schemes that are activated (*hyperactivated* in the authors' terms) either by mental attention or spontaneous attention following Pascual-Leone and Johnson's (2011) terms. Mental attention is the result of four organismic operators called E, M, I, and F. The operator E is the set of executive schemes evoked above that mobilize and allocate the operators M and I that can be seen as two attentional resources. Operator M, corresponding to attentional activation, is the M operator that we presented in this section with a size k evolving from 1 to 7 action schemes that can be simultaneously activated, whereas I corresponds to attentional inhibition or interruption that deactivates irrelevant schemes, as in the traditional Stroop task in which the meaning of the written word must be discarded to name its colour. The coordinated application of operators E, M, and I to action schemes produces the content of mental attention named focal centration or M-centration by Pascual-Leone. The notion of F-operator (for Field) is more muddled. It corresponds to the field effects, as the Gestalt laws for perception with the principles of proximity or closure, and facilitates the activation of the simplest possible representations and the selection of the appropriate figurative schemes. The status of this operator remains unclear because, while the F-operator is part of the spontaneous attention, the effortless

16 The role of working memory in development

form of attention driven by novel or salient stimuli in the environment (but also by affects and emotions, or mind wandering), it is also presented as a system pertaining to endogenous mental attention that inhibits schemes outside of the focal or M-centration. This depends on the nature of the situation. In misleading situations, operator F spontaneously recruits salient but irrelevant schemes (e.g. the length of the row in the number conservation task) that have to be inhibited by the operator I for correct performance, but in most everyday circumstances, it helps to limit M-centration to the simplest representation of the environment.

Overall, beyond the successive elaborations of the TCO, the M-operator model has remained largely unchanged, with the main idea that cognitive development and stage transitions are better understood as resulting from the age-related increase in an M space able to simultaneously activate an increasing number of schemes than from some equilibration process. Importantly, the theory makes strong assumptions about the size k of this mental space, increasing of one unit every two years from one at age 3 to seven at age 15. As we will see, it is this metric that attracted the strongest criticisms.

Evaluation and appraisals of Pascual-Leone's model

Validation of the M-*operator model*

As it is often the case, Pascual-Leone's (1970) article was followed by a first wave of validation. Pascual-Leone's theory assumes that the capacity of M, which results from epigenetic and maturational factors, determines the maximum number of schemes that children can mobilize at any given time. Consequently, this capacity should not be restricted to the CSVI task, but should be task-independent. Case (1972) tested this hypothesis by introducing a new measure through an original digit placement task. In this task, children aged 6, 8, and 10 were presented with an apparatus in which a row of doors concealed a series of numbers in ascending order (e.g. 3, 9, 18). From left to right, these doors were successively open for 1.5 s and closed by the experimenter before opening the next door, children being asked to read each unveiled number aloud. On the right hand of this display was a door concealing a final target number (e.g. 11). After having read this target number and its door having been closed, the task of the children was to indicate where this number belonged in the row. Following our example, there are four possible places, on the left of the first, leftmost, door, between the first and the second door, between the second and the third, which is the correct response as 11 stands between 9 and 18, and on the right of the third door. Because each door was closed before opening the next one, children saw the numbers one at a time and had consequently to remember the series as well as the target number for finding its place. The total number of numbers in the display (including the target number), called n, was set to k in a first series of five trials, and to $k+1$ in a second series of five further trials, with $k=2$, 3, and 4, for children aged 6, 8, and 10 respectively (e.g. 8-year-old children were presented with problems involving either three or four numbers). These values were set according to a task analysis. First, it was assumed that each number required the activation of the appropriate figurative scheme for its representation in such a way that the n numbers require a mental space of n. Second, it could have been assumed that the ordering operation for finding the appropriate place of the final number would have required at least an additional scheme. However, Case assumed that the training that preceded the experimental task would have created in each child an overlearned executive scheme that would leave unaffected the capacity k as executive schemes are assumed to be fuelled by the constant a (or e in further elaborations of the theory, see Equation 1.1). Consequently, it was predicted that the majority of children would pass when n equals the size k of their M space, but fail when $n = k + 1$. This is what occurred (e.g. a majority of 8-year-old children succeeded with problems involving 3 numbers, but not 4). For each value of n from 2 to 5, a theoretical distribution of scores was calculated for each value of k from 2 to 4, and it was observed that the empirical data fitted the theoretical distributions corresponding to the predicted values of k.

In a further study, Case (1974) investigated the effects of reducing the M demand of the task by allowing children of the same ages to open the doors themselves. It appeared that some children began by opening the rightmost door that concealed the target number. Theoretically, this strategy would reduce the M demand to $a + 2$, because children can now keep in mind the number to be placed, and compare it with each number unveiled in the series, thus keeping in mind only two numbers at a time at any moment. Accordingly, children who adopted spontaneously this right–left strategy achieved high-level performance as the M demand of the task never exceeded their capacity (which is already 2 in 6-year-old children). In a second experiment, Case instructed children to use this right–left strategy in opening the doors. Their performance corresponded to what the theory would predict for a task with an M demand of $a + 3$ and not $a + 2$. This was explained by the fact that implementing the newly acquired and not yet automatic right–left strategy requires some M-centration, because exploring the display from right to left would oblige the child to supersede the overlearned tendency to explore arrays from left to right in our culture, a type of situation classified by Pascual-Leone as field misleading (see above).

Many other tasks have been designed by Pascual-Leone and his collaborators to assess M capacity. For example, in the figural intersection task (FIT), children have to find the intersection of an increasing number of overlapping shapes (Morra, 1994; Pennings & Hessels, 1996). The colour matching task (CMT) is a 1-back task in which children are presented with successive sets of colours and have to judge whether each set of colours is the same as in trial $n - 1$ (Arsalidou, Pascual-Leone, & Johnson, 2010). The mental attention memory task (MAM) is a modified verbal span measure in which children read series of consonants and recall them aloud while dialling each consonant in an old-fashioned rotary telephone (Pascual-Leone & Johnson, 2011). In the direction following task (DFT; Pascual-Leone & Johnson, 2011), children follow directions of increasing complexity (e.g. 'Place a small blue

18 The role of working memory in development

square on a yellow space'). In each of these tasks, children passed items the M demand of which did not exceed their theoretical M capacity, but otherwise failed. Moreover, scores on different tasks (e.g. CMT and FIT) are very close to each other at each age studied and conform to the predictions of the theory (Pascual-Leone & Johnson, 2011).

Appraisals and criticisms

Pascual-Leone's model and experimental method for assessing k did not, however, remain uncriticized. Trabasso and Foellinger (1978) ran what is probably the most detailed investigation of Pascual-Leone's (1970) claims and methods. Recall that, in this latter study, Pascual-Leone introduced the CSVI task in which children learnt a set of S-R units and were then asked to produce the motoric response associated with each of the n cues nested in a compound stimulus, n varying from 2 to 8. Trabasso and Foellinger (1978) noted that, in Pascual-Leone's study, the total number of actions requested was confounded with the age of the participants (older children were presented with stimuli involving more cues). Moreover, the rate of correct responses varied from one S-R unit to another and this difficulty interacted with age. Indeed, the youngest groups were confronted with the most difficult S-R units. Thus, the developmental increase in the number of responses observed by Pascual-Leone could have resulted from the fact that older children were presented with more and easier cues to process. Finally, Trabasso and Foellinger noted that Pascual-Leone had not statistically tested the adequacy of his model to the data.

The aim of Trabasso and Foellinger was to test Pascual-Leone's assumption that the estimate of cognitive capacity k is independent of n. For this purpose, they ran a study in which the age was held constant by using only 8-year-old children, while the number n of cues presented was varied in exactly the same way as Pascual-Leone did (i.e. four groups were created that studied stimuli containing up to five, six, seven, or eight cues). The task was modified and consisted of a short-term memory task in which the experimenter demonstrated a series of actions in succession, children being asked to reproduce them. To test the assumption that k is independent of n, Trabasso and Foellinger used Equation 1.2 proposed by Pascual-Leone[7] and goodness-of-fit tests to find the best estimate of k for each value of n in their data. The results revealed that not only k estimates varied with n, but the model was rejected by large margins for almost all the n values. Moreover, when applying Pascual-Leone's model to his own data, χ^2 goodness-of-fit test rejected the model in 10 of the 19 experimental conditions studied by Pascual-Leone. Actually, a simple model assuming that each additional action requested in Trabasso and Foellinger's task leads to a constant decrease in the probability of recalling previously requested actions provided a better fit of the data than Pascual-Leone's model.

In the ensuing debate, Pascual-Leone (1978) argued that Trabasso's criticisms resulted from divergences between the rationalist and empiricist epistemologies, whereas Trabasso (1978) retorted that from his point of view, the issue was one of falsifiability (Popper, 1968) of Pascual-Leone's claims and model. We must admit that this question of falsifiability seems to us of paramount importance, especially when considering the critical points of task analysis and computation of the number of schemes a given task requires. Case (1985), evoking a personal communication from Klahr, noted that this number depends on the *grain* at which the task is analysed. But even when the level of analysis remains approximately constant, surprising variations occur in the way Pascual-Leone assesses the M demand of the tasks he uses (i.e. the minimal amount of M capacity needed to solve it). Consider for example the CSVI task. It is clear from Pascual-Leone's (1970) analyses that each response to a given cue requires the activation of a scheme in such a way that the M demand of the task corresponds to the number of cues nested in the compound stimulus (in fact, children with a capacity $k = x$ are expected to be able to give a maximum of x responses at each attending act). It is the same in Case's digit placement task. The M demand corresponds to the number of digits to be held in short-term memory, because the scheme needed for ordering the digits is assumed to be part of the executive schemes fuelled by the a capacity and not by k. However, this is not the case in the FIT task, in which the operative scheme needed to search and find the common intersection of all the shapes is assumed to require M space. Nonetheless, the M demand corresponds to the number of shapes (and not this number plus one due to the operative scheme), because it is assumed that participants take one of the shapes as a background for visual exploring, the corresponding scheme becoming over-learned and no longer requiring additional boosting by M capacity. In the MAM task in which children dial previously read consonants in a rotary telephone, M demand corresponds to the number of consonants with no additional capacity needed by the operative scheme involved in recalling and searching the consonant on dial (noted OPi). Indeed, it is assumed that a consonant is already chunked with this operative scheme, 'because this search-of-consonants process is well-practiced enough to have a built-in place for the currently searched consonant' (Pascual-Leone & Johnson, 2011, p. 31). By contrast, in the CMT task that requires comparing sets of colours, the M demand for a set of n colours corresponds to $2 + n$ because, at each step of the comparison, the target colour that children are trying to match against the set previously seen adds one to-be-activated scheme to the n colours of the previous set that have to be maintained in an active state for comparison, while the operative scheme needed to scan and identify the searched colour in the set constitutes a second scheme to be added. Thus, in assessing the M demand of each task, the operative schemes involved are either added or not to the number of items to be processed for reasons that remain unclear. Other examples of task analyses in terms of number of schemes required are detailed in Morra et al. (2008), but it is sometimes difficult to escape the feeling that these analyses are driven, maybe unconsciously, by what the authors already know about the age at which children usually solve the task, looking for the predicted number of schemes depending on the age of success.

20 The role of working memory in development

As Trabasso (1978) noted at the end of his reply to Pascual-Leone (1978):

> I believe that mental capabilities increase with age and experience but I am, nonetheless, compelled by the present evidence not to accept the claim that capacity can be measured and follows the growth pattern claimed by Pascual-Leone. I should also add that one should beware of a confirmatory bias in one's theorizing.
>
> *(Trabasso, 1978, p. 45)*

Illustrative of the difficulty of predicting precisely quantitative age-related increases in capacity is the study by Globerson (1983b), who administered M capacity tasks like the CSVI test and what she called short-term memory tests, among which was the digit placement task described above, to children aged 8, 10, and 12. Although mean scores at the CSVI test were 2.75 and 3.55 in 8- and 10-year-olds respectively, not so far from the 3 and 4 predicted, 12-year-old children reached a mean score of 4.1, and not 5, as Pascual-Leone's theory would have predicted. Moreover, the scores observed with the digit placement task were at each age at least one unit higher than predicted and observed by Case (1972).

Conclusion

The advent of the information processing approach, allied with the complexity of Piaget's theory and his difficulties in accounting for stage transitions through the concept of equilibration, naturally led psychologists to reformulate cognitive development in terms of an increased capacity to process information. It is interesting to note that, after early attempts to capture the increasing complexity of children's thought in terms of more and more complex programs, the first general theory linking cognitive development with the amount of information that children were able to integrate conceived this increase in capacity as the increase in size of some central computing space. Although the phrase 'working memory' does not appear in Pascual-Leone (1970), the central space M is clearly a working memory in which all cognitive processing is assumed to occur as Case and Globerson (1974) noted. Considering the historical and scientific context of elaboration of Pascual-Leone's theory, it does not come as a surprise that the units activated in this mental space were conceived as Piagetian schemes, and that their maximum number was set to Miller's magical number seven. Although the concept of scheme has nowadays fallen in disuse and the upper limit of seven has been called into question (Cowan, 2001), most of Pascual-Leone's proposals are still part of the modern conception of working memory, such as the notions of activation, of a limited number of chunks of information constituting the span of attention, or the distinction between figurative and operative schemes that prefigured the opposition between declarative and procedural knowledge. As early as the middle of the 1970s, and long before the creation of the first working memory span tasks by Daneman and Carpenter (1980) and Turner and Engle (1989), correlations were observed between the measures of

M space and analytic intelligence (nowadays called Gf; Case & Globerson, 1974), prefiguring modern studies (e.g. Cowan, Fristoe, Elliott, Brunner, & Saults, 2006; Engle, Tuholski, Laughlin, & Conway, 1999; Kane et al., 2004; Kyllonen & Christal, 1990). Relations with other constructs less prominent in modern psychology such as mental effort as conceived by Kahneman (1973), and field-dependence/independence were also documented (Globerson, 1983a, 1985). Thus, even if the strict correspondence Pascual-Leone (1970) hypothesized between age, Piagetian substages, and the size k of the M space has not been universally endorsed, his work was pioneering in introducing the age-related increase in working memory capacity as the main factor of cognitive development. Importantly, Pascual-Leone's work set the stage for a series of theories known as neo-Piagetian in which the age-related increase in working memory capacity is seen as a key problem of cognitive development.

Notes

1 For example, in the well-known task of number conservation, a child who assumes that one row contains more objects because 'it is longer' does certainly not evoke the same property of length (resulting from the sum of the successive intervals between objects) as we use as adults, because if that was the case, he or she would not produce the error, but would understand that increasing the length of the row by spreading the objects does not modify their number.
2 The fact that two behaviours theoretically underpinned by the same structure appear with a systematic developmental lag such as the conservations of matter and weight.
3 What is described by Pascual-Leone as 'operative supercheme ϕ_{zi}' was previously referred to as an 'operative subscheme'.
4 What we would call nowadays 'task set'.
5 Actually, and following Pascual-Leone's reasoning, the total number of energy units used after k attending acts should be $k + (k-1) + (k-2) + \ldots + (k-k)$, that is $k(k+1)/2$ and not k^2.
6 Field dependence defines a personality trait to which people are influenced by the inner (field-independence) or environmental (field-dependence) cues. It differs from the later conception of high and low working memory capacity individuals.
7 In their model, Trabasso and Foellinger (1978) corrected the equation by replacing k^2 by $k(k-1)/2$ (see note 5).

2
WORKING MEMORY IN NEO-PIAGETIAN THEORIES

According to Case (1985), the two postulates of Piaget's theory that encountered the greatest difficulties were the ideas that children's development is underpinned by the construction of general structures organizing mental operations in a logical way, and that this construction results from the equilibration process described in Chapter 1. Moreover, the explanatory power of the stage notion itself, at least as it was theorized by Piaget, was called into doubt and the notion of equilibration criticized for its vagueness and lack of heuristic power (Brainerd, 1978). Brainerd argued that to be really explanatory, a stage theory should describe real age changes in behaviour, specify some antecedent variables that are believed to cause these changes, and perhaps more importantly 'should provide methods whereby these variables can be measured independently of the changes they purport to explain' (Brainerd, 1978, p. 209). The programme developed by Pascual-Leone might be seen as an attempt to take up the challenge of identifying an antecedent variable susceptible to cause the developmental changes occurring at stage transition (i.e. the endogenous increase in capacity of a central computing system for activating schemes simultaneously) and to propose a way of measuring this capacity (i.e. the M-capacity tasks). However, Pascual-Leone did not remain isolated in his attempt to establish a bridge between the information processing approach and Piaget's genetic psychology, and his work gave birth to a series of so-called neo-Piagetian theories (Case, 1978, 1985, 1992; Case & Okamoto, 1996; Chapman, 1987; Demetriou, Efklides, & Platsidou, 1993; Demetriou & Mouyi, 2011; Demetriou & Raftopoulos, 1999; Fischer, 1980; Halford, 1982, 1993; Halford et al., 2014). With Piaget's, these theories share a constructivist stance and the division of the developmental period into stages that differ with each other in a qualitative way. However, although they also share with Piaget the assumption of the existence of general structures, they characterize these structures as information processing systems of increasing complexity instead of logically organized assemblies of operations. More importantly for our purpose, they suppose that the complexity of these structures is, across different domains, subject to a common ceiling that results from a limitation in working memory capacity, the age-related increase of which would consequently play a major role in cognitive development. Our purpose in this chapter is not to give a detailed account of these neo-Piagetian theories – we invite interested readers to consult the excellent book by Morra and colleagues (2008) – but to illustrate the role of working memory in cognitive development that these theories postulate. For this purpose, we will focus on two of these theories that have elaborated theoretical conceptions about what is working memory and how it develops, namely Case's and Halford's theories.

Growth in short-term storage space and cognitive development: Cases's theory

Case (1985) presented his theory as an attempt to solve the dilemma that, according to him, developmental psychology was facing at the end of the 1970s. On the one hand, the post-Piagetian theories that had been proposed to solve the problems that plagued Piaget's theory did so by focusing on the *process* of intellectual development rather than its *structure*, leading to a series of domain-specific theories.[1] On the other hand, there was a lack of general approach able to organize the new data supplied by these theories and to determine the subjectively appropriate grain of analysis for different tasks that would have permitted the provision of a coherent and global picture of cognitive development, something that the classical structural theory did. Consequently, Case (1978, 1985) proposed a new theory in which children build structures that permit an executive control of their cognitive and affective experiences by temporally organizing sequences of figurative and operative schemes. This sequence connects some figurative schemes representing the current state of affairs by which the child is confronted (i.e. the problem representation), to some other figurative schemes representing a desired state of affairs, for it has a higher affective or cognitive value (i.e. the objectives), and finally to a sequence of operations to go from the first to the latter state (i.e. the strategies). Of interest for our purpose is the assumption that the maximum complexity that these executive control structures can attain at a given developmental level is constrained by working memory capacity. Although this proposal seems to echo Pascual-Leone's theory, there are sharp differences between the two approaches.

From 7 to 4: beyond the age-related increase in M capacity

Pascual-Leone's explanation of a transition from one Piagetian stage to the next by an increase in M capacity posed, according to Case (1985), a series of difficulties, at both the theoretical and empirical levels. The theoretical problems have been already evoked. They refer to the identification of the correct level (the *grain*) of task analysis in evaluating the M demand of a given task, and to the fact that major qualitative changes *between* stages (e.g. from the pre-operational to the operational

24 The role of working memory in development

period) were assumed to result from the same increase in M capacity as more minor changes *within* stages (e.g. from the early to the late period of the concrete operational stage). At the empirical level, several short-term memory spans did not asymptote at 7, even when involving overlearned material such as letters or words, while 5-year-old children proved able to recall more than two items (Dempster, 1981). Finally, the most disputable aspect of Pascual-Leone's theory was the tacit assumption that any scheme requires the same M capacity, and that this capacity remains unchanged over the developmental period, changes in capacity being only conceived as involving the number of schemes that can be activated and not the amount of attention each of these schemes requires. However, in contradiction with this idea, a host of studies had reported at this time age-related increases in processing speed for basic operations such as visual search, naming, or same/different judgements, suggesting a strong age-related decrease in cognitive demand (e.g. Chi & Klahr, 1975; Enns & Girgus, 1985; Manis, Keating, & Morrison, 1980; Mansfield, 1977; Nelson & Kosslyn, 1975).

Going back to Piaget, the solution adopted by Case (1985) was to assume that the operative schemes coordinated in the executive control structures differed in nature from one developmental stage to another, being successively sensorimotor, relational, dimensional, and vectorial for infancy, pre-school age, primary school period, and adolescence respectively. Whereas the units of thought from birth to 18 months are sensory objects and actions, these basic units become relationships between these actions and objects in the following stage from 18 months to 5 years, while coordinating these relationships results in the construction of dimensions between 5 and 11 years (e.g. the dimension of weight or length). Finally, integrating dimensions with each other results in complex concepts that Case calls vectors, which are expressed as ratios between dimensions such as density and speed in the physical domain or analogy in the verbal domain. This later achievement corresponds to adolescence. In line with Piaget's integrative conception of stage transition, each executive control structure at a given stage was assumed to result from the integration of two previously existing structures that served a qualitatively different purpose at the previous stage.

However, more original was the idea that, within each of these stages, the executive control structures undergo a universal sequence of three substages of unifocal, bifocal, and elaborated coordination differentiated by the number of elements they involve and the way these elements are organized. Figure 2.1 illustrates this progression during the dimensional stage for the problem of the balance beam. This task, first introduced by Inhelder and Piaget (1958), was given a more detailed description and analysis by Siegler (1976). The substage 0 (operational consolidation) corresponds to the last substage of the previous relational stage during which dimensions emerge from the coordination of relations. Figure 2.1 represents at the dimensional level the basic executive control structures for the dimensions of weight and number. Substage 1 of unifocal coordination is characterized by the construction of executive control structures that coordinate the two dimensions, resulting in the exclusive focusing on the weight dimension for predicting the

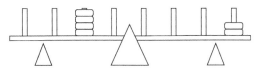

Substage 0: Operational consolidation (3½–5 years)

Problem situation
- Balance beam with an object on each arm

Objective
- Determine which side will go down

Strategy
- Look at each side. Predict that the one which looks *heavy* will go down, the *light* one up

Problem situation
- Set of objects at X and Y

Objective
- Determine which set has the big number

Strategy
- Count each set; note one with big number

Substage 1: Unifocal coordination is (5–7 years)

Problem situation
- Balance beam with stacks of objects on each arm
- Each stack composed of a number of identical units

Objective
- Predict which side will go down
- Determine which side has larger number of units

Strategy
1. Count each set of units; note which side has the bigger number
2. Pick side with bigger number as the one which will weigh more (and therefore go down)

Substage 2: Bifocal coordination (7–9 years)

Problem situation
- Balance beam with stacks of objects on each arm
- Each stack composed of a number of identical units
- Each object at a specifiable distance from fulcrum

Objective
- Predict which side will go down
- Determine with greater number of objects
- Determine side with weight at greater distance

Strategy
1. Count each set of units; note which side has the bigger number
2. Repeat 1 for distance pegs
3. If weights equal, predict side with greater distance will go down. Otherwise predict side with greater weight will go down

Substage 3: Elaborated coordination (9–11 years)

Problem situation
- Balance beam with stacks of weights at various distances
- Action of weight and distance in opposite directions
- Each stack composed of equal units

Objective
- Predict which side will go down
- Determine whether weight or distance has a greater effect
- Determine relative number of weights on each side
- Determine relative distance in each side

Strategy
1. Count each distance; note size as well as direction of difference
2. Repeat step 1 for weight
3. Compare the magnitude of the results in steps 1 and 2
4. Focus on dimension of greater difference. Pick side with higher value as one which will go down

FIGURE 2.1 Apparatus used by Case for studying the balance beam problem and illustration of the successive executive control structures constructed by children at the four substages of the dimensional developmental stage for this problem in Case's theory

Source: R. Case (1985). *Intellectual development: Birth to adulthood*, pp. 102–106. New York, NY: Academic Press, adapted with permission.

26 The role of working memory in development

outcome. This developmental level corresponds to the use of the Rule I identified by Siegler (1976, 1978), children systematically judging that the greater weight will go down. Substage 2 of bifocal coordination involves the additional dimension of distance, but with only a partial integration corresponding to Siegler's Rule II by which children take the distance into account, but only when weights are equal. Finally, the substage 3 of elaborated coordination reflects a genuine integration of the two dimensions, yet at a qualitative level, that corresponds to the Rule III identified by Siegler.[2] Case described the same sequence of three substages for each of the sensorimotor, relational, dimensional, and vectorial stages in a variety of domains spanning social cognition, language, scientific, causal, spatial, and verbal reasoning, including infant's interactions with inanimate objects and other human beings. The elaborate coordination at stage n was assumed to constitute an elementary building block at stage $n + 1$ (e.g. the basic dimension of weight is assumed to correspond, at the relational level, to a complex and elaborated coordination of relations between the objects on the two arms and the movements that these objects impart to the balance beam). The hierarchical integration leading from one developmental level to the next was assumed to be mediated by four general processes that are problem solving, exploration, imitation, and mutual regulation (e.g. instruction).

However, Case (1985) noted that hierarchical integration alone could not account for cognitive development, and that some maturational factor should be at work to explain why this development takes so long, why it stops at about the age of 18 years, and why it decelerates from birth to the end of adolescence at approximately the same rate as physical development. The maturational factor invoked was the increase in executive processing space, the maximum number of schemes that a child can keep simultaneously in a full activation while working toward a goal. At each developmental stage, from sensorimotor to vectorial, Case conducted a functional analysis of the tasks mastered by children at the unifocal, bifocal, and elaborated coordination levels in order to determine the maximum executive processing load (EPL) they involve. It resulted from these analyses that this maximum EPL increases by one unit at each substage and corresponds to the number of entries in the list of objectives of the executive control structure. This number equals the operating space OP required to reach the objective ranked at the lowest level in the objective's stack, plus one unit S of storage for each of the higher-order objectives. For example, in our example of elaborated coordination in Figure 2.1, the maximum EPL is 4, with the operating space OP required to count each distance, while maintaining three higher-order objectives (determining the relative number of weights, whether weight or distance will have the greater effect, and predicting the side that will go down). Thus, for each level of executive control structures, the maximum EPL can be formalized as $OP_x + nS$ in which x corresponds to the level of operation to a given stage (i.e. sensorimotor, relational, dimensional, or vectorial) and n to the level of the substage from 0 to 3 (see Figure 2.1). For example, the maximum EPL at the dimensional stage would successively be $OP_{dimensional}$, $OP_{dimensional} + S$, $OP_{dimensional} + 2S$, and $OP_{dimensional} + 3S$ from the substage 0 of consolidation to the final substage 3 of elaborated coordination. Consequently, at each developmental stage, the maximum executive processing demand varies from one to four schemes to be simultaneously activated.

The short-term storage space development

The analysis of the executive demand associated with each level of executive control structure suggested that what increases with age under maturational influence is the number of figurative schemes (called S above) that can be stored while performing an operative scheme, what Case (1978, 1985) called children's short-term storage space (STSS). The size of this STSS was hypothesized to evolve during each stage from 0 to 3, limiting the complexity of the problems that can be analysed and solved. This hypothesis was tested at each developmental stage by designing tasks involving a series of identical operations and requiring the storage of pointers to each prior operation in such a way that the EPL increases at each step. For example, for testing STSS increase in infancy, a task was created in which infants were presented with an apparatus in which four pegs could be pulled to produce a chime sound. An experimenter first demonstrated how to produce these sounds, and pulled in immediate succession a number of pegs that varied from one to four, inviting infants to imitate. The infant's score was the maximum number of pegs he or she was able to pull on any trial. From the analysis outlined above, it was assumed that monitoring the experimenter's demonstration and imitating him required an operative scheme $OP_{sensorimotor} + S$ for each peg. Thus, the space for ringing three bells was assumed to be $OP_{sensorimotor} + 3S$, corresponding to the maximum capacity of infants able to assemble elaborated coordination at the substage 3 of the sensorimotor stage. In line with the predictions of the theory, the mean scores in infants aged 6, 10, and 15 months, assumed to pertain to substages 1, 2, and 3 respectively, were 1.3, 2.3, and 3.3 respectively, very close to the predicted scores of 1, 2, and 3.

The tasks used for assessing STSS in early childhood involved relational operations and consisted of a word span task, in which children were asked to repeat series of words in correct order, and an action span task. The apparatus for this latter task consisted of a box from which five different objects protruded. Each of these objects might be manipulated in two different ways, producing distinct outcomes (e.g. one of these objects was a small door that could either be opened, revealing a set of bright polka dots, or closed, revealing nothing). In both tasks, the children's span was the maximum number of words they were able to repeat or of actions they were able to reproduce in correct order. The corresponding tasks for the dimensional stage were the counting span and the CUCUI tasks. In the former, children were presented with a series of cards displaying sets of dots to be counted aloud, the number of cards increasing until the point is reached where they were unable to keep track of all the totals and to recall them in correct order. The CUCUI task involved spatial localization. Children were shown a clown figure with some body parts painted a bright colour and asked, after the figure had been removed and replaced with an exact replica with no colour, to point to the parts

28 The role of working memory in development

that were painted in the figure previously shown. For adolescents was designed a ratio span task that resembled the counting span task. The cards displayed green and yellow dots, children being asked to determine how many green dots there were for each yellow dot on each card.

For each of these three stages, four groups of children corresponding to the theoretical age ranges of the successive substages were tested. The theory predicts a recursive progression of STSS from 0 at the first substage 0 of consolidation to 3S at substage 3 of elaborated coordination, resulting in predicted working memory spans from 1 to 4. Observed mean spans fitted reasonably well the predictions (Table 2.1).

Explaining working memory development

Having observed the predicted increases in STSS, a central question became to identify what produces this increase. Although Case (1985) acknowledged that factors often invoked in the 1970s such as knowledge (Chi, 1976, 1978) or strategies (Belmont & Butterfield, 1971; Flavell, 1971) accounted for a substantial part of the age-related growth in short-term memory, he also claimed that these factors are not all the story, as the STSS increases described in the previous section were observed while obvious sources of strategies or chunking were controlled. Of course, an available option was provided by Pascual-Leone's hypothesis of a maturationally based increase in some total processing space (TPS). However, another possibility was to assume a decrease in the space required for executing the basic operation (noted OP above) that is characteristic of each stage. The two models are illustrated in Figure 2.2. Both models assume that working memory capacity can be flexibly allocated either to execute operations, which requires some operating space (OS), or to maintain the products of previous operations in short-term storage, which requires STSS. Thus, both models assume that

$$TPS = OS + STSS \qquad (2.1)$$

but the *TPS increase model* explains the STSS increase by some continuous growth in capacity while OS remains constant for a given stage, whereas the *OS decrease model* assumes that STSS increases because the space needed to execute the operations at a given stage decreases during this stage, while TPS remains constant from birth to adulthood. It does not come as a surprise that Case favoured the second term of the alternative as we have already evoked his dissatisfaction with Pascual-Leone's assumption of the unchanged capacity needed by a given scheme over the developmental period. As we have seen, Case concluded from the well-documented age-related increase in processing speed of several basic cognitive processes that the demand of cognitive operations decreases with age. From the postulate that the time needed to execute an operation is an index of its cognitive demand (with faster processes being less demanding), Case developed a series of studies to test the *OS decrease model*. All the experiments had the same rationale. If it is true that STSS

TABLE 2.1 Hypothesized short-term storage space (STSS) and mean spans in STSS measures reported by Case (1985) for the relational, dimension, and vectorial stages

Substage	Hypothesized STSS	Expected mean span	Relational stage (1.5–5 years) Word span	Dimensional stage (3.5–11 years) Counting span	Vectorial stage (9–15+ years) Ratio span
0	0	1	1.0 (1–1.5 years)	1.1 (3.5–5 years)	1.3 (9–11 years)
1	S	2	2.4 (1.5–2 years)	2.5 (5–7 years)	2.1 (11–13 years)
2	2S	3	3.1 (2–3.5 years)	3.3 (7–9 years)	— (13–15 years)
3	3S	4	4.0 (3.5–5 years)	3.8 (9–11 years)	4.0 (15+ years)

30 The role of working memory in development

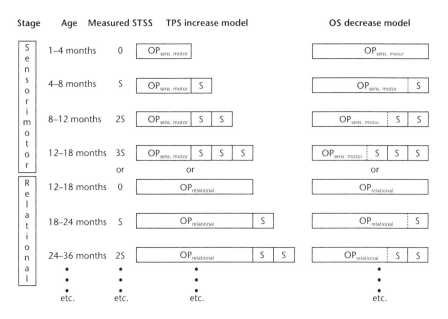

FIGURE 2.2 Schematic illustration of two hypotheses about the mechanism governing the developmental increase in short-term storage space (STSS) according to Pascual-Leone (1970) and Case (1985).

Source: R. Case (1985). *Intellectual development: Birth to adulthood*, pp. 352–353. New York, NY: Academic Press, adapted with permission.

Note
In Pascual-Leone's (1970) model the increase results from an increase in total processing space (TPS; TPS increase model, left panel); in Case's (1985) model it emerges from the decrease of the operating space (OS; OS increase model, right panel). Only the four substages of the sensorimotor stage and the three first substages of the relational stage are illustrated here.

increases because executing the operations characteristic of a given developmental stage consumes less and less working memory capacity with age, and assuming that the time needed to execute these operations is an index of the capacity they require, the size of STSS should be a direct function of processing speed.

This hypothesis was tested at three developmental levels: sensorimotor, relational, and dimensional stages. At the sensorimotor stage, STSS measure was provided by the peg-pulling task described above, while the operation the speed of which was measured was reaching, because reaching was the major operation involved in pulling pegs. Reaching speed was assessed independently from the peg-pulling task in 6, 10, 15, and 22-month-old infants who were shown objects in a box and encouraged to pick them up. As the *OS decrease model* predicts, STSS measures increased linearly with speed of reaching. The same method was applied for the relational and dimensional stages by Case, Kurland, and Goldberg (1982). Measures of STSS at the relational level was the word span already mentioned, while the operation was word repetition, the latency of which was measured in 3-, 4-, 5-, and 6-year-old children. For the dimensional stage, the counting span described above provided a measure of STSS in children from age 6 to 12, while operational efficiency was assessed through the maximum counting speed that each child was able to reach. Once more, a linear trend related speed of counting to counting span, demonstrating that STSS increases as processing time and supposedly OS decrease. We have already presented these studies in detail elsewhere (see Barrouillet & Camos, 2015, Chapter 2).

One of the strengths of Case et al.'s (1982) study, above and beyond providing empirical evidence for the trade-off between STSS and OS, was to lend support to the hypothesis that TPS remains constant through age. In a first study, adults were subjected to a word span and word repetition task as children from the relational stage were, but they had to perform these tasks with two types of nonsense syllables. The first type corresponded to close approximations to English and referred to as English Nonsense list (*loats, thaid, flim, brup, meeth, zarch, and dast*). The second type, referred to as Foreign Nonsense list, was more remote from English and involved some phonemes from other languages (*tsitk, lloach, chatz, llemph, pfluch, mfaffl, tkipf*). As expected, repetition times in adults were far longer for these two sets of nonsense syllables as they would have been for English words, and commensurate with the repetition times observed previously in young children. In line with the hypothesis of a constant TPS through age, when adults' mean spans with these nonsense syllables were plotted against repetition times, the point fell close to the children's regression line (Figure 2.3a). Concerning the dimensional stage, adult participants were taught a new counting language with which they performed the counting speed and counting span tasks. As expected, their counting speed was significantly decreased and fell close to 7-year-old children's performance. As predicted, their counting span was also reduced to the level of those children who achieve a comparable level of operational efficiency (Figure 2.3b). Overall, these results lent strong support to the hypothesis of a trade-off between STSS and OS, the former increasing as the latter decreases while TPS remains constant, as the *OS decrease model* assumes.

The sources of working memory development

The fact that adult performance in span tasks falls to the level of young children when differences in practice are eliminated could have led to the conclusion that practice is the underlying factor of increase in operational efficiency, OS decrease, and the corollary STSS increase. However, Case (1978, 1985) surmised that specific experience and practice should not be sufficient and that maturation probably plays a greater role. Training studies were used to establish this point. For example, first-graders received intensive training in speeded counting at a rate of 20 minutes per day during 3 months, resulting in children counting more than 5,000 arrays of dots (the equivalent of somewhere between 2.5 and 5 years of natural practice in counting, according to the author). Of course, counting speed in the experimental group increased, but rather moderately, never exceeding the level of second-graders

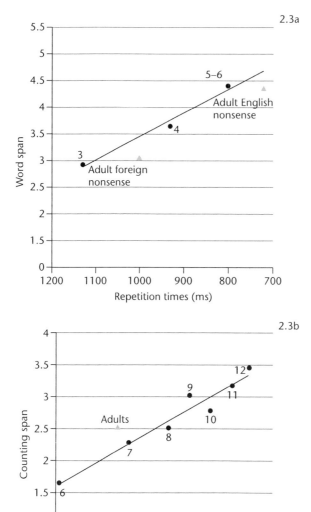

FIGURE 2.3 Relationship between repetition latencies and word span in children aged 3 to 6 (Figure 2.3a) and between counting speed and counting span in children aged 6 to 12 (Figure 2.3b) with linear regression lines

Source: Adapted from R. Case, D. M. Kurland, and J. Goldberg (1982). Operational efficiency and the growth of short-term memory span. *Journal of Experimental Child Psychology, 33*, pp. 394 and 398, with permission from Elsevier.

Note
Both panels display performance in adults when equated in processing efficiency with young children.

who did not receive any particular training, and still lagging far behind adult controls (about 300 ms vs. 200 ms per dot). Thus, Case (1985) suggested that maturation, and more precisely changes in the degree of neuronal myelinization, underpins OS decrease and the development of STSS. This would in the first place speed up linear neuronal transmission, but also decrease the amount of lateral transmission and diminish the amount of resulting interference. This process of myelinization was assumed to take place in cycles, successive waves of myelinization occurring in different neurological systems subserving different psychological functions. The idea here was that successively higher levels of cognitive operations that determine the four developmental stages would be controlled by successively higher systems in the brain, the degree of myelinization of a given system determining the maximum value of STSS that might be reached at this point in development.

Further developments

Case (1992; Case and Okamoto, 1996) subsequently extended his model by introducing the notion of central conceptual structures (CCSs). These CCSs were defined as internal networks of concepts and conceptual relations that permit children to think about a range of situations within a given domain at a new epistemic level by permitting the construction of the executive control structures we described above. According to Case, this notion of central conceptual structure is very close to the notion of domain-specific theory as described by Carey (1985). This theoretical move might be seen as an attempt to introduce domain-specificity in cognitive development, because the CCSs were presented as constituting the outcome of the innate core domains described by neo-nativist theories (Fodor, 1982; Gelman, 1990; Spelke, 1988) and organizing modular contents. Thus, the number of domains for which a CCS exists is necessarily limited, Case and Okamoto (1996) tentatively listing eight of them (number, logical analysis, language, space, social, motor, musical, interpersonal).

However, and more interestingly for our purpose, Case stressed that the structures themselves 'reflect a set of principles and constraints that are system-wide in their nature and that change with age in a predictable fashion' (Case & Okamoto, 1996, p. 5). Among the general set of developments that constrain these structures are changes in speed of processing or working memory, the growth in children's working memory capacity exerting a 'strong facilitating influence on the growth of their central conceptual structures' (Case & Okamoto, 1996, p. 205). Overall, the new theorizing was presented more as an expansion than a replacement of the previous theory, the later writings leaving unchanged what was previously said about the nature and underpinnings of working memory development.

Cognitive complexity and increase in capacity in Halford's theory

Halford (1993) shares with the other neo-Piagetian authors the idea that the notion of processing capacity can account for observations formerly attributed to stages.

However, his approach differs from other neo-Piagetian authors in a critical aspect that explains many of the characteristics of his model. One of the main tenets of Piaget's theory was the idea that development consists of the simultaneous and reciprocal construction of the subject, thought of as a structured set of schemes, and the object of knowledge, considered as a coherent set of defined attributes. The cognitivist revolution that we evoked in introducing this book, with its emphasis on problem solving and real time cognition, did not appear at a first glance incompatible with the 'subject' side of Piaget's theory, and explicit attempts to merge the cognitivist and Piagetian constructivist approaches were made by the Genevan school itself (e.g. Inhelder & Cellerier, 1992). Pascual-Leone's (1970), Chapman's (1987), or Case's (1985) theories can be seen as good examples of this endeavour. Within this conception, cognitive demand is a function of the number of schemes that must be simultaneously activated or of the number of embedded subgoals and related procedures that can be held in mind to solve the problem at hand. The demise of Piaget's constructivism came from the accumulating evidence that the hypothesis of cognitive operations structured in a logical way was untenable. However, it also resulted from a re-assessment of the other side of the constructivist project and the assumption that reality was progressively constructed in a dialectical exchange between a subject in development and a reality initially undifferentiated and perceived as chaotic. Far from being laboriously constructed, the basic concepts by which children organize and understand the world were assumed to be innate (Gelman, 1990; Spelke, 1988), evolving into naive theories (Carey, 1985; Carey, Zaitchik, & Bascandziev, 2015). Case's notion of central conceptual structure can be seen as an integration of the object or conceptual side of constructivism into his theory, the subtitle of his 1992 book *The mind's staircase* being *Exploring the conceptual underpinnings of children's thought and knowledge*. Halford (1993) explicitly focuses on this other side of the constructivist project, the conceptual side, his theory giving a central role to children's understanding, the concepts children understand having 'a strong influence on the strategies, skills, and competencies they can develop' (p. xi).[3] One of the main hypotheses of Halford's theory is that working memory capacity constrains the complexity of the concepts that children can represent and understand.

Conceptual complexity and development

Halford assumes that understanding a concept or a situation entails having a mental model of the structure of that concept or situation (Halford, 1982; Halford & Wilson, 1980). Mental model refers here to a type of representation hypothesized by Johnson-Laird (1983) and Gentner and Stevens (1983). A mental model is not necessarily accurate and can be even incomplete or approximate, but is in structural correspondence to its referent in such a way that it can generate predictions about the environment and guide action to solve problems. Thus, Halford (1993) suggests to consider cognitive representations as the mapping of an internal structure onto the structure of a segment of environment, establishing a structural correspondence that preserves the relevant relations. Based on seminal studies by Baillargeon (1986, 1987) about object permanence in infants, Halford assumes that representations are available in children at least from 4 months of age.

However, an infant's capacity to construct representations does not mean that representations do not evolve with age. Certain concepts require for their representation a more complex mapping than others as they involve a higher number of interconnected elements. This is what Halford (1993) calls *dimensionality* of concepts, which varies from one to four. One-dimensional concepts are defined as predicates with one argument or as unary relations (e.g. 'Fido is a dog', or 'This dress is blue'). For example, the type of representation needed to avoid the A–not-B error would be such a unary relation. Recall that the A–not-B error discovered by Piaget occurs when infants who have retrieved an object hidden by the experimenter at location A right in front of their eyes persist in searching for the object in this location even when they had watched the experimenter hiding it in a different location B, the error disappearing about the end of the first year. The avoidance of this error would be associated, according to Halford, to the capacity to maintain and update the binding between the object and its location, which is a unary relation (Andrews & Halford, 2011; Halford, Andrews, Phillips, & Wilson, 2013). Binary relations such as *larger than* (e.g. elephants are larger than flies) involve predicates with two arguments (e.g. the notion of larger involves a comparison between at least two things) and two-dimensional concepts. Predicates with three arguments or ternary relations correspond to three-dimensional concepts. Among these concepts are those acquired at the concrete operational stage in Piaget's theory such as transitivity or inclusion. Understanding transitivity requires the simultaneous consideration of three entities (e.g. a, b, and c in 'if a > b and b > c, then a > c'), while understanding that dogs are included within animals requires one to coordinate the relations between three classes, the animals, the subclass of dogs, and its complement. Arithmetic operations are also typical three-dimensional concepts that involve ordered triplets of numbers $(3,4 \rightarrow 7)$. Finally, four-dimensional concepts involve quaternary relations or predicates with four arguments. Compositions of binary operations such as $a(b + c) = d$ or proportions (2 is in the same ratio to 6 as 3 is to 9) are examples of four-dimensional concepts.

These four types of concept require four different levels of mapping that Halford (1993) defines as element, relational, system, and multiple-system mappings for concepts with one, two, three, and four dimensions respectively. This increasing complexity of mental models was subsequently theorized as a relational complexity, with the idea that not only the dimensions but also the relations that these dimensions entertain have to be represented for a genuine understanding (Halford, Wilson, & Phillips, 1998), cognitive development being characterized as 'the ability to construct mental models that involve more complex relations' (Andrews & Halford, 2011, p. 47). The four levels of complexity described above are attained at 1, 2, 5, and 11 years for the unary, binary, ternary, and quaternary relations respectively, these ages corresponding roughly to the preconceptual (i.e. the last three substages of the sensorimotor period), intuitive, concrete operational, and formal operational stages in Piaget's theory.

36 The role of working memory in development

The relational complexity theory has been tested in a variety of domains. For example, Andrews and Halford (2002) presented binary-relational and ternary-relational problems of transitive inference, hierarchical classification, class inclusion, cardinality, hypothesis testing, and relative clause sentence comprehension to children aged 3 to 8 years.[4] Not only relational complexity had a strong effect on transitive inference, as Andrews and Halford (1998) had already observed, but this was true for all the domains and there were substantial cross-task correlations, all tasks loading on a single factor of relational complexity. While even the younger children were able, as predicted by the theory, to solve binary-relational problems, ternary-relational problems were only mastered approximately from age 5 onward. The relational complexity factor accounted for 80 per cent of variance in fluid intelligence Gf (Culture Fair test, Cattell, 1950). Relational complexity analyses have been successfully applied to a range of other domains such as balance scale problems (Halford, Andrews, Dalton, Boag, & Zielinski, 2002), theory of mind (Andrews, Halford, Bunch, Bowden, & Jones, 2003), or deductive reasoning (Halford & Andrews, 2004), including tasks involving what is called hot cognition, such as the gambling task (Bunch, Andrews, & Halford, 2007). Overall, Andrews and Halford (2011) concluded that 'the Relational Complexity theory provides a viable alternative to normative logic as a criterion for cognitive development' (p. 64).

As other neo-Piagetian theories, Halford's theory assumes that the capacity to understand concepts of increasing complexity, or to solve problems involving an increased relational complexity, is of course due to acquisition of knowledge, but more importantly to an increase in cognitive capacity. Nonetheless, Halford develops an original conception of this capacity that departs from Pacual-Leone's or Case's theories.

Cognitive capacity

Halford (1993) developed an interesting reflexion about the notions of cognitive load, resources, and capacity, pointing out that a task can be difficult independently of cognitive load. Indeed, it can be made difficult by the high number of steps it involves, the lack of the required knowledge to solve it, the difficulty to frame it through the appropriate hypothesis (as in insight problems), or some extrinsic processing load reducing the clarity of the stimuli or task demands. Processing load, according to Halford (1993), must also be distinguished from short-term memory storage load 'because the information is not actively constraining decision making while it is stored' (p. 88). Instead, processing load is related to conceptual or relational complexity: the cognitive load of a task is assumed to depend on its intrinsic structural complexity, defined as the number of independent dimensions, or units of information, to be processed in parallel, these dimensions or units of information being similar to chunks.

The maximum number of dimensions individuals are able to take simultaneously into account was studied by Halford, Baker, McCredden, and Bain (2005) who asked adults to interpret graphically displayed statistical interactions. Understanding an interaction requires integrating the different independent variables into a single complex concept the dimension of which varies with the number of variables. Results revealed that adults were able to interpret, though with difficulty, four-way interactions, suggesting that a structure or concept defined on four variables or dimensions is at the limits of human processing capacity, whereas performance with five-way interactions were at chance level. This estimate of human capacity around four echoes the limit of mental storage capacity proposed by Cowan (2001). Using tasks in which children were asked to recognize correspondences between structures of varying complexity, Halford (1978; Halford & Wilson, 1980) found evidence that the number of dimensions that children can process in parallel reaches three at approximately 5 years and the adult level of four at approximately 11 years. It can be observed that these estimates match what could be expected from the developmental levels of relational complexity described above, lending support to the hypothesis that the maximum conceptual or relational complexity that children can reach is constrained by their cognitive capacity evolving from one to four chunks between the end of the first year and adulthood.

Capacity, short-term, and working memory spans

As we mentioned above, one of the originalities of Halford's conception of capacity is to distinguish it from the capacity of the short-term store, thus departing from a tradition that can be traced back to Miller (1956). Halford reports in his 1993 book that, initially, he found this idea attractive (Halford, 1982), until he performed working memory experiments that consistently failed to support the hypothesis of a trade-off between processing and storage at the basis of Case's model. We summarize below some of these studies.

Halford, Bain, and Maybery (1984) addressed the same question as Baddeley and Hitch (1974), wondering whether a concurrent memory load interferes with reasoning. For this purpose, they had adult participants solving arithmetic problems involving ternary or quaternary relations such as:

$(7[?]3)/4 = 1$ (ternary)

$(7[?]3)[?]4 = 1$ (quaternary)

in which the operation(s) that the question marks replaced had to be found while rehearsing aloud series of consonants at span -3 to span $+1$. The results revealed that memory load interacted with problem difficulty, but only when this memory load was at span or higher. The fact that there was no effect of infra-span memory loads on concurrent reasoning was interpreted as demonstrating that it is active processing of the memoranda through encoding or rehearsal (at supra-span levels) instead of pure storage that produced the interference with the reasoning task. In a subsequent study, the same authors observed that transitive reasoning interacted

38 The role of working memory in development

only with the encoding of a memory load, but not with its mere retention (Halford et al., 1984). Halford (1993) concluded from these findings and others (Klapp, Marshburn, & Lester, 1983) that the trade-off is between one process and another (e.g. encoding while reasoning), rather than between processing and storage.

The independence of processing and storage was further explored by Halford, Maybery, O'Hare, and Grant (1994) who tested the hypothesis that short-term memory is the workspace of higher cognitive processes and more precisely the Case's hypothesis of a trade-off between OS and STSS within a TPS of constant capacity through age. The rationale of their study was to present children with a preload, ask them to process an interpolated task varying in cognitive demand, and then to recall the preload. Two experiments involving numerical and transitive reasoning tasks failed to reveal the strong effect of cognitive load on memory performance predicted by the trade-off hypothesis.[5] A further experiment tested the hypothesis that spans increase with age due to a smaller OS demand in older children. Children aged 5, 9, and 12 were asked to maintain and recall preload lists of digits of increasing length while counting either zero, one, two, three, or four cards as those used in Case et al.'s (1982) counting span task. Of course, increasing the number of cards to be counted resulted in lower and lower recall performance, but contrary to the *OS decrease* model, the rate of loss of preload information as a function of cards counted was the same in each age group, whereas the *OS decrease* model would have predicted lower rate of loss in older children who need less operating space for performing the counting operation. Halford et al. (1994) concluded that their results cast doubt on the idea that short-term memory and working memory constitute a single system. Rather, they favoured Baddeley's (1986; Baddeley & Hitch, 1974) distinction between a short-term store specialized for processing phonological information (the phonological loop) and some processor 'that forms the workspace of higher cognitive processes' (Halford et al., 1994, p. 1341). Thus, age-related increases in short-term memory or working memory spans could not account for the growth of central processing capacity.

The distinction between span measures and central capacity in Halford's theorizing can be illustrated by Andrews, Birney, and Halford (2006). In three experiments, they observed that tasks assessing relational processing capacity were better predictors of the understanding of object-extracted relative clause sentences (e.g. It was the cook that the king sent the man to) than working memory span tasks such as the backward digit span or the well-known Daneman and Carpenter's (1980) reading span task. For example, among the relational processing capacity tasks is the Latin square task (Birney, Halford, & Andrews, 2006), in which participants have to determine which of four elements should fill a target cell in an incomplete 4×4 matrix so that the conditions of the Latin square are satisfied with only one of the four possible elements occurring in each row and column of the matrix (Figure 2.4).

In summary, contrary to Case who hypothesized that the total processing space remains unchanged, Halford (1993) assumes that processing capacity changes with age. Despite the fact that there is probably more than one capacity, he conjectures

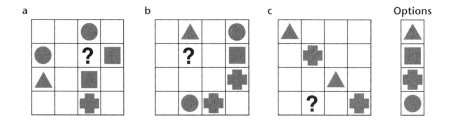

FIGURE 2.4 Illustration of three trials of the Latin square task

Source: Adapted from G. Andrews, D. Birney, and G. S. Halford (2006). Relational processing and working memory capacity in comprehension of relative clause sentences. *Memory and Cognition, 34*, p. 1334, with permission from Springer.

that there is probably a central general-purpose system operating on representations to reason and produce knowledge, the dimensionality of which increases with age from 1 to 4. It is this increase that is the main developmental factor.

Conclusion: working memory constraints and development in neo-Piagetian theories

In introducing this chapter, we stated that one of the main tenets of neo-Piagetian theories is that cognitive development depends at least in part on an age-related increase in working memory capacity (see also Morra et al., 2008). However, our rapid overview in these two first chapters of the role and nature of working memory in some of the main theories of this approach reveals a surprising, and somewhat disheartening, diversity. Conceptions differ not only on the maximum capacity that working memory reaches at its final developmental state, but also on the nature of its content, and consequently on the grain at which the information that working memory holds must be analysed, on the determinants of its development, and even on its main functions and its connexions with short-term memory.

The magical number four

We saw in Chapter 1 that when conjecturing the maximum size of working memory, Pascual-Leone quite naturally endorsed the widespread estimate of seven. Indeed, it was rather natural to assume that a working memory able to hold seven chunks of information, as Miller (1956) assumed, could activate the same number of schemes. Pascual-Leone distinguishes, within each scheme, a subpart consisting of a figural scheme that approximately corresponds to a chunk of information susceptible to trigger an action, rendering sound the hypothesis that a working memory able to hold seven chunks could activate seven schemes. However, subsequent neo-Piagetian theories abandoned the magical number seven for the magical number four, as did subsequent re-evaluations of verbal (Sperling, 1960) and visuo-spatial (Luck & Vogel, 1997) working memory. Illustrating this move, the executive

40 The role of working memory in development

control structures hypothesized by Case can hold a maximum of four goals and subgoals, while the number of independent dimensions that can be coordinated in Halford's theory is also four. This number, advocated by Cowan (2001; Chen & Cowan, 2009; Saults & Cowan, 2007) as the size of the focus of attention, has been claimed to be even smaller, and reduced to one (Garavan, 1998; McElree, 1998; Oberauer, 2002) or two (Oberauer & Bialkova, 2009). It becomes uneasy in these conditions to base a developmental theory of cognition and a quantified description of the cognitive system characterizing the final stage of development on some estimate of working memory capacity, which is assumed to determine the maximum complexity that these systems or structures could reach. This problem is made even more complex by the uncertainty about the nature of the units of cognition that this working memory is assumed to hold.

The grain of working memory

The strong influence of Piaget's theory during the previous century naturally led Pascual-Leone to assume that the units held in the mental space he hypothesized were schemes. However, from its very inception, this idea was fraught with problems. Miller (1956), though he favoured the notion of chunks, based his estimate of short-term capacity mainly in adult's digit and letter spans, and it could be argued that maintaining simple and overlearned units such as letters or digits has little to do with activating and coordinating schemes. We mentioned in Chapter 1 the difficulties encountered by Pascual-Leone in establishing how many schemes the different tasks he studied involved, a problem referred to as the *grain* of task analysis by Case (1985). It must be admitted that, despite the abandonment of the scheme as unit of behaviour, this problem has not yet been settled. Beyond their convergence on an estimate of four, it remains uncertain that the units favoured by Case (i.e. a number of stored goals and subgoals, possibly associated with the observables from which they were generated) can be compared to the conceptual dimensions advocated by Halford, or the chunks evoked by Cowan, even if remarkable attempts have been made in this direction (Halford et al., 2007). To take the example of Case's theorizing, is verifying that a child can hold three digits in mind while enumerating a collection of dots sufficient to infer his or her capacity to maintain the same number of subgoals in a task? And maybe more importantly, do all the subgoals, all the chunks, or all the independent dimensions require the same mental space, the same cognitive capacity, or the same amount of attention for their activation and maintenance? Moreover, as our review of neo-Piagetian theories made clear, uncertainties remain about what evolves with age.

Increase in capacity or in processing efficiency?

The seven schemes that adults would be able to simultaneously activate according to Pascual-Leone were assumed to be indifferently figurative or operative in nature, the figurative schemes being in charge of constructing representations of the situation, whereas the operative schemes aim at operating on these representations. Thus, the mental space in Pascual-Leone's theory was indifferently devoted to either store or process information. Accordingly, the increase in M space hypothesized by Pascual-Leone can be understood as a global increase of what Case refers to as the Total Processing Space. However, the undeniable increase in processing efficiency with age means that a same set of schemes needed to complete a given task cannot be considered as involving the same cognitive demand in children of different ages, hence the solution adopted by Case of a Total Processing Space remaining constant through age whereas OS decreases in older children. It is worth noting that any age-related increase in processing efficiency does not mean in itself that some global capacity does not increase at the same time. Indeed, even in Case's theory, each developmental stage has a maximum STSS of four, but the nature of the items held in working memory evolves with age, becoming more abstract and complex. Another way to escape the conundrum of the complex relations between processing efficiency and global capacity is to assume that there is no trade-off between processing and storage, as Halford (1993) does, and that working memory must be understood as a kind of mental space for constructing representations, its capacity being defined by the number of independent dimensions these representations can coordinate. Once more, though appealing, this solution faces the same problem of the alleged invariance with age of the cognitive demand resulting from the representation of a given dimension. We will see in the remainder of this book that, as Cowan (2015) stressed, the question of the factors of working memory development is probably among the more complex of developmental psychology.

Is working memory a memory?

Finally, the real nature of working memory itself remains uncertain. The M space theorized by Pascual-Leone, able to hold figurative and operative schemes, can be indifferently described as a short-term memory (it has the same capacity) or as some central executive as described by Baddeley (1986) if it is assumed that M space coordinates and controls processing. The same option seems to be favoured by Case. In both theories, a single mental space hosts the different components hypothesized by Baddeley (1986), the slave systems devoted to storage as well as the central executive. Things become more complex with Halford's approach. The central general-purpose system he hypothesizes resembles the focus of attention described by Cowan (2005), at least in its maximum capacity. However, this general-purpose system is explicitly compared by Halford et al. (1994) with a central executive, whereas in Cowan's approach, the focus of attention and the central executive are two different constructs. The central capacity hypothesized by Halford seems to be closer to the controlled attention in Engle's (2002) conception of working memory. Thus, contrary to Pascual-Leone's and Case's views, the general-purpose system described by Halford is not a memory, and its capacity cannot be properly estimated by short-term memory spans. However, and contrary to Engle's theorizing, even working memory spans such as the reading or the counting span are claimed

42 The role of working memory in development

to be inappropriate to measure relational processing capacity. Thus, although neo-Piagetian theoreticians agree that goal-directed and controlled cognition takes place in some mental space or central system, the nature and function of this space or system remains a debated issue.

Coda

At a first sight, it probably seemed rather straightforward to overcome the inadequacies of Piaget's theory of equilibration when equipped with the theoretical toolbox of cognitivism and information processing approach. This theoretical framework seemed especially appropriate to give body to the intuition shared by all neo-Piagetian theoreticians that brain maturation results in the increase of some mental capacity or mental space for holding and processing relevant information. This endeavour proved more difficult than expected when the structure and function of this central system had to be made explicit, generating a proliferation of divergent and often contradictory theoretical proposals. As the remainder of this book will illustrate, the problems encountered by neo-Piagetian theoreticians have not yet been solved. Nonetheless, the hypothesis that working memory growth, whatever the precise meaning that authors give to this concept, underpins developmental changes has been endorsed in a variety of areas. The next chapter illustrates this approach in a some of these domains.

Notes

1 A good illustration of this focusing on processes is the book edited by Siegler (1978) entitled *Children's thinking: What develops?*
2 Note that the correspondence is not perfect because children using Rule III in Siegler's (1976) model are guessing when differences in weight on the one hand and distance on the other lead to opposite predictions.
3 We are grateful to Bob Siegler for having suggested to us during an informal discussion in March 2015 the existence of two distinct Piagetian legacies, one revolving around problem solving and real time cognition, the other concerning world construction and conceptual development.
4 For example, with a display containing four green and three yellow circles, a binary-relational problem for inclusion consists of comparing the two subclasses ('Are there more green or more yellow things?'), whereas a ternary-relational problem requires comparing the superordinate class with the major subclass ('Are there more circles than green things?'). For transitive inferences, ternary-relational problem requires the integration of two premises (e.g. inferring *green* > *blue* from *red* > *blue* and *green* > *red*), while a binary-relational problem requires consideration of a single premise relation (e.g. finding what comes after *red* from *blue* > *purple*, *red* > *blue*, *yellow* > *green*, and *green* > *red*). For sentence comprehension, binary- and ternary-relational problems involved understanding two-role object relative (*Sally saw the gorilla that the zebra kicked*) and three-role object relative sentences (*The duck that the monkey touched sat*), respectively.
5 The effect of processing difficulty was actually significant in Experiment 1, but deemed as 'small'.

3

WORKING MEMORY IN DOMAIN-SPECIFIC DEVELOPMENTAL THEORIES

The difficulties encountered by universal theories of cognitive development such as Piaget's often led modern developmental psychologists, with the notable exception of neo-Piagetian theorists, to abandon the aim of constructing general theories of development for proposing and testing local models for the development in specific domains. As we noted in the previous chapter, one of the first signals for this tendency was the book edited by Robert Siegler in 1978 entitled *Children's thinking: What develops?* A strong assumption of the information processing approach is the simplicity hypothesis put forward initially by Simon (1969), who assumed that thinking human beings, viewed as behaving systems, are quite simple. According to this hypothesis, their adaptive behaviour would mainly reflect characteristics of the outer environment, revealing 'only a few limiting properties of the inner environment of the physiological machinery that enables a person to think' (Simon, 1969, p. 53). Memory limitations were among these few limitations that attracted attention in explaining children's failures in Piagetian tasks (e.g. Trabasso, 1975a), Brainerd (1983, p. 168), assuming that 'cognitive development can, in fact, be reduced to memory development', adding that 'the development of memory is the childhood of cognition; the development of cognition is the adulthood of memory'.

In this chapter, we review some of these local models in which working memory plays a pivotal role in explaining development, from reasoning to problem solving, concept formation or language. These examples illustrate how the simplicity hypothesis that governed, at least implicitly, the first and more modern attempts to assimilate cognitive development with working memory development is in fact insufficient for fully understanding development, even in specific and restricted domains.

44 The role of working memory in development

Probability judgements: an attempt to reduce cognitive development to working memory development

One of the main aims of Piaget's work was to provide evidence that human rationality is a progressive construction from an initial state of egocentrism characterized by the lack of logical competence, the first forms of logical thinking emerging around the age 7 only through the construction of new structures of cognitive operations. Contrary to this hypothesis of structural discontinuity, the information processing approach of cognition views cognitive development as essentially continuous and qualitatively similar to the adult model. Development is seen within this context as resulting from the continuous increase in efficiency of a system that codes information from the environment, stores this information for immediate use or subsequent retrieval, and transforms this information to reach solutions for the problem at hand. What was considered by Piaget as a lack of logical competence is, in this view, the consequence of the limitations of children's short-term or working memory.

This view was perfectly illustrated by Brainerd (1983) who made explicit, in a chapter entitled 'Working-memory systems and cognitive development', the aim to reduce cognitive development to the development of working memory. He stated that 'the objective of any working-memory analysis is to explain all the age-related variation in performance on the target tasks, at least within permissible statistical error' (p. 195). The task studied by Brainerd (1981, 1983) to illustrate the role of working memory in cognitive development was inspired by the studies introduced by Piaget about probability judgements (Piaget & Inhelder, 1951). In the Piagetian task, children were asked to count and place in an opaque container a certain number of tokens of different colours (e.g. eight red and three blue tokens). Then, the experimenter randomized the content of the container by vigorously shaking it. Children were asked to predict the colour of tokens successively drawn at random from the container by the experimenter, these draws being made with or without replacement. In the former case, the relative frequencies of colours in the container remain unchanged over the successive samples, and the correct response is always to predict the colour of the larger set (i.e. red), despite the fallacious insight leading to assume that previous samples have an impact on forthcoming results. In the latter case, without replacement, the successive draws modify the relative frequencies of colours in the container, something critical if children are informed of the result of each draw.

Three main findings arose from Piaget and Inhelder's (1951) study. First, before age 7 or 8, children rarely base their predictions on the relative frequencies of the colours and tend to respond at random. Second, during the concrete operational stage (i.e. between 7 or 8 and 11 or 12), children base on these frequencies their responses to the first, but not to the subsequent trials in the sequence. Finally, it is only when reaching the formal operational stage (after age 12) that children and adolescents base all their predictions on the frequencies that governed the filling of the container. Subsequent studies tended to confirm these conclusions (Pire, 1958).

It is often assumed that empirical findings contradicted the first Piagetian observation and that young children are often correct in the first trial (Brainerd, 1981), a claim that has become frequent in the modern literature (Girotto, 2014). Actually, Brainerd (1981) observed 66 per cent of correct responses in 5;5-year-old children in the first trial of a task inspired by Piaget and Inhelder, while Girotto and Gonzalez (2008) report 61 per cent of correct decisions in children of the same age (66 per cent at 6;4 years). It is worth noting that, when corrected for guessing, these rates barely exceed 30 per cent at best, and do not seem to be at odds with Piaget's assumption that young children rarely base their responses on the relative frequencies of the colours. From the developmental tradition to which Piaget pertained in which a capacity is attributed to a given age when a large majority of children exhibit it, Girotto and Gonzalez's claim that children, from the age of 5, are able to assess prior probability is overstated.[1]

The research strategy used by Brainerd (1981, 1983) was to introduce in a task inspired by Piaget a sequence of experimental manipulations, each of them designed to isolate the role of one or more working memory factors. In these tasks, the tokens introduced in the opaque container bore pictures of familiar animals (horses, birds, rabbits, etc.). Depending on experiments, there were either two types of animals with frequencies of 7 and 3 for the High and the Low class, respectively, or three types of animals with frequencies of 8, 5, and 2 for the High, the Medium, and the Low class respectively. Each experiment involved five problems. Children were asked to deposit the appropriate numbers of animals in the container, and to predict the result of a sequence of five successive one-element draws.

A first experiment with two types of animals in each problem and no replacement or feedback established that, after the first trial in which they made 66 per cent of correct predictions, 5-year-old children adopted on the four following trials of each problem a simple alternation rule, predicting on trial $n + 1$ the class they had not selected on trial n. This neglect of the relative frequencies was not due to a failure in encoding or maintenance. Indeed, even when frequencies were made available by placing in front of the container the same numbers of tokens that were deposited inside, performance did not improve. This suggested that children's difficulties were due to a retrieval failure as they do not use the appropriate retrieval cues, the salient previous response interfering with the relevant information. The retrieval failure hypothesis was corroborated by an experiment in which children were given feedbacks in such a way that the most recently encoded information was this feedback and not the response to the preceding draw. Under this procedure, the response alternation disappeared, a strong tendency appearing for a stimulus perseveration bias; children predicted on trial $n + 1$ the same outcome that occurred on trial n.

The fact that children use the most frequently encoded information (i.e. their last response, or the feedback) led to the prediction that the introduction of probes for frequency information before each prediction should greatly increase performance, provided that children have correctly stored frequencies. Consequently, in a further experiment, before each prediction, children were asked questions such as

46 The role of working memory in development

'Did we have more horses or more rabbits when we started?' or 'Do you think that there are more horses or more rabbits in here now?'. Children aged 5;8 years answered correctly 89 per cent of the probes on Trial 1 and 86 per cent on the subsequent trials, with 94 and 86 per cent of correct predictions, respectively. Brainerd (1983) concluded from these findings that 'the principal locus of working memory failures in these children is a tendency to use the most recently encoded information in short-term memory as a basis for retrieval' (p. 208).

A second series of experiments tested the hypothesis that age improvements in probability judgements should primarily result from an increased reliance on frequency-based retrieval cues. For example, when presented with three-class problems, although 9-year-old children still exhibited a tendency to alternate responses, they systematically favoured the larger class between those that they did not select in the previous trial, indicating that they process frequency information, something that was not observed in 5-year-old children. In the same way, memory for irrelevant stimulus information (e.g. the outcome of a recent draw from another container) was better in third-graders than kindergartners. Finally, Brainerd replicated in third-graders aged 8;9 years the frequency probe study in which children were asked to recall which was the larger class before each prediction. While kindergartners correctly answered 89 per cent of the frequency probes on Trial 1 and 86 per cent on further trials, these rates increased to 99 and 96 per cent, respectively, in third-graders.

Brainerd concluded from these two series of experiments that the key factor in the development of probability judgements is the development of retrieval, resulting from age-related changes in the capacity of working memory rather than in knowledge about the pertinence of frequency information or in the efficiency in processing this information.

Working memory in reasoning development

The hypothesis that cognitive development can, in fact, be reduced to memory development did not only inspire Brainerd's (1981, 1983) work on probability judgements. It also motivated Bryant and Trabasso (1971) to reassess what was at this time a received conclusion, namely that young children are unable to perform transitive inferences before having reached the concrete operational stage at about 7 years of age (Piaget, 1937/1954).

Transitive inferences and working memory limitations

A transitive inference is an instance of relational reasoning which occurs when premises of the form $A\,r\,B$ and $B\,r\,C$ are coordinated to reach the conclusion $A\,r\,C$ in which r stands for a relation (Wright, 2001, 2012). For example, if rod A is taller than rod B ($A > B$), and rod B is taller than rod C ($B > C$), it can be concluded without further empirical test that A is taller than C ($A > C$). This form of reasoning governs a variety of activities from the understanding of measurement (Castle &

Needham, 2007) to inferences from class inclusion relations (Barrouillet, 1996; Favrel & Barrouillet, 2000) or risk taking in decision making (Reyna & Farley, 2006). Most of the interest of psychologists for transitive inference comes from the fact that Piaget claimed that this form of reasoning was beyond the capacities of young children at the pre-operational stage. In a well-known and highly commented study, Bryant and Trabasso (1971) argued that Piaget's claim about a lack of logical competence in young children was unjustified, their failure to produce transitive inferences resulting from their incapacity to remember the to-be-coordinated premises. Bryant and Trabasso provided evidence of young children's inferential capacity by first ensuring the memorization of the differences in length between five coloured wooden rods (A > B, B > C, C > D, D > E) through training. In a first training phase, these adjacent pairs were learned in order from the tallest to the smallest or vice versa to a criterion of eight out of ten successful choices. In a second training phase, the same pairs were presented in random order. At test, children were asked what was the taller or shorter rod in the ten possible pairs of colours. Two experiments revealed that when the premises (i.e. the pairs from AB to DE) were correctly memorized, young children including 4-year-olds were able to correctly respond to the inferential pairs AD and CE, and even to the critical pair BD that does not contain any extreme term, each rod of this pair having been the larger and the smaller in the initially learned comparisons (but see Boysson-Bardies & O'Regan, 1973, for a discussion of this assumption). The authors concluded from these findings that young children can make genuine transitive inferences, although not perfectly because the critical BD pair elicited lower performance than the other pairs. Trabasso (1975a) reviewed 29 conditions in various experiments based on the paradigm introduced by Bryant and Trabasso, establishing that the correlation between the performance on the premises BC and CD on the one hand, and the inference test BD on the other was highly significant ($r = .80$), clearly indicating that the ability to make inferences is more a matter of memory for the premises than logical competence per se.

Subsequent studies (Luktus & Trabasso, 1974; Riley & Trabasso, 1974; Trabasso, Riley, & Wilson, 1975) established that children, like adults, store a linear ordering of the terms instead of separated, ordered pairs, as testified by the fact that response times are faster for pairs requiring more inferential steps, something that is only possible if participants read out responses from a linearly ordered and spatialized representation in which more distant terms are easier to discriminate and to order. Moreover, the stability of the slope of the relation between number of inferential steps and response times between age 6 and adulthood suggested that the internal representations of the linear order were the same across age groups as well as in mentally retarded adolescents (Trabasso, 1975a).

It is worth noting that, beyond the debate about the existence of logical capacities in young children, Riley and Trabasso (1974) themselves noted that if something like reading an ordered representation underpins performance in the Bryant and Trabasso procedure, then this procedure is irrelevant as far as Piaget's theory and the existence of a logical inferential capacity are concerned, since this procedure

48 The role of working memory in development

does not measure operational transitivity. Indeed, constructing a spatially ordered array of the terms through associative learning of pairs orderly presented at training (i.e. beginning by AB, then presenting BC, and so on) and scanning this representation at test does not require operational transitivity in Piaget's terms, even if Riley and Trabasso (1974) assumed that some notion of transitivity is needed for constructing the ordinal scale in the first place.[2] More important for our purpose is the fact that Trabasso (1975b, p. 336) assumed that the processes involved in constructing and reading the spatialized representation like encoding, representing, ordering, listing, scanning, and retrieving are 'part of what we mean by memory as a general information-processing system'. Accordingly, Trabasso (1975b) reviewed several studies demonstrating that inferential responding was related to memory of the premises, concluding that 'holding of the information in working memory via symbols is a critical limitation for the younger child' (Trabasso, 1975b, 362), a conclusion extended to adults by Trabasso (1977).

Although the conclusions of Bryant and Trabasso (1971) have been largely endorsed and the extensive-training paradigm they introduced became dominant in the field, further studies and analyses cast doubt on the possibility of reducing the development of transitive reasoning to a mere problem of memory. The in-depth review of the literature conducted by Wright (2012) clearly shows that inferential capacities in 4-year-old children seem limited to the extensive-training paradigm in which premise pairs are orderly presented. Although Pears and Bryant (1990) claimed having observed 4-year-olds to be logical in a paradigm that did not involve training, Markovits, Dumas, and Malfait (1995, see also Wright, Robertson, & Hadfield, 2011) demonstrated that young children did not perform above chance on inferential pairs in Pears and Bryant's task when non-transitive strategies such as categorical labelling and absolute cued solutions were made unavailable. In fact, the three-term problem introduced by Piaget (i.e. concluding $A\,r\,C$ from $A\,r\,B$ and $B\,r\,C$ in a non-training procedure) proved to be never solved by young children beyond age 7 or 8, even with everyday material (Markovits & Dumas, 1999) or when memory for premises was ensured (Wright & Dowker, 2002; see also Wright, 2006). Moreover, transitive responding using the extensive-training paradigm has been observed in non-humans ranging from monkeys (McGonigle & Chalmers, 1992) to pigeons (Couvillon & Bitterman, 1986; von Fersen, Wynne, Delius, & Staddon, 1991; but see Markovits & Dumas, 1992) and even baby chicks (Daisley et al., 2009). Moreover, it has been established that transitive responding in this paradigm is accompanied by hippocampal activations in both humans and non-humans (Greene, Spellman, Dusek, Eichenbaum, & Levy, 2001; Hanlon et al., 2011), suggesting the involvement of long-term rather than working memory. By contrast, the three-term task without training activates the prefrontal cortex (Goel, Makale, & Grafman, 2004), suggesting the involvement of working memory for integrating premises. From these findings, Wright (2012) proposes a dual-process theory of transitive reasoning with an intuitive, unconscious/automatic mode for reaching transitive conclusions from heavily memorized information (e.g. those that young children acquire in the extensive-training paradigm), and an analytic mode for new and novel situations like in the three-term non-training paradigm. The former would not rely much on working memory whereas the latter does, especially for premise integration (Andrews & Halford, 1998; Halford et al., 1984).

In summary, despite initial claims, the possibility of reducing the development of transitive reasoning to the development of memory remains uncertain. Of course, what is considered by certain authors (Markovits & Dumas, 1999; Wright, 2012) as a genuine logical transitive responding requires integrative processes relying on working memory, and it could be assumed that the age at which this responding emerges (i.e. 7 or 8) coincides with an increase in working memory capacity allowing for this integration, as suggested by Halford, Wilson, and Phillips (1998, 2010). However, such an account differs strongly from the seminal Bryant and Trabasso's (1971) intuition. These authors surmised that young children fail to solve the three-term Piagetian problem simply because they do not correctly remember the premise pairs, their integration being implicitly considered as unproblematic. This account refers to working memory limitations in terms of the capacity and efficiency of a short-term storage device to hold premises. The explanation provided by the analysis of the relational complexity of the integrative process in Halford et al.'s (1998, 2010) approach refers to a working memory capacity in terms of number of entities that can be related in a unified mental model. This latter conception goes beyond 'holding of the information in working memory' as Trabasso (1975b) assumed and is closer to concepts like the capacity for binding elements (Oberauer, 2002) in a focus of attention (Cowan, 2005) rather than some short-term storage space for maintaining premises. The main difference is that, contrary to Bryant and Trabasso's endeavour, the intrinsic complexity of the three-term transitive reasoning task cannot be reduced and developmental differences abolished by a perfect memorization of the premises. If Wright (2012) is correct, contrary to what Bryant and Trabasso (1971) claimed, young children cannot make transitive inferences, even when precautions are taken to prevent deficits of memory from being confused with inferential deficits. If inferential capacities depend on memory, it is another sort of memory than a mere short-term repository.

The development of conditional reasoning and working memory

Along with transitive inferences, conditional reasoning permitted by the connective *If* is especially important for human thinking as it expresses hypothetical thinking that permits humans to imagine and analyse non-existing but possible states of the world (Evans & Over, 2004). As such, it is involved in scientific hypothesis testing (Kuhn, Amsel, & O'Loughlin, 1988), in the development of causal learning (Gopnik et al., 2004; Kushnir & Gopnik, 2007), and also in understanding of social rules and conventions (Harris & Nuñez, 1996; Light, Blaye, Gilly, & Girotto, 1989).

Traditional theories suggested that the human mind is endowed with inferential rules constituting a mental logic, these rules being automatically triggered by the

50 The role of working memory in development

syntactic structure of the information at hand (Braine, 1990; Braine & O'Brien, 1991; Rips, 1994). For example, one of these rules for *If* would correspond to *Modus Ponens*: When two propositions with a syntactic form *if p then q* and *p* are available, a mental rule would be triggered, delivering a conclusion of the form *q*. Importantly, most of the rules hypothesized by these mental logic theories were assumed to be universal, innate, and consequently available early in childhood. The forms of reasoning appearing later in development were considered as constituting a set of secondary (as opposed to primary) skills, which would not consequently be part of the mental logic (Braine, 1990). As such, and contrary to Piaget's theory with which they have often been erroneously assimilated, the mental logic theories offered little room for a development of reasoning capacities, and the triggering of the rules being automatic would not involve working memory.

Things are different with alternative accounts such as the mental model theory proposed by Johnson-Laird and Byrne (1991, 2002; Johnson-Laird, Byrne, & Schaeken, 1992). This theory assumes that individuals reason by constructing and manipulating mental models of the possible state of affairs to which the available premises refer. For example, understanding the sentence *There is an orange or a pear* would lead to the construction of a complex representation involving a model for each of the possible worlds when the sentence is true, that is a first model representing the occurrence of an orange with no pear, a second model representing the occurrence of a pear with no orange, and a third model representing the co-occurrence of both fruits if the disjunction is interpreted in an inclusive way. As far as conditional statements are concerned, the theory predicts that a sentence of the form *if p then q* would lead to a mental model of the form

$$p \quad q$$

$$\ldots$$

in which the first line refers to the possibility in which the propositions p and q are verified, the second line referring to an implicit model, a mental footnote indicating that there are other possibilities. These other possibilities could be made explicit by a fleshing-out process adding alternative cases when p is false, resulting in the following set of models

$$p \quad q$$

$$\neg p \quad \neg q$$

$$\neg p \quad q$$

in which the $\neg$ sign corresponds to a mental tag for negation. For example, the conditional *If the animal is a dog, then it has four legs* is compatible with dogs having four legs, non-dogs that don't have four legs (i.e. the $\neg p \quad \neg q$ case, for example, snakes), but also non-dogs that nonetheless have four legs (i.e. the $\neg p$ q case, for example, cows).

What is interesting for our purpose is that mental models are not retrieved from long-term memory, but are transient representations held in working memory in such a way that working memory load increases with the number of different models that must be held (Johnson-Laird & Byrne, 1991; 2002). For example, the initial representation containing only the p q model is assumed to involve a lower working memory load than the completely fleshed-out three-model representation of the conditional. Moreover, the fleshing-out process itself is assumed to be demanding. Barrouillet and Lecas (1998; see also Markovits & Barrouillet, 2002) derived from these assumptions a model for the development of conditional understanding and reasoning, assuming that the complexity of the representation children and adolescents are able to construct and maintain should evolve with the development of working memory capacity. Namely, they hypothesized that a first level of understanding of *If … then …* sentences would correspond to the construction of a single model corresponding to the explicit part of the initial model described above that represents the co-occurrence p q. Such a representation would lead to a conjunctive interpretation of the conditional. A second level would result from the addition of a second model of the form $\neg p$ $\neg q$ leading to a representation Barrouillet and Lecas (1998) called 'complete' as it establishes a one-to-one correspondence between the values of p on the one hand and those of q on the other:

$$p \quad q$$

$$\neg p \quad \neg q$$

Such a representation supports a biconditional interpretation of *If … then …* in which q results from p and $\neg q$ from $\neg p$. Finally, the construction of the three-model representation described above would be possible, resulting in what is called a conditional interpretation of *If*. The prediction issuing from the hypothesis of a developmental increase in working memory capacity was therefore an age-related evolution from a conjunctive to a biconditional and finally a conditional interpretation. This prediction was verified in several studies using a variety of tasks such as the identification of cases violating a conditional rule, the production of the case compatible with the rule, the production and verification of inferences, the judgement of truth-value of conditional sentences from available evidence (Barrouillet, Gauffroy, & Lecas, 2008; Barrouillet, Grosset, & Lecas, 2000; Barrouillet & Lecas, 1998, 2002; Barrouillet, Markovits, & Quinn, 2001; Gauffroy & Barrouillet, 2009, 2014; Lecas & Barrouillet, 1999), and even the evaluation of the probability of conditional sentences to be true or false (Barrouillet & Gauffroy, 2015). Usually, for conditional sentences involving unfamiliar relations between the propositions p and q, school-aged children mainly exhibit a conjunctive interpretation, whereas young adolescents predominantly adopt a biconditional reading whereas older adolescents and adults reach a conditional understanding. The semantic nature of the propositions

52 The role of working memory in development

embedded in the sentences to be processed as well as the context of their enunciation can affect interpretation (Barrouillet & Lecas, 1998, 2002), variations in task difficulty can delay the transition between the successive developmental levels (Gauffroy & Barrouillet, 2011), but their order of appearance remains immutable. Importantly, Barrouillet and Lecas (1999) verified that working memory capacity is a better predictor than age of the level at which children and adolescents understand conditionals. This relationship was explained by assuming that mental models for conditionals take the form of the relational schemas described in Halford's theory, the complexity of these schemas increasing with the number of elements to be bound together (Markovits & Barrouillet, 2002). Thus, working memory would exert the same constrains on conditional and transitive reasoning by limiting the complexity of the mental models that can be constructed.

It is worth noting that the developmental trend we just described only concerns conditional sentences with unfamiliar relations between p and q, for example 'If the piece is a square, then it is red', for which there exists no relevant knowledge that could be retrieved from long-term memory. Things are different with familiar relations, and it has been shown that even young children aged 6 or 7 correctly reason from categorical premises (Markovits, 2000; Markovits et al., 1996; Markovits & Thompson, 2008). When given premises such as 'If an animal is a dog, then it has four legs' and 'An animal has four legs', they correctly conclude that there is no certain conclusion (cows have four legs too), whereas even adults who are given the same problem with abstract content (e.g. 'If the piece is a square, then it is red' and 'The piece is red') often erroneously conclude to the truth of the antecedent (i.e. the piece is a square). These correct responses of uncertainty in young children require the retrieval from long-term memory of alternative antecedents of the form $\neg p \quad q$ (non-dog animals with four legs) that are, in Barrouillet and Lecas' (1998) theory, only accessible at the latest stage of development, that is the three-model conditional interpretation. Interestingly, correctly reasoning from familiar causal premises of the form *If cause P, then effect Q* (e.g. 'If a rock is thrown at a window, the window will break') is a latest achievement (Janveau-Brennan & Markovits, 1999). Markovits (2013) suggests that this is because it is more difficult to retrieve alternative antecedents for effects, which requires in our example to construct the ad hoc category (Barsalou, 1983) of those things that can break a window, than to access in long-term memory the category of four-legged animals. Of course, it is even more difficult to evoke, instead of retrieve, alternative antecedents when confronted with abstract conditionals for which no knowledge base is available (Markovits & Lortie-Forgues, 2011). According to Markovits (2013), the representational redescription model of Karmiloff-Smith (1995) could provide an explanation of how children and adolescents move from reasoning with familiar content to abstract reasoning through the construction of a developmental sequence of increasingly abstract deductive reasoning processes. This development would culminate with the capacity to evoke all the possibilities compatible with an abstract conditional for which there is no available knowledge stored in long-term memory (e.g. spontaneously imagining that a red triangle is compatible with the rule 'If the piece is a square, then it is red').

The studies by Barrouillet and colleagues we evoked above showed that working memory capacities strongly constrain the output of the most abstract reasoning schemas needed to understand unfamiliar conditionals. However, working memory development seems to be only a part of the story and complex processes are probably involved in the transitions that lead children from concrete to abstract conditional reasoning. Thus, as we concluded from the studies about transitive reasoning, the development of conditional reasoning resists the simplicity hypothesis and cannot be accounted for by the development of memory alone, even if working memory is a factor of this development.

Can working memory development explain cognitive development?

The previous sections of this chapter reviewed some attempts in the domain of reasoning and judgement to corroborate Brainerd's (1983) assertion that cognitive development can be reduced to memory development. As Brainerd and Reyna (1993) noted, memory has long been regarded as the most important of the elementary processes that could underlie the acquisition of reasoning abilities, giving body to Simon's (1969) simplicity hypothesis in one of the most complex achievements of human cognition. Trabasso's studies on transitive inferences as well as Brainerd's investigations on probability judgements seemed to corroborate a view that has, according to Brainerd and Reyna, 'the aura of common sense and, to many, self-evidence', which is that the retention of relevant information is a necessary and possibly sufficient precondition for successful reasoning (Brainerd & Reyna, 1993, p. 43). According to this memory-enables-reasoning hypothesis, limitations in working memory would place insurmountable constraints on reasoning that can only be alleviated by working memory development. However, in most of the reasoning tasks that have been considered as benchmarks for cognitive development, such as transitive inference, probability judgements, conservations, class inclusion, or story inference, empirical evidence contradicts the memory-enables-reasoning hypothesis and points towards a reasoning–memory independence.

The first evidence for this counterintuitive finding was provided by Brainerd and Kingma (1984) who used a probe paradigm along with the standard procedure for studying transitive inference. After having been presented with the premises $A > B$ and $B > C$ and asked to answer the transitivity question 'Which is longer, A or C?', children's memory for the premises was assessed using probe-recognition tests 'Which is longer A or B?', 'Which is longer B or C?'. Brainerd and Kingma tested the reasoning–memory dependence hypothesis in the following way. If $P(T)$ and $P(M)$ are the probabilities of correct responses to transitivity and probe tests respectively, the dependency hypothesis predicts that the conditional probability $P(T/M)$ of correctly responding to transitivity tests when correctly responding to memory tests should be higher than the unconditional probability $P(T)$. In other words, the probability of correct reasoning increases when memory for premises is perfect. In the same way, the conditional probability of remembering the premises

54 The role of working memory in development

when correctly responding to transitivity tests P(M/T) should be higher than the unconditional probability of remembering the premises P(M). Contrary to these predictions, there was no difference between conditional and unconditional probabilities in kindergartners (aged 5;8 years) and second-graders (aged 7;10 years), a finding that was replicated even when memory for the premises was tested before, and not after, the transitivity tests were administered. The fact that children's reasoning performance was stochastically independent of their memory for the premises was also found when reanalysing data from other studies on transitive inference (Halford & Galloway, 1977; Russell, 1981). The stochastic independence of short-term memory and reasoning was subsequently extended by Brainerd and Kingma (1985) to class inclusion problems,[3] conservation of liquid quantity, probability judgements, and story inference (verify the inference 'The cat is under the bird' from the premises 'The cage is on the table', 'The bird is in the cage', and 'The cat is under the table'). For both kindergartners and second-graders, and in all of these tasks, performance on reasoning items was independent of short-term memory retention of the critical facts presented prior to these items. As Brainerd and Kingma emphasized, the fact that the independence effect was observed at two age levels suggests that improvements in reasoning on the one hand and short-term memory on the other that occur during childhood are independent of each other.

Moreover, Brainerd and Kingma (1985) tested the hypothesis that two separate types of traces are stored in working memory, one type retrieved in memory tests and the other type used to answer reasoning questions. In line with the hypothesis of separate traces, manipulations that are known to improve reasoning performance left short-term memory for critical background facts unaffected. For example, in the class inclusion problem, the use of a superordinate term referring to collections vs. classes (e.g. 'tribe' instead of 'Indians' for the union of the sets 'chiefs' and 'braves') that makes part-whole comparisons easier (Markman, 1979) improved class inclusion performance but did not affect memory for background facts. In the same way, the introduction of visual illusions in transitivity tasks (e.g. the Müller-Lyer illusion) proved to strongly impair responses on transitivity items while leaving memory probes unaffected. In the other way round, manipulations that increase short-term memory performance, such as providing external stores during probability judgements (see above) or conservation, dramatically increased memory probes but did not improve reasoning.

The independence between short-term memory and information processing led Brainerd and Kingma (1985) to speculate on the structure of working memory. Are working memory and short-term memory functionally independent systems or are there two types of traces stored in working memory? Brainerd and Kingma favoured the idea of a single working memory system in which resources are adapted to perform different functions on separate memory traces. Detailed verbatim traces would serve as a basis for responding to short-term memory probes, while degraded gist-type traces would serve as a basis for information processing and reasoning. Nonetheless, contrary to the information processing assumptions, the independence of reasoning and remembering calls into question the idea that reasoning tasks are processed in limited-capacity working memory because, if that was the case, reasoning and memory would necessarily be dependent (Reyna & Brainerd, 1994). The solution for the dilemma created by what is called the independence effect (Brainerd & Reyna, 1992) was to develop a Fuzzy-Trace Theory (Brainerd & Reyna, 2004, 2015; Reyna & Brainerd, 1995, 2011) based on three main tenets. The first is that gist and verbatim traces are stored simultaneously through a parallel gistification. While verbatim traces store the surface form of the input and are rich in details and contextual cues, the same background inputs function as retrieval cues for semantic knowledge stored in long-term memory. This results in vague and patternlike representations that preserve the meaning of the inputs. The second tenet concerns the fuzzy-processing preference (Brainerd & Reyna, 1990). Because verbatim and gist traces are stored in parallel, a variety of task-relevant representations are available for processing during reasoning or problem solving, ranging from very detailed verbatim traces to fuzzy and skeletal gist traces that preserve meaning. It is assumed that there is a cognitive preference to reason intuitively from representations that present the most simplified information by calibrating reasoning to the lowest level of precision permitted to solve the task (e.g. in probability judgements, information about the relative instead of absolute magnitude of the two sets – there are more red than blue tokens – suffices to correctly predict the outcome of the next draw). This is due partly to the fact that gist representations are more stable and less prone to decay and interference than verbatim traces that tend to rapidly fade away from working memory. Moreover, this fuzzy-processing preference is assumed to become more marked with development (Brainerd & Reyna, 1992; Gomes & Brainerd, 2013). Finally, a representational independence is assumed between verbatim and gist traces, which is the source of the reasoning–memory independence effect, individuals relying on verbatim traces when probed for memory of background facts, but on gist traces when asked to draw inferences from these facts. Interestingly, when experimental manipulations lead children to process the same gist representations or the same verbatim traces to solve reasoning problems and answer memory questions, the independence effect disappears (Brainerd & Reyna, 1993).

The Fuzzy-Trace Theory departs radically from the two main traditional approaches of cognitive development, the Piagetian theory and the information processing view of cognition, but also from the modern dual-process theories. Whereas Piaget assumed that intuitions in young children were progressively supplanted by logical operations, the Fuzzy-Trace Theory suggests that thinking is fundamentally intuitive and based on gist processing. Contrary to the information processing approach in which more elaborate thinking results from processing more information stored in increasingly accurate and detailed representations, the Fuzzy-Trace Theory suggests that the intuitive processing that characterizes advanced thinking trades off precision and simplicity. While the modern dual-process theories of cognition view development as an increasing reliance on analytic over intuitive processing as working memory capacity increases with age (Barrouillet, 2011a, 2011b), the fuzzy-processing preference postulated by the Fuzzy-Trace Theory

56 The role of working memory in development

implies that developing human minds rely more and more on sophisticated intuition rather than on step-by-step analytic computations.

The increasing reliance on gist means that cognitive development no longer depends on some increase in working memory capacity, as Reyna and Brainerd (1994, p. 262) made explicit when stating that 'studying variations in working memory for "bits" of information is unlikely to illuminate the origins of intelligent behaviour'. Rather, 'development of particular reasoning skills depends on the emerging abilities to retrieve, edit, and process pertinent forms of gist' (Brainerd & Reyna, 1993, p. 48). Thus, the main source of age changes must be found in the more and more well-articulated semantic networks from which gists are retrieved and edited through automatic processes akin to those described in Kintsch's (1988) construction-integration model. However, despite the attractiveness of this approach and its heuristic power, a question remains: Even if the emergence of intelligent behaviour is not a matter of maintaining a greater number of bits in working memory, should we abandon the venerable hypothesis that working memory development determines cognitive development, at least in certain domains? The next section provides some hints for a (negative) response.

Are working memory and cognitive development independent?

The independence effect decisively weakens the idea that reasoning failures necessarily result from breakdowns occurring in an overloaded memory, and there is no doubt that advanced thinking and decision making relies more often on sophisticated intuitions than on the analytic processing of numerical data (Brainerd & Reyna, 2015; Reyna & Brainerd, 2011; Reyna & Farley, 2006; Reyna et al., 2011). Nonetheless, we would argue that these incontrovertible pieces of evidence are not necessarily sufficient to definitely discard the hypothesis of a causal link between working memory development and cognitive development. It is worth noting that what the independence effect reveals is that reasoning performance is not dependent on verbatim short-term memory of background information. However, two remarks can be made. First, such a verbatim memory is not needed to solve several of the problems studied by Brainerd and Kingma (1985). For example, there is no need to remember the precise number of cows and horses to know that there are more animals than cows, and it has been demonstrated that those children who rely on numerical information to solve this problem are more prone than others to err when given many additional cows and asked whether something can be done to have more cows than animals on the table (see Barrouillet & Poirier, 1997, for a Piagetian account of this error). In the same way, as we noted above, a perfect memory of numerical values is not needed to make correct predictions in the probability judgement task. Second, as we will see in the next chapter, modern theorizing of the role and functions of working memory goes beyond the mere short-term memory maintenance. Two main functions are of interest here that have been assumed to depend on working memory capacity: representation (understanding) of concepts and storage of knowledge in long-term memory. Cowan (2017a) assumes that one basis of the importance of working memory capacity in cognition is that it limits the number of items that can be associated deliberately or incidentally. This would have a direct impact on the nature of the concepts that children can represent and consequently understand, as Halford (1993; Halford et al., 2014) assumes. For example, representing three-term inclusion or transitive relations would involve more complex concepts and a higher cognitive capacity than representing two-term simple relations like 'larger than'. The gist representations that integrate elements retrieved from semantic networks in the Fuzzy-Trace Theory could depend on working memory capacity conceived in this way. Moreover, it has also been suggested that working memory has a function of chunking and learning, those elements that are concurrently held in working memory being associated and stored in long-term memory as a chunk (Cowan, 1999; Ericsson & Simon, 1980, 2005; Miller, 1956). In this case, maintaining and storing verbatim traces may have, as we will see, a critical importance for learning. We will close this chapter with two examples in the domain of mental arithmetic and language acquisition.

Working memory and acquisition of arithmetic facts

Developmental studies on mental arithmetic were launched by Groen and Parkman (1972) who studied solution times in first-graders when solving small additions with operands from 1 to 5, and observed that the best predictor of response times was the smaller of the two operands. This finding pointed towards a model called *Min* in which a counting procedure starts from the larger addend and counts on by one for the value of the smaller addend (e.g. for $2 + 3$, starting from 3 and counting 4, 5; see also Baroody & Ginsburg, 1986; Fuson, 1982, Geary & Burlingham-Dubree, 1989; Siegler & Robinson, 1982; for further evidence of counting strategies in young children). Subsequent studies revealed that the best predictor of response times in older children and adults was no longer the smaller of the two addends but the square of their sum, which was interpreted as reflecting a strategy of direct retrieval of the answer from long-term memory through a tabular search (Ashcraft, 1992; Ashcraft & Battaglia, 1978; Ashcraft & Stazyk, 1981). A popular account of this developmental counting-retrieval shift assumes that problem solving leaves footprints in long-term memory in the form of operand–answer associations that progressively strengthen as a result of the repeated use of algorithms up to the point the answer can be directly retrieved (Siegler & Shrager, 1984). Interestingly, it has been repeatedly observed that children with mathematical disabilities have difficulties in retrieving basic arithmetic facts from long-term memory (Geary, Hoard, Byrd-Craven, & DeSoto, 2004; see also Barrouillet, Fayol, & Lathulière, 1997; Geary, 1990; Jordan, Hanich, & Kaplan, 2003) and exhibit poorer performance than their same-age peers in working memory tasks (Bull & Scerif, 2001; Bull et al., 2008; Geary, 2011; Geary, Hoard, & Hamson, 1999; McLean & Hitch, 1999). Geary et al. (2004) suggested that the two findings could be related, because children who have low working memory capacities could be slower in executing the algorithmic counting procedures, slower counting resulting in degraded working memory traces that leave weak associations in long-term memory unable to support direct retrieval (Thevenot, Barrouillet, & Fayol, 2001).

Geary et al.'s (2004) hypothesis leads to straightforward predictions. If lower working memory resources result in weaker long-term memory associations, solving additions by retrieving the answer from long-term memory should be less frequent in children with low working memory capacities. Moreover, assuming a frequent use of the *Min* strategy, this difference in retrieval use should increase as the smaller operand is larger and brings about longer algorithmic solution times. Barrouillet and Lépine (2005) verified both hypotheses in 9-year-old children with either high or low working memory capacities who solved small additions $(a+b \leq 10)$. Whereas both working memory groups mainly relied on retrieval for additions with a smaller addend of 1, the difference in retrieval use increased dramatically with the size of the smaller addend, children with low working memory (WM) capacity relying more often on counting than retrieval for additions with a smaller addend of 4 (Figure 3.1). These findings suggest that working

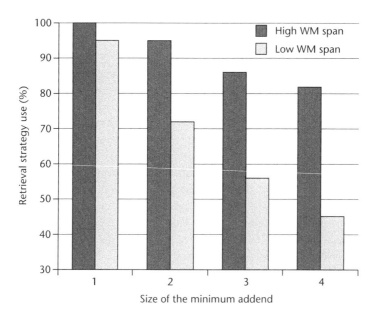

FIGURE 3.1 Percentage of retrieval uses by 9-year-old children to solve additions as a function of the size of the minimum addend and working memory capacity

Source: Adapted from P. Barrouillet and R. Lépine (2005). Working memory and children's use of retrieval to solve addition problems. *Journal of Experimental Child Psychology, 91*, p. 196, with permission from Elsevier.

Note
The figure shows that low-span children rely less often than high-span children on direct retrieval of the answer from long-term memory, this trend increasing with the size of the minimum addend.

memory capacity could constrain and delay the developmental shift from counting to retrieval and affect the type of strategies that children, and probably adults, can use (for similar findings in numerical transcoding, see Camos, 2008). It is worth noting here that what working memory must maintain to form valid and retrievable associations for exact calculation are verbatim and not gist traces.

Working memory and language learning

Another domain in which working memory has been assumed to play the role of a learning device is language development. Because working memory is usually defined as a system for maintaining information in view of its on-line processing, its critical role in language comprehension might seem self-evident due to the ephemeral nature of the oral language input. Despite its intuitive appeal and correlations found between working memory capacity and language comprehension (Daneman & Merikle, 1996), this hypothesis has received little empirical support, leading Caplan and Waters (1999) to suggest that the syntactic and semantic structures of sentences are interpreted by a resource independent from working memory. By contrast, the contribution of verbal working memory to language learning, and more precisely to vocabulary acquisition, has often been suggested (see Gathercole, 1998; Szmalec, Brysbaert, & Duyck, 2011, for reviews). Language development is primarily related to the ability to learn new words. Baddeley, Gathercole, and Papagno (1998) advanced the idea that verbal working memory, and more specifically the phonological loop (the slave system devoted to the storage and maintenance of verbal information in Baddeley's multi-component model, see next chapter) supports the long-term learning of the sound patterns of new words. Indeed, several studies had revealed a strong relation between measures of verbal short-term memory like digit span or immediate repetition of non-words (e.g. *woogalamic* or *loodemaypish*) and vocabulary size in children (see Gathercole, 2006, for a review). Page and Norris (1998) in their primacy model have suggested that learning a new word like *artecey* involves memorizing its components *ar*, *te*, and *cey* and their order in the same way as the sequence of letters RTC is maintained in the phonological loop for serial recall. The repeated occurrence of a word in a child's environment would result in the development of a lexical representation in the same way as the repetition across trials of an ordered sequence of letters in an immediate serial recall task leads to a stable long-term memory trace that improves its recall relative to unrepeated sequences (an effect known as the Hebb repetition effect). In line with this hypothesis, Mosse and Jarrold (2008) found in 5- to 6-year-old children a correlation between the speed at which this Hebb effect builds up and their performance in a paired-associate learning task with non-words. Another piece of evidence in favour of the role of verbal working memory in language learning comes from studies of Specific Language Impairment (SLI), a developmental condition in which children experience great difficulties in learning words and grammatical structures. Children with SLI manifest a severe impairment in non-word repetition (Gathercole & Baddeley, 1990; see Roy & Chiat, 2004, for a

60 The role of working memory in development

review) that has been adopted as a clinical diagnostic indicator of the condition (Conti-Ramsden, 2003).

Although the existence of a causal relation between verbal working memory deficits and developmental lag in vocabulary acquisition is a matter of dispute (e.g. Bowey, 1996; Masterson et al., 2005; Snowling, Chiat, & Hulme, 1991), we think that this hypothesis constitutes an enlightening illustration of the way working memory can be conceived as a learning mechanism. In this domain, as it was the case for arithmetic facts, the key for a successful learning of new words is the maintenance of verbatim traces.

Conclusion

Can cognitive development be reduced to memory development, as Brainerd (1983) surmised? Although initial attempts to support this hypothesis seemed successful (Brainerd, 1981; Bryant & Trabasso, 1971), it rapidly appeared that developmental changes are too complex to be explained by the mere increase in capacity of a single system, as central and important as it can be. This chapter gave examples from studies on transitive and conditional reasoning, and we have seen that theories like the Fuzzy-Trace Theory assume that the development of key functions like reasoning can be dissociated from the development of working memory, at least when understood as a short-term store for the maintenance of verbatim premises. It is also worth noting that alternatives to the Piagetian conception of development have been proposed without resorting to working memory development, such as Siegler's (1996) overlapping waves model (see Barrouillet & Camos, 2017, for an analysis).

Nonetheless, it is not because cognitive development cannot be reduced to working memory development that it can be understood and explained without it. It has been known for a long time that working memory capacity is strongly related with reasoning abilities (Kyllonen & Christal, 1990) and, as the last part of the present chapter suggests, working memory constitutes a powerful learning device the efficiency of which constrains development in several areas. Accordingly, learning difficulties of various types have been repeatedly shown to be associated with poor working memory capacities (e.g. Cain, Oakhill, & Bryant, 2004; Peng, Namkung, Barnes, & Sun, 2016; Pickering, 2006; Raghubar, Barnes, & Hecht, 2010; Swanson, 2011), and measures of working memory capacities prove to be a better predictor of academic achievement than IQ (Alloway & Alloway, 2010). As Cowan (2014) assumes, 'working memory underpins cognitive development, learning, and education'. As such, how and why working memory itself develops is of crucial importance for child development. The second part of this book addresses these questions.

Notes

1 In Girotto and Gonzalez (2008, Exp. 1) who tested children from preschool to fourth grade, the rate of correct decisions when corrected for guessing barely reached 50 per

cent (46 per cent) in second-graders (mean age of 7;11 years), this rate reaching 82 per cent in fourth grade.

2 Note that Bryant (1977) did not share Trabasso's prudence and still claimed that transitivity as revealed by the Bryant and Trabasso procedure is logical in nature.

3 Children were shown, for example, a card with pictures of seven robins and three blue jays. They were first asked to count all the robins, all the blue jays, and all the 'birds', and the card was turned face down. The reasoning questions involved the comparison of the superordinate class with the larger of the subclasses 'Are there more robins or more birds?', 'Are there less robins or less birds?'. The probe questions were of the form 'How many birds were there in this picture, 10 or 3?', 'How many robins were there in this picture, 7 or 3?', 'How many blue jays were there in this picture, 10 or 3?'.

PART II

The development of working memory

The chapters of Part I of this book reviewed several developmental theories and models that appealed to working memory development as an explanatory concept. However, the attentive reader probably noticed that the conception of working memory itself strongly evolves from one theory to the other. Miller's (1956) short-term memory store able to hold seven (plus or minus two) elements that inspired Pascual-Leone's (1970) central computing space M strongly differs from Case's (1985) total processing space, which differs in turn from the working memory hypothesized by Halford (1993), in which a maximum of four independent dimensions can be simultaneously held and integrated. In Chapter 3, working memory, the development of which was assumed to account for the age-related increase in a variety of functions and processes, was sometimes conceived in turn as a short-term store for maintaining premises, a space for the construction and simultaneous manipulation of an increasing number of representations, a system for creating associations in long-term memory and acquiring new knowledge, or an attentional system the capacity of which increases with age. These various conceptions result from the evolution of the concept of working memory itself and the diversity of the theories that have been proposed to describe its structure and functioning. The following Chapter 4 presents this evolution and describes some of these theories. Not surprisingly, the first model of working memory, the multi-component model delineated by Baddeley and Hitch (1974) and afterwards fully developed by Baddeley (1986, 2000; Baddeley & Logie, 1999), has been of paramount importance in cognitive psychology. The fractionation of working memory proposed by this model into a central attentional component devoted to executive control on the one hand, and slave systems for storage purpose on the other, has led to two distinct streams of developmental research. One is dedicated to the age-related increase in short-term maintenance capacities, whereas the other examines the development of what is nowadays called executive functions. Accordingly, Chapter 5 will be

64 The development of working memory

devoted to the studies that have addressed the age-related increase in maintenance capacities for both verbal and visuospatial working memory, whereas Chapter 6 reviews the studies that have examined the development of the executive control through the study of the executive functions. We close this second part with the analysis in Chapter 7 of the main sources of working memory development.

4

THE EVOLVING CONCEPT OF WORKING MEMORY

The various conceptions of cognitive development presented in Part I in which working memory is assumed to play a key role manifestly use different acceptations of the term 'working memory'. As we noted above, the working memory studied by Brainerd (1981), which resembles a short-term store, differs from the structure theorized by Case (1985) in which processing and storage share a common mental space, which in turn differs from the working memory hypothesized by Barrouillet and Lépine (2005) in which operand-answer associations are created and deposited in long-term memory. This diversity reflects both the evolution of the notion during the last 60 years and the proliferation of theories intended to describe the same cognitive system. In a recent enlightening review, Cowan (2017b) has distinguished no less than nine different definitions that, implicitly or explicitly, have guided theoretical endeavours and empirical research. Our aim in this chapter is not to provide an exhaustive review of the different models of working memory that have been proposed (see the books by Shah & Miyake, 1999 and, more recently, Baddeley, Eysenck, & Anderson, 2015, for excellent reviews). We will instead concentrate on three models, namely Baddeley (1986, 2000; Baddeley & Logie, 1999), Cowan (1995, 2005), and Engle (2002; Engle et al., 1999) that, in our view, privilege different aspects of working memory on which developmental studies have mainly focused and that will be presented in Chapters 5 and 6.

The multi-component model: towards the fractionation between storage and executive control

Baddeley's model is, without any doubt, the most popular model of working memory. Most often, authors who refer to the concept of working memory have in mind the multi-component model proposed by Baddeley (1986). We noted in Chapter 1 that the limitation of the M space hypothesized by Pascual-Leone (1970)

66 The development of working memory

to a maximum of seven schemes that could be activated simultaneously was evidently inspired by the size of the immediate memory described by Miller (1956) in his famous article. This estimate in Miller's review came from adults' performance on memory span procedures (more precisely, the digit span task). As Cowan (2017b) emphasizes, this immediate memory was subsequently labelled short-term memory in several models (e.g. Broadbent, 1958; Waugh & Norman, 1965) that were synthesized by Atkinson and Shiffrin (1968) in a model called the modal model. Importantly, Atkinson and Shiffrin assumed that the short-term store they hypothesized between the sensory stores and the long-term store fulfilled the function of a working memory, a variety of control processes coding the incoming information, maintaining items through rehearsal, copying them into long-term memory, retrieving information from long-term memory, and making decisions for action.

It is precisely this hypothesis of the short-term store as a working memory that Baddeley and Hitch (1974) tested in their so-often cited chapter. They reasoned that if the short-term store, which is capacity limited, were a working memory in charge of both the storage and treatment of information like reasoning or comprehension, absorbing some of its capacity by a memory load should have a detrimental effect on concurrent processing. Their empirical investigations revealed that maintaining, for example, digits for further recall had some disruptive effect on reasoning performance, but they also noted that this effect was 'far from massive' (Baddeley & Hitch, 1974, p. 75). For example, a three-item memory load had no effect on concurrent processing whereas a six-item load had some effect. Moreover, Baddeley and Lewis, in a study reported by Baddeley (1986), observed that even when the capacity of short-term memory was virtually exhausted by a memory load of eight digits, adults' accuracy in a verbal reasoning task remained almost unaffected. These findings led Baddeley and Hitch (1974) to assume some independence between the short-term store described by Atkinson and Shiffrin, the capacity of which was assessed through span measures, and the system in charge of the cognitive processes underpinning reasoning, learning, or comprehension. They consequently suggested that a separate component that they called the central executive was in charge of both the control processing demands and some storage space to supplement the short-term store when needed, this latter structure being conceived of as a passive phonemic buffer. Although remaining unexplored in this seminal study, a distinct storage system for visuospatial information was already envisioned. In other words, it was suggested that working memory does not involve a single short-term store but several components.

These ideas were extended by Baddeley (1986) who described the central executive as a system devoted to the control of attention akin to the Supervisory Attentional System (SAS) described by Norman and Shallice (1986), whereas its possible role as a storage device was no longer mentioned. The fractionation between the functions of storage on the one hand, and executive control on the other, was consummated in Baddeley and Logie (1999) where any storage capacity for the central executive was explicitly abandoned. Based on studies by Duff and Logie (1999; see also Duff & Logie, 2001), who observed that varying the number of words to be maintained for further recall had virtually no effect on a concurrently performed arithmetic task, Baddeley and Logie concluded that processing and storage were fuelled by separate cognitive resources. Storage was assumed to depend on domain-specific systems, a phonological buffer for the verbal material and a sketchpad for the visuospatial information. These buffers were assumed to be passive stores in which information is prone to temporal decay. However, dedicated mechanisms of maintenance conceived as loops, namely the articulatory loop and the inner scribe, were supposed to reactivate memory items by recirculating them in the phonological buffer and the visuospatial sketchpad, respectively. The capacity of these passive stores was assumed to depend on the efficiency of these mechanisms of maintenance. For example, Hulme, Thomson, Muir, and Lawrence (1984) established that children aged 4, 7, and 10 and adults are able to recall as many words as they are able to articulate in 1.5 s.

Besides these storing components, a central executive would be in charge of processing. Baddeley (1996) postulated some of the processes that the central executive would perform. Apart from the control and coordination of the short-term stores (the phonological loop and the visuospatial sketchpad) described as slave systems, the central executive would also be in charge of a number of other executive functions such as the capacity to carry out two tasks simultaneously, to focus attention and select relevant information, to switch attention from one element to another, or to activate information from long-term memory. Baddeley (2000; Baddeley, Allen, & Hitch, 2010, 2011; Repovs & Baddeley, 2006) subsequently completed this multi-component model by adding an episodic buffer assumed to hold multi-modal representations in an integrated format.

The fractionation of working memory proposed by the multi-component model into separate systems dedicated to either the control of attention or the storage of different types of information had important consequences regarding further theorizing as well as empirical approaches for studying working memory development. Before addressing developmental questions in the next chapters, the remaining of this chapter presents two models of working memory that mainly focus on one of the two main working memory functions. The first is primarily concerned with the storage function, accounting for its limitations and their evolution with age. This model also elaborates on the relationships between working and long-term memory and, consequently, accounts for the fact that working memory is also a powerful learning device (Cowan, 1995, 1999, 2005). The second model concentrates on the executive rather than the storage function of working memory, assuming that working memory capacity is the capacity to control attention in face of interference and distraction (Engle, 2002; Engle, Kane, & Tuholski, 1999).

The embedded-process model of working memory

According to Cowan (1999, p. 62), 'working memory refers to cognitive processes that retain information in an unusually accessible state, suitable for carrying out any task with a mental component', such as language comprehension or production,

68 The development of working memory

problem solving, decision making, or other thought. Cowan emphasizes that this is a functional definition in that any process contributing to bring information to this state of accessibility can be considered as being part of working memory. Thus, 'the mnemonic functions preserving information that can be used to do the necessary work collectively make up working memory' (Cowan, 1999, p. 63). These mnemonic functions form what Cowan (1999) called an *embedded-process model*, which is derived from the information processing system previously proposed by Cowan (1988).

This information processing system assumes that stimulus information enters brief sensory stores where it is coded for only some hundreds of milliseconds before contacting and activating features stored in long-term memory, this activation lasting several seconds. Importantly, the nature and number of activated features depends on whether the stimulus is attended to or not. Whereas the activation is only partial and mainly concentrated on physical features for unattended stimuli, more features are activated if stimuli, or their after-image, are attended to, this activation extending to semantic features and resulting in more stable representations. Accordingly, subsequent studies established that attention to the stimuli is needed for activating semantic features (Conway, Cowan, & Bunting, 2001). Interestingly, Cowan (1988) assumed that there is no need in his system for an attentional filter (as for example in Broadbent, 1958). Stimuli that remain physically unchanged in the environment would become habituated and no longer elicit attention, except if they are especially significant. By contrast, novel or changing stimuli would be attended to, resulting in deeper encoding. Moreover, attention could also be voluntarily directed towards stimuli, even habituated, by a central executive that is also in charge of the control of voluntary processing. The central executive could direct attention outward to stimuli, but also inward for activating information stored in long-term memory.

Contrary to what Baddeley (1986) suggested, the embedded-process model posits that there is only one storage system that contains features and features combinations corresponding to information about past stimuli, in other words a long-term memory. Within this long-term memory is the subset of items and features that have received activation and constitute what is called short-term memory. Importantly, activated information can prime associated items, possibly irrelevant for the task at hand, that receive activation and become part of short-term memory too. Moreover, within the activated part of long-term memory is a limited subset of items that are within the focus of attention and correspond to the content of conscious awareness. This introduces an important distinction between activation and attention, not all of the activated memory being in the focus of attention. Cowan (1999) suggests that this focus of attention corresponds to the primary memory hypothesized by James (1890), whereas the entire set of activated items and features, including the focus of attention, might correspond to the active cells assembly described by Hebb (1949).

It should be noted that this conception departs from both the theories that assume a short-term memory distinct from long-term memory (e.g. Atkinson &

Shiffrin, 1968; Baddeley, 1986, 2000; Baddeley & Logie, 1999) and what Cowan (2017b) calls the monistic view (Crowder, 1993), which denies the existence of separate stores and assumes that what is usually called short-term memory is governed by the same processes as long-term memory. In Cowan's theory, there is only one store, long-term memory, with a short-term memory embedded in it, but this short-term memory is functionally distinct from long-term memory as it results from the processes of activation and attention. These processes are of importance because they determine the two limitations of working memory. Contrary to other theories like that of Anderson, Reder, and Lebière (1996), Cowan assumes that there is no limitation in the available amount of activation, but activation is temporally limited and decays with time within about 10s to 20s unless items are reactivated. Moreover, interference from incoming similar items would also limit the size of the activated portion of long-term memory (Cowan, 2005). By contrast, the limit in the focus of attention is not a temporal, but a capacity limit. The focus could only hold about three or four unrelated items in young adults, but less in children (Cowan, 2001, 2005).

It is important to note that the capacity limit of the focus of attention to three to four elements does not necessarily concern isolated items, but chunks of information. For example, the letters P, S, G, O, and M will probably be encoded as unrelated items by north American participants, resulting in five chunks, but French football fans will identify in this list acronyms of famous football clubs (PSG and OM) and encode the same letters into two instead of five chunks. A study by Chen and Cowan (2009; see also Chen & Cowan, 2005) nicely illustrates the limit in terms of chunks, and not items. Adult participants were presented with lists of 4, 6, 8, or 12 words presented in pairs for immediate recall, the familiarity of the participants with the stimuli being manipulated using various study procedures. In a no-study condition, participants studied pairs made of words they had not seen before. In a second condition, the pairs were made of words that had been seen before, but individually (the singleton condition), whereas in a third condition, the presented pairs had been learned before in such a way that they should be recognized during test and encoded as a single chunk. Moreover, in order to obtain a more accurate estimate of the capacity of the focus of attention, any intervention of verbal rehearsal that could inflate this estimate was prevented by asking participants to perform the memory task under articulatory suppression, continuously repeating a nonsense syllable. The authors adopted a lenient scoring that does not take recall order into account and computed the number of chunks recalled. When a learned pair was correctly recalled, it counted as one two-word chunk. In the singleton and no-study conditions in which participants had not been familiarized with the pairs before the test, each word recalled counted as a one-word chunk. The hypothesis of a limitation of the focus of attention to three to four chunks led to predict that the number of chunks recalled should be constant across list lengths for both the singleton and the learned-pair conditions. In line with this expectation, in all the conditions and for all list lengths, participants recalled approximately three chunks. For example, when six learned pairs were presented, participants recalled three pairs

70 The development of working memory

(i.e. six words), whereas when presented with 12 singletons constituting six pairs, they recalled approximately three words. This estimate of three or four chunks, considered as a central capacity limit expressed by Cowan as the k value (Cowan, 2001), was found not only for verbal but also for visuospatial stimuli (Rouder et al., 2008), for a combination of both types of information (Saults & Cowan, 2007), and even for non-verbal auditory items, though the estimate is lower for stimuli that are difficult to categorize (Li, Cowan, & Saults, 2013). It is worth noting that this estimate corresponds to a maximal capacity. The scope of attention could be zoomed in a single item (e.g. the goal of a difficult task in a highly interfering context) or zoomed out for simultaneously apprehending a maximum of four items (Cowan, 2005).[1]

This cursory presentation of Cowan's model was intended to illustrate how the way working memory is conceived and theorized, evolving from the first model proposed by Baddeley and Hitch (1974). One of the main differences concerns the unitary nature of working memory. Whereas Baddeley and Hitch (1974) assumed different short-term stores for verbal and visuospatial information, the embedded-process model assumes that there is a single store in which memory traces consist of the integration of a variety of codes. As Cowan (2005) noted, this allows for the introduction of other important distinctions in the type of information that working memory must process, such as auditory versus verbal versus tactile information, to which could be added other distinctions concerning musical, kinaesthetic, or olfactory stimulations. Thus, in the embedded-process model, there is no phonological loop or visuospatial sketchpad that are just conceived as two varieties of memory activation, and the processes intended to reactivate memory traces in Baddeley's model (verbal rehearsal for the phonological loop, visualization within the inner scribe) are just processes that can be initiated by the central executive, but that can become automatized. Cowan (2005) noted that the addition by Baddeley of the episodic buffer for integrating multi-modal representations has strongly reduced the difference between the multi-component and the embedded-process models, a difference that is 'not very large and is probably best viewed as one of the level of analysis' (Cowan, 2005, p. 48). It is true that the representations postulated by Baddeley in the episodic buffer are akin in nature to the feature combinations that constitute representations in Cowan's approach, and Baddeley (2000) has suggested that representations in the episodic buffer are maintained through attention by the central executive in the same way as the items within the focus of attention continuously receive activation. However, important differences remain concerning the existence of a separate short-term memory and the relationships between the functions of processing and storage.

The short-term stores in Baddeley's theory are structurally and not simply functionally distinct from long-term memory as in the embedded-process model. This makes working memory an entity distinct from long-term memory. This could have important implications for our understanding of working memory development. Considering short-term store or stores as separate from long-term memory opens the possibility to imagine developmental changes in the capacity of these stores themselves, such as the maximum number of slots they contain that can be filled by items, or the development of specific mechanisms devoted to these separate stores (e.g. verbal rehearsal for the phonological loop). By contrast, if the locus of the distinction between short-term (working) memory and long-term memory is a matter of general processes such as activation and attention in the embedded-process model, the development of working memory should depend on the development of these processes themselves. This would make working memory development a consequence of the development of more general mechanisms.

Another diverging point concerns the relationships between processing and storage. We noted above that Baddeley and Logie (1999) completed the fractionation of working memory into subcomponents specifically dedicated to storage (the slave systems) or processing (the central executive) fuelled by their own pool of resources, explaining that Duff and Logie (1999, 2001) did not observe any trade-off between the two functions.[2] By contrast, the embedded-process model does not predict such independence (Cowan, 2005). Because complex and difficult tasks involve the focus of attention, processing might interfere with storage as long as it requires itself the focus of attention (e.g. when verbal storage requirements exceed the capacity of the phonological loop). In the same way, while memory loads held in distinct slave systems are assumed to not interfere in the multi-component model, the embedded-process model predicts such an interference as long as both memory sets require the focus of attention. Accordingly, Morey and Cowan (2004, 2005) observed interference between visual and verbal memories. More generally, the hypothesis of a unique store in which a focus of attention helps to maintain items in a privileged state of accessibility predicts that maintenance of a variety of memory items should require general attention, something that was verified in several studies (e.g. Barrouillet et al., 2007; Morey & Bieler, 2013; Vergauwe et al., 2009, 2010).

Within the different definitions of working memory distinguished by Cowan (2017b), the embedded-process model pertains to a definition he calls *generic* that 'refers to the ensemble of components of the mind that hold a limited amount of information temporarily in a heightened state of availability for use in on-going information processing' (Cowan, 2017b, p. 1159). As this definition makes clear, this view puts the emphasis on the storage function of working memory (the ensemble of components of the mind that hold a limited amount of information). However, other models adopt a different view, privileging the control function of working memory over its storage function. This is the case of Engle's approach.

Working memory as controlled attention

Engle et al. (1999, p. 102) define working memory as 'a system consisting of those long-term memory traces active above threshold, the procedures and skills necessary to achieve and maintain that activation, and limited-capacity, controlled attention'. At first glance, this definition does not strongly differ from Cowan's conception developed in the previous section and suggests that both approaches focus on the memory part of working memory. However, this is not the case, probably because the questions motivating their scientific quest differ. While the

72 The development of working memory

model proposed by Cowan issued from his reflection about the relationships between attention and memory with the objective of designing an integrated information processing system, Engle's reflexion originates from questions concerning individual differences in working memory capacity as they are measured through working memory complex span tasks.

We have already evoked in the previous chapters the reading span task, the first working memory task designed by Daneman and Carpenter (1980), in which participants are invited to read successive unrelated sentences while retaining their last word. This dual requirement of processing and storage was intended to conform to the definition of working memory proposed by Baddeley and Hitch (1974). The *reading span*, the maximum number of unrelated words that can be recalled in correct order under this procedure, proved to be a far better predictor of reading comprehension than short-term memory spans such as the word span (Daneman & Carpenter, 1980). Importantly, Turner and Engle (1989) established that the correlation between reading span and reading comprehension was not due to the reading component of the task created by Daneman and Carpenter. When Turner and Engle replaced the sentences to be read by equations to be verified, each equation being followed by a to-be-remembered word (Is $4/2 + 3 = 6$? DOG), the resulting *operation span* still correlated with reading comprehension. This suggested that working memory span tasks such as the reading span task, the operation span task, or the counting span task described in Chapter 2 measure some domain-general capacity that is important for high-level cognition. Accordingly, Engle et al. (1999; see also Engle and Kane, 2004) listed a series of studies having established that working memory capacity, when measured in this way, predicts performance in activities as varied as vocabulary learning (Daneman & Green, 1986), following directions (Engle, Carullo, & Collins, 1991), reasoning (Kyllonen & Christal, 1990), and even bridge playing (Clarkson-Smith & Hartley, 1990). What do complex span tasks measure that is so important for complex cognition? What do studies on individual differences tell us about the nature of working memory? These are the two questions that guide Engle's studies.

In response to these questions, Engle et al. (1999) proposed to distinguish three components in working memory: a short-term memory made, as in Cowan's approach, of the activated part of long-term memory; a repertoire of grouping skills, coding strategies, and procedures for maintaining activation; and controlled attention. However, the authors emphasized that when referring to working memory capacity, they mean the capacity of only one element, controlled attention, that can be understood as the capacity of the central executive in Baddeley's theory. For clarifying this theoretical stance, they added 'working memory capacity is not really about storage or memory per se, but about the capacity for controlled, sustained attention in the face of interference or distraction' (Engle et al., 1999, p. 104). The isomorphism between working memory capacity and the capacity for controlled processing implies a close relationship of working memory capacity with general fluid intelligence or gF, the ability to solve novel problems. As mentioned in Engle et al. (1999), this relationship was elegantly demonstrated in an unpublished manuscript by Kane and Engle (1998) who reasoned in the following way. If complex spans provided by working memory tasks reflect a controlled attention component in addition to the short-term memory component, and if the relationship between working memory capacity and fluid intelligence is principally mediated by controlled attention, then this relationship at the latent variable level should remain highly significant when the variance common to working memory and short-term memory is partialled out. For this purpose, adult participants performed three short-term memory tasks (a word span with phonologically similar words, a word span with dissimilar words, and a backward word span), three complex span tasks (reading span, operation span, and counting span), along with the Raven's Standard Progressive Matrices (Raven, Court, & Raven, 1977) and the Cattell Culture Fair test as gF measures. Results indicated that working memory and short-term memory latent variables share a substantive part of variance, but when this common variance is removed, the correlation between the residual of working memory and gF is high and highly significant, whereas the correlation between the residual of short-term memory and gF does not reach significance.[3] Kane and Engle concluded that the component of working memory performance important for high-level cognition is separate from short-term memory and corresponds to controlled attention.

Further studies were devoted to the direct measure of the relationship between working memory capacity and controlled executive attention. For example, Kane, Bleckley, Conway, and Engle (2001) compared individuals with high and low working memory capacities in an antisaccade task in which participants have to identify a target that briefly appears at one side of a visual display just after an attention-attracting cue that appears systematically in the other side. The difficulty of the task lies in the fact that processing the target before its disappearance requires resisting the automatic attraction that the cue exerts on attention. Kane et al. (2001) observed that individuals with high working memory capacity are better able than others to control their attention and resist attraction, whereas no working-memory-related difference was observed when the cue appeared in the same location as the target (i.e. saccade task). In the same way, individuals with high working memory capacity are less prone to errors than others in the well-known Stroop task in which participants are asked to name the colour of the ink in which colour words are printed (Kane & Engle, 2003). The task is easy when the word matches the colour of the ink (e.g. the word 'blue' printed in blue, a congruent trial), but far more difficult when it does not (e.g. the word 'red' printed in blue, an incongruent trial). In this latter case, the tendency to say the word must be resisted by maintaining the goal of naming the colour of the ink. More errors were committed by individuals with low than high working memory capacities, but only when incongruent trials were rare (25 per cent). Kane and Engle explained this finding by assuming that it is only when incongruent trials are rare that it is difficult to maintain the goal of naming the colour of the ink, because the vast majority of trials that are congruent trials can be achieved by reading the word. The greater ability of individuals with high working memory capacities to control their attention is also apparent in their

74 The development of working memory

higher capacity to resist proactive interference (the intrusion in memory of previously learned, but now irrelevant, material, Kane & Engle, 2000; Rosen & Engle, 1997) or to block distracting information in a dichotic-listening task (Conway et al., 2001).

Engle and Kane (2004) proposed a two-factor model of the executive control for explaining these findings. One of these factors was assumed to be the maintenance of the task goals in active memory. Low-span individuals would sometimes fail to maintain the current goal active and, more often than high-span individuals, read the word in the Stroop task or shift their attention toward the cue in the antisaccade task. The other factor would be the resolution of competition or conflict, for example between prepotent natural responses and the task goals in the antisaccade and Stroop tasks, or between relevant and irrelevant information, as in situations of proactive interference or dichotic listening. This conception was further refined in a recent article by Shipstead, Harrison, and Engle (2016) who proposed to clarify their conception of the relationships between working memory capacity and fluid intelligence. The former would not be a determinant of the latter, as it is often assumed (e.g. Shipstead, Redick, Hicks, & Engle, 2012; Sternberg, 2008). Instead, both working memory capacity and fluid intelligence would arise from two similar general cognitive mechanisms by which top-down executive attention controls behaviour. Within this recent conceptualization, these mechanisms would be *intentional maintenance*, which focuses attention on relevant information, and *disengagement*, which removes irrelevant or no-longer relevant information from active processing. According to Shipstead and colleagues, working memory capacity and fluid intelligence are correlated because intentional maintenance and disengagement facilitate performance in the tasks used to measure these constructs (e.g. the operation span task and the Raven's matrices task). Nonetheless, they remain distinct because they place a different emphasis on the two mechanisms, working memory capacity relying to a greater extent on maintenance and fluid intelligence on disengagement, though the difference is only one of degree. It could be surmised that this new theorizing turns Engle's views into a memory-based conception of working memory, but this is not the case. As Shipstead et al. (2016) make clear, individual differences in the amount of information maintained does not reflect the capacity limits of a storage system, but are the by-product of aptitude for stabilizing attentional resources on goal-relevant information through the interplay between maintenance and disengagement.

Engle's conception of working memory is one that explicitly puts the emphasis on the central executive. Of course, several theories, including Cowan's (1999), assume the existence of a central executive, but it remains often in neglect and its structure and functioning largely unexplored. We have tried to illustrate in this section the sustained and fruitful efforts of Engle and his colleagues to analyse the functions of the central executive and to explain why complex spans correlate so strongly with high-level cognition, a correlation that demonstrates how working memory is important in cognition and its development.

Conclusions

This rapid overview of some leading theories of working memory reveals a surprising diversity. As Cowan (2017b) emphasizes in his recent analysis, the frequent reference in the working memory literature to Baddeley and Hitch (1974) accompanied by the processing-plus-storage definition is often followed by largely divergent conceptions. This renders any attempt to account for working memory development arduous. Should we focus on the age-related changes in the capacity to maintain information, or should we broaden the scope of our inquiry to address developmental changes in executive attention? It is worth recalling that what made working memory different from short-term memory in Baddeley and Hitch (1974), in other words what made for these authors the specificity of working memory, is the central executive. Thus, it is not coincidence that Engle and his colleagues argue that working memory capacity reflects executive attention, the central executive component in Baddeley's (1986) model, and not short-term memory. Keeping in mind that Baddeley (1986; Baddeley & Logie, 1999) assumes that storage and executive control are supported by distinct components and fuelled by separate resources, accounting for working memory development requires taking into account the development of both aspects. This is why Chapter 5 will be devoted to the development of the processes and structures responsible for the maintenance of information in the short term, while a separate chapter (Chapter 6) will address the development of the executive control, which is also called executive functions.

Notes

1 Other models assuming that working memory is the activated part of long-term memory postulate a focus of attention restricted to a single element. For example, in Oberauer's (2002) model, there is within the activated part of long-term memory a subset of a maximum of four items highly activated and available for immediate processing called the *region of direct access*. Within this region, the focus of attention would select a single item at a time for processing.
2 For an extensive discussion of the problem of resource-sharing and the existence of a trade-off between processing and storage, see Barrrouillet and Camos (2015) as well as Chapter 8 in this volume.
3 The correlation between working memory and fluid intelligence has subsequently been found in several studies (see Chuderski, 2013, or Shipstead, Lindsey, Marshall, & Engle, 2014, for recent examples).

5

AGE-RELATED INCREASES IN SHORT-TERM MAINTENANCE

Using short-term storage and working memory tasks in children, Bayliss, Jarrold, Gunn, and Baddeley (2003; Bayliss, Jarrold, Baddeley, Gunn, & Leigh, 2005) found that both a domain-general processing component and several domain-specific storage components account for working memory performance in 7- to 9-year-olds. Gathercole, Pickering, Ambridge, and Wearing (2004; Gathercole & Pickering, 2000) extended these findings as this processing/storage dissociation is in place in children as young as 6 years of age and remains across childhood up to 15 years. In accordance with Baddeley's model in which distinct storage systems sustain short-term maintenance, Alloway, Gathercole, and Pickering (2006) confirmed the relative independence of verbal and visuospatial short-term memory from an executive component in 4- to 11-year-old children (see also, Alloway, Gathercole, Willis, & Adams, 2004; Giofre, Mammarella, & Cornoldi, 2013; Hornung, Brunner, Reuter, & Martin, 2011; Michalczyk et al., 2013; Nadler & Archibald, 2014). Confirming these findings, a recent large study involving more than 2,000 participants from 6 to 66 years showed that the factors underlying performance in complex span tasks were similar across ages, although some differentiation appears between verbal and visuospatial domains (Swanson, 2017). Thus, from an early age, short-term maintenance processes are distinct from executive functions, and among the processes in charge of maintenance, at least two main domains are dissociable, the verbal and the visuospatial domains. This chapter examines the development of short-term maintenance and the next chapter will be dedicated to the development of executive functions.

Overall, the maintenance of information in the short term is characterized by an important age-related increase. This increase is observed in infancy as well as throughout childhood. However, the difference in paradigms between infants and children studies renders the comparison across these two age periods very difficult. Because memory research in infancy presents also some other specificities that we will detail below, we will present them first before exposing the development of short-term maintenance in childhood for verbal and visuospatial information.

Short-term memory in infancy

As we discussed in the previous chapter, theoretical approaches differ on their conception of the relationships between short-term and working memory, and a sharp distinction between the two concepts is often difficult to draw. This distinction is even more tenuous in the study of infants' memory and questions what is the most appropriate label for the short-term storage in infants. While some authors like Reznick (2007, 2014) favour the idea that it is all about working memory, others (e.g. Oakes, Ross-Sheehy, & Luck, 2006; Oakes & Luck, 2014) prefer to name it short-term memory. Here we consider short-term memory as the storage function of a working memory system in charge of all types of processing (including storage) in the short term.

The study of short-term memory in infants could be traced back to the question raised by Piaget (1937/1954) about object permanence; since then, other paradigms have been developed to specifically assess infants' short-term memory. After describing these different paradigms and discussing some important methodological issues, we will see that the capacity of short-term memory develops during infancy in terms of duration and amount of memory traces infants can store.

Which paradigms to study infants' short-term memory?

The challenge for building paradigms to study infants' short-term memory is to ensure that the response is not based on information that had been acquired previously, i.e. stored in long-term memory. Various procedures have been created and could be categorized into three types: hide-find, observe-perform, and familiarize-recognize procedures (Reznick, 2007).

The *hide-find* procedure is among the oldest paradigms used to study infants' memory. It allows the assessment of spatial short-term memory, and the delayed-response task introduced by Hunter (1913) is considered as the canonical procedure (Goldman-Rakic, 1987). Many findings in the study of infants' memory are based on it (for a review, see Pelphrey & Reznick, 2003). The Piagetian A–not-B task is derived from this paradigm. In this task, the participant is given a cue that specifies which location among various is the correct one. This cue could be a light above the location (Hunter, 1913) or the hiding of an attractive object under a cloth or in a box (e.g. Diamond & Doar, 1989; Huttenlocher, Newcombe, & Sandberg, 1994; Piaget, 1937/1954). After a delay and some distraction, participant is allowed to make a choice, for example, to find in the correct location the hidden attractive object. The aim of the delay and distraction is to break participant's attention to the location. Instead of passively attending to the cued location, participant is engaged in some other processes while retaining it. This assures that correct findings of the attractive object are based on an active choice to maintain relevant information.

78 The development of working memory

However, these findings in the hide-find task could also be accounted for by long-term memory.

Indeed, Moore and Meltzoff (2004) observed that 14-month-old infants can retain and search for an attractive object (a bell) in the adequate location (a drawer) 24 hours after seeing where it was hidden. With such a long delay of retention, the information was not maintained in a short-term but in a long-term memory. Thus, appropriate demonstration of short-term storage should rule out any alternative account in terms of long-term memory. Reznick (2007) proposed that one way to rule out the implication of long-term memory is to present several successive trials to the participant and to hide the object in a different location in each trial. The participant could encode in long-term memory the different locations, but the correct answer can only be based on the short-term maintenance of the correct location in that particular trial.

Another important concern with this paradigm is that infants are sensitive to violation of expectations. Indeed, infants are attentive to an event that violates the bounds of the possible. This is at the root of the violation-of-expectation paradigm that was and still is used in many studies to examine infants' expectation about dimensions of the world (cf. Baillargeon, 1995). For example, when an object is hidden in a location, 10-week-old infants can be 'surprised' when this object is retrieved from an impossible location (i.e. another location) after 5 seconds (Wilcox, Nadel, & Rosser, 1996). This delay increases with age, with a surprise reaction after a 50-second delay at 5 months and 70 seconds at 8 months (Baillargeon, DeVos, & Graber, 1989; Baillargeon & Graber, 1988; Newcombe, Huttenlocher, & Learmonth, 1999). These results could also be taken as evidence for an early short-term maintenance capacity, but they can also reflect long-term memory. The violation-of-expectation paradigm leads also to interesting findings that question the impact of modality of responses in the hide-find procedure.

In the classic A-not-B task, the experimenter hides a toy at location A, allows the infant to reach it, and then hides the toy at a different location, B. Piaget described how 8- to 12-month-old infants make a perseveration error and search for the toy at location A, what is known as the A-not-B error. However, using similar design but a violation-of-expectation paradigm in which looking times to locations A and B are measured, Ahmed and Ruffman (1998) have shown that infants looked longer to the impossible event (i.e. when the toy is found in A though hidden in B). This result is at odds with the A-not-B error observed in Piaget's task in which infants have to reach the hidden object. It indicates that infants have some knowledge of where the toy was actually hidden, and this knowledge could be uncovered because the violation-of-expectation paradigm has the advantage of not requiring an explicit response from the infant (Ahmed & Ruffman, 1998). However, if we agree that the specificity of working memory representations is to direct action (cf. Baddeley, 2007; previous chapter), performance in the violation-of-expectation paradigm may not be so informative about the content of working memory. Alternatively, responses could be triggered by long-term memory, with episodic representations giving enough information to affect looking times.

Actually, one can consider that the discrepancy observed between looking and reaching behaviours in the A-not-B task indexes the difference in memory traces stored in either long-term or working memory. It should be noted that in the violation-of-expectation paradigm, infants are not exhibiting a visual response in the sense of directing their gaze to an expected event (e.g. the particular location where an object should appear). Thus, infants are not actually carrying out any action or, as Ahmed and Ruffman (1998) said, 'it is more of a reaction than a response, as the infants are not required to attend to the correct location themselves' (p. 452). Congruently with the idea that looking and reaching behaviours rely on different memory traces, Ahmed and Ruffman (1998) suggested that 'the violation-of-expectation task involves a reaction to an event, using a form of recognition memory rather than a response using recall memory' and looking times 'reveal a different form of knowledge, which may not be the full conceptual understanding needed for correct direction of reach' (p. 452). Alternatively, it can be suggested that object concepts are not all-or-nothing, but graded memory representations that varied in strength and accessibility (Munakata, 2001; Munakata, McClelland, Johnson, & Siegler, 1997; see next chapter). Lower threshold may be enough for driving looking behaviour, while reaching responses would require stronger memory representations. However, it should not be forgotten that Piaget himself considered such a discrepancy in behaviour when defining *horizontal décalage*, i.e. when an infant is able to demonstrate knowledge of the existence of hidden object through eye movement and later through hand movement when grasping the hidden object (Piaget, 1941).

Another type of procedure, the *observe-perform* task, asks participants to repeat, after a delay, a sequence of actions previously observed. Probably the most well-known task of this type is the Corsi block test (Corsi, 1972; Milner, 1971) in which participants reproduce a sequence of tapping blocks in a nine-block complex configuration. Memory capacity is assessed by increasing the length of the sequence. Such a task is based on the ability to reproduce actions, i.e. to imitate at a later time, and infants are able to imitate (Bauer, 2002; Meltzoff, 1985; Piaget, 1945/1962), though it is still unclear how exactly they are able to do so (Anisfeld, 1991; Meltzoff & Moore, 1983). Recall that Case (1985) used such a task to assess the development of STSS in infants (Chapter 2). Thus, this type of task is a promising tool for studying infants' short-term memory. However, the same concern as for the hide-find procedure exists: infants' behaviours can reflect the implication of a long-term storage more than the capacity of their working memory.

Finally, based on adults' tasks, the *familiarize-recognize* procedure tests the ability to recognize if a probe was previously presented. For example, after the presentation of a series of digits, adults would decide if a digit (the probe) was in the series originally presented. This procedure is adapted to infants because they are able to differentiate between familiar and unfamiliar stimuli (Fantz, 1956), and their preference for the unfamiliar is at the root of the famous habituation paradigm so often used to test infants' knowledge. De Saint Victor, Smith, and Loboschefski (1997) showed that the fixation to a familiarized stimulus when presented with a novel stimulus was a function of the familiarization set size in 10-month-old infants (see

80 The development of working memory

also Rose et al., 2003, 2011, for similar findings). This suggests that infants scan one by one the content of their memory to determine if the presented stimulus is familiar or not. As for the other procedures, an important issue for such a task is to discriminate between the two types of memory. Indeed, an infant could discriminate the familiar stimulus immediately after presentation of the familiarization set, but also hours or days later. Thus, this procedure, like all those previously mentioned, faces the same challenge of discriminating between short- and long-term memory. In addition to this issue, the familiarize-recognize procedure necessitates some level of representation to distinguish familiar from unfamiliar stimuli. Discriminating the novel vs. familiar stimulus could be either due to the recognition of the familiar stimulus based on the maintenance of its representation or to the feeling of familiarity encountered at the presentation of a known stimulus, without the maintenance in short-term memory of its representation. This is rather similar to the point made about the discrepancy between looking and reaching behaviour in the A-not-B task. The difference between these two processes explains why it is often easier to recognize than to recall information. Though some issues remain to be solved, the use of these paradigms gave raise to an important finding, the age-related increase in duration and size of the memory traces stored at short term during infancy.

An increase in duration and size

It is now considered that 5 to 6 months of age is the *onset* of short-term storage. A delayed-response paradigm can be used to determine this onset age. An experimenter appears at one of two windows in front of an infant and then disappears for 1–2 seconds behind a curtain. When the curtain opens, the first gaze gives an indication if the infant attempts to localize the experimenter. Reznick, Morrow, Goldman, and Snyder (2004) have shown that most infants reach performance above chance in their sixth month.

Later during the *first year* of life, infants will be able to maintain information through longer delays (Pelphrey & Reznick, 2003) increasing linearly at a rate of 2 seconds per month from 6 to 12 months of age (Bell & Fox, 1992; Diamond, 1985; Diamond & Doar, 1989). The estimate of storage capacity is nevertheless affected by the valence and the distinctiveness of the stimulus. For example, infants in delayed-response tasks would more likely search for their mother than for a toy, or for a person than an object (Bell, 1970; Schwartz & Reznick, 1999). There is also clear impact of the response modality on storage capacity. Generally, infants exhibit better performance in a delayed-response task when they are allowed to gaze than to reach the correct location, as mentioned previously (Diamond, 1985; Hofstadter & Reznick, 1996). This response modality effect is largely discussed to account for the difference between Piaget's classic findings in the A-not-B task and the very good performance of infants in the delayed-response task. It has been suggested that the level of processing required for gaze control differs from those needed to control actions. Diamond (2001) suggested that the maturation of the dorsolateral prefrontal cortex and its corollary improvement of inhibitory control are major contributors to both A-not-B and delayed-response task. Accordingly, Diamond (1990) showed identical developmental progression on both tasks from 7 to 12 months.

Besides this increase in duration, the number of items that can be stored also increases during the first year of life. As mentioned previously, while 6-month-old infants could maintain one stimulus for some delay, older infants from 8 months onward could exhibit good performance in tasks with several stimuli to be stored (Feigenson, 2007; Kibbe, 2015; Oakes & Luck, 2014; Zosh & Feigenson, 2015). This was shown with two types of tasks. First, in a modified Luck and Vogel's (1997) change detection paradigm, two arrays of simple objects were simultaneously presented to infants. They appeared and disappeared at a regular pace (500 ms on and 250 ms off screen). While all objects remained identical for one array, one object changed colour for the other. Because infants have a preference for novel stimuli, they should prefer looking to the changing condition if they are able to maintain the identity of the objects. By increasing the number of objects in the array, Ross-Sheehy, Oakes, and Luck (2011) have shown that 10-month-old infants preferred the changing condition when arrays contained one to four objects, but they showed no preference in case of six-object arrays. The authors concluded that infants could not represent or store more than four objects presented simultaneously. Using a more naturalistic context, Feigenson and collaborators reached similar conclusion about the number of objects infants would be able to store in short-term memory (Feigenson & Carey, 2003, 2005; Feigenson, Carey, & Hauser, 2002). For example, infants search for one to four hidden balls an experimenter has placed one by one in an opaque box. Unknown to the infants, some balls were removed from the box before they start searching. By measuring the search time and comparing it to a base-line measure when the box was empty, the authors assessed infants' ability to remember that there were some balls in the box. They showed that 12- and 14-month-olds search longer when two balls instead of one were hidden, and for three instead of two balls. However, no significant difference in search times appears in comparisons between one and four and between two and four balls. Thus, experiments based on different paradigms yield similar conclusions. Infants can represent about three to four objects in memory. The three items apparently become individuated sometime around the end of the first year (Kibbe & Leslie, 2013).

It is rather intriguing to consider that infants older than 8 months appear to have a capacity of about three items, which is an adult-like capacity if one accepts the infant and adult procedures as equivalent. This raises numerous questions. Does the same performance at different ages indicate the same underlying competence? Do identical outputs necessarily mean that the task is performed in the same way at different ages? Indeed, as Cowan (2007) noted, children at the beginning of elementary school display a smaller capacity, around two items, which gradually raises with age to the limit of three-to-four observed in adults. This makes clear that the various tests of capacity cannot be considered as pure measures of storage capacity.

Across *toddler years*, short-term memory capacity continues to improve. Scoring memory for locations, Kagan (1981) observed a steep improvement during the second year of life followed by a plateau (see also, Reznick, Corley, & Robinson,

82 The development of working memory

1997). Though studies during childhood also showed an improvement in children older than 6 or 7 years (see next section), the 1- to 3-year age range is poorly documented. Indeed, procedures effective with younger and older children are not appropriate for this age range. This is an important gap to understand the development of short-term memory, especially because these years give rise to a wide range of age-related changes both in cognitive and social development.

Contrary to infant studies in which working memory is assessed through looking or reaching behaviour, evaluation of working memory capacity in later childhood relies on the recall of previously presented information. Following the dissociation introduced by Baddeley between a verbal and a visuospatial store in charge of different types of information, we present the development of the short-term maintenance of these two types of memory items.

Maintenance of verbal information and its childhood development

Since age 2 to end of childhood, the number of verbal items (either digits, letters, or words) a child can maintain in the short term increases steadily (Dempster, 1981, 1985; Henry & Millar, 1993, for review). For example, while a child at 5 years can repeat back three words that were auditorily presented to her, she would recall four words at 9 and five words at 11 (Hitch, Halliday, Dodd, & Littler, 1989). As we have seen in Chapter 3, this ability to maintain verbal items is often considered as an important ability because it sustains achievements in many cognitive tasks and learning of numerous academic skills (language, arithmetic). It is also related to general intellectual ability, and measure of verbal span (i.e. the maximum number of recalled verbal items) is included in IQ tests such as the Wechsler Intelligence Scale for Children (WISC). In Baddeley's model of working memory, verbal items are stored in a specific storage system, named the phonological loop. This loop is thought to rely on language processes to store this information under a phonological format and on a particular mechanism of articulatory rehearsal that recirculates the information through the subvocal repetition of the memory items by our inner speech to preserve memory traces from forgetting (for a similar proposal, see Glanzer & Clark, 1963). Accordingly, research on verbal maintenance focuses on three main questions: Does the age-related increase in articulation rate account for the developmental change in verbal memory span? When are children able to code to-be-maintained information phonologically? Do changes in the use of rehearsal constitute a determinant factor of development in verbal working memory? In the three next sections, we summarize the main findings concerning these three issues.

Articulation rate and increase in the number of verbal items maintained in working memory

The articulation rate is the speed at which one can repeat verbal material over and over again. It can be measured through the repetition of single words or pairs or triads of words, or even non-words that are presented either visually (in this case they are read – reading rate), or auditorily (especially in the case of young illiterate children). It should be noted that the method of measuring articulation rate could have an impact on subsequent correlations with working memory. Importantly, Henry (2012) noted that asking children to repeat two or three words (or even a single multisyllabic word) runs the risk of exceeding their memory span. In other words, the repetition in itself requires maintaining information in working memory. To avoid memory demand, articulation rate should be assessed through repetition of individual words. Supporting this view, Ferguson, Bowey, and Tilley (2002) have shown that two distinct articulation rates can be segregated in accounting for verbal span in 7- and 9-year-olds: one included measures of triads of words and single long words, and the other included articulation of single one-syllable words.

In adults, Baddeley, Thomson, and Buchanan (1975) have shown that verbal memory span (i.e. the maximum number of words recalled in the serial order they were presented) is correlated with the rate at which the words are read. More specifically, adults are able to recall as many words as they can read in two seconds. These authors suggested that reading rate reflects the speed of the internal articulation rate at which words can be repeated subvocally by a rehearsal mechanism. In accordance with this suggestion, adults with a faster reading rate exhibit higher memory spans, lists of short words that are faster to repeat are better recalled than lists of long words, and memory span is higher in languages with a fast articulation rate (Ellis & Hennelly, 1980). In children, the idea emerged that the developmental increase in memory span observed through childhood could be related to age-related changes in articulation rate.

Nicolson (1981) and Hulme et al. (1984) provided evidence that memory span in children depends on their speed of articulation. By measuring reading rate in 8-, 10- and 12-year-old children, or articulation rate in 4-, 7- and 10-year-olds, these authors reported a linear relationship between the speed at which words can be repeated and memory span across age groups (Figure 5.1). Several other studies replicated this finding (Cohen & Heath, 1990; Cowan, Keller, Hulme, Roodenrys, McDougall, & Rack, 1994; Henry, 1994; Hitch, Halliday, Dodd, & Littler, 1989; Hitch, Halliday, & Littler, 1989, 1993; Hulme & Tordoff, 1989; Standing & Curtis, 1989). Though the studies by Nicolson and Hulme et al. led to the same finding that age-related increase in memory span is related to the change in the rate of repetition, the authors diverged in their conclusion. Hulme et al. (1984) interpreted this as supporting Baddeley's phonological loop proposal, and concluded that articulation rate was responsible for the developmental increase in memory span. However, Nicolson (1981) proposed that the reading rate is in fact an index of speed of processing and developmental increase in memory span is due to changes in processing speed, a proposal akin to Case's or Kail's model (Case et al., 1982; Kail, 1997; cf. Chapter 2).

Beyond this divergence in theoretical perspective, it is worth noting that these previous findings rely on correlational evidence based on averaged data across

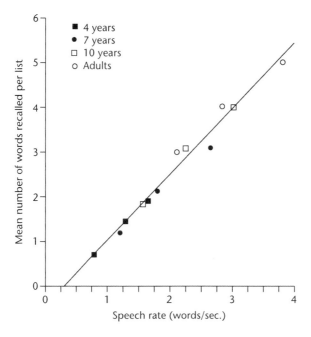

FIGURE 5.1 Relationship between number of words recalled and articulation rate in different age groups with linear regression line

Source: Adapted from C. Hulme, N. Thompson, C. Muir, and A. Lawrence (1984). Speech rate and the development of short-term memory span. *Journal of Experimental Child Psychology, 38*, p. 244, with permission from Elsevier.

individuals of same age. A strong reading of Baddeley's proposal predicts that such a correlation between articulation rate and memory span should emerge at individual level. Kail (1992) and Kail and Park (1994) examined this point, studying either two age groups (9-year-olds and young adults), or a large sample from 7 to adulthood, respectively. Both studies reported relatively modest correlations between individual articulation rate and memory span, ranging between .32 and .36. Though these significant correlations support the phonological loop proposal, they also pointed towards other factors to account for memory span. Kail and Park (1994) speculated that long-term memory knowledge of the to-be-maintained material or efficacy of memory strategy use could be relevant factors (see Chapter 7).

Concerning efficacy of memory strategy use, Henry (1994) noted that the older participants involved in Kail's study could have more often used subvocal rehearsal than the younger ones. However, the fact that the correlation analysis did not segregate participants by age could not permit examining changes in strategy. Thus, Henry (1994) did a similar study in three age groups (5, 7 and 10) to examine correlation at individual level across age groups but also in each age group. Though she replicated the high correlation between articulation rate and memory span across age groups ($r = .60$), this correlation was no longer significant when age was partialled out ($r = .15$) as well as in each age group (r ranging from .18 to .24; see Ferguson et al., 2002, for similar findings). Similarly, no significant correlation appears in younger children aged between 2 and 4 (Gathercole & Adams, 1993; Gathercole, Adams, & Hitch, 1994). Another way to study the impact of articulation rate on developmental change in memory span is to train children to repeat words more quickly and to examine the effect of this training on span. Unfortunately, attempts to train articulation rate in 7-year-old children resulted on small improvements of this rate and it was thus not possible to test any impact on span (Hulme & Muir, 1985). However, in a slightly different way, Cowan, Elliott, Saults, Nugent, Bomb, and Hismjatullina (2006) tested the same idea. They asked 8-year-olds to speed up their response at recall phase. Though children were able to increase their speech rate to the point where they were even faster than adults, this did not result in any improvement in memory span. Finally, an alternative way to examine the role of articulation rate on span is to match children of different age on their articulation rate by presenting different words to old and young children. Doing so, it appears that the classic age difference in span observed between 5- and 7-year-olds became non-significant (Henry & Millar, 1991).

Concerning the second factor mentioned by Kail and Partk (1994), the role of long-term memory, Roodenrys, Hulme, and Brown (1993) assessed memory span and speech rate in 6- to 10-year-olds. They showed that, for both words and pronounceable non-words, the articulation rate was linearly related to memory span but data were better described by two regression lines with words better recalled than non-words. These authors suggested that two factors account for memory span: speech rate and availability of long-term memory phonological representations. In a subsequent study, Kail (1997) extended his own work by introducing measures of phonological skills and also processing speed in 6- to 10-year-olds. Replicating Kail and Park (1994), he showed that articulation rate was correlated with processing speed. But more importantly, span was fully accounted for by articulation rate and phonological skills, while age was not a significant predictor of span. Similar findings were reported by Ferguson and Bowey (2005) in 5- to 13-year-olds, who also observed weaker correlation between articulation rate and span than between phonological skills and span. Elaborating on Roodenrys et al.'s proposal, Kail suggested that as children develop, they process information more rapidly and then can articulate the to-be-maintained items faster, thus improving their maintenance in the phonological loop. However, children's phonological skills also improve, and when memory traces decay in working memory, older children can more efficiently search in long-term memory for information to reconstruct the degraded memory traces (see the redintegration hypothesis by Hulme et al., 1997). Though this could explain both Kail and Roodenrys et al.'s findings, this cannot be applied to preschoolers' working memory in which speech rate and span are not correlated (Gathercole & Adams, 1993; Gathercole et al., 1994). Moreover, when examining the impact of redintegration in children from 5 to 10 years of age, Turner and collaborators found that the familiarity of the memory items had no

86 The development of working memory

effect in the 5-year-olds, though affecting recall in older children as well as in adults (Turner, Henry, Brown, & Smith, 2004; Turner, Henry, & Smith, 2000). They also reported that the advantage for familiar (vs. unfamiliar) words increases with age in spoken recall task, but decreases with age when recalling the position of items was required. Long-term memory knowledge could also be beneficial in the recall of non-words. For example, children better recall non-words made from combinations of sounds that are common rather than uncommon in English, or non-words with large (rather than small) neighbourhood (Gathercole, Frankish, Pickering, & Peaker, 1999; Gathercole, Pickering, Hall, & Peaker, 2001; Thomson, Richardson, & Goswami, 2005).

Finally, others have suggested that another important factor could account for the developmental increase in verbal memory span, i.e. the speed of overt response at recall (Cowan et al., 1994; Cowan, Wood, Wood, Keller, Nugent, & Keller, 1998; Henry, 1991). In the same way as memory traces can decay during the maintenance period and the speed of rehearsal accounts for recall, memory traces can also decay during recall phase. In this case, the speed at which children articulate their response would affect span because it impacts the duration of the recall phase. Accordingly, the duration of pauses between words at recall is related to memory span (Cowan, 1992; Cowan et al., 1998), individuals with shorter pauses having higher spans. Moreover, Cowan and collaborators (1994, 1998) showed that the speed of spoken responses at recall dramatically increases with age during childhood (see Cowan et al., 2003). Importantly, although measures of articulation rate and output pause duration both correlate with memory span, these two speech timing measures do not relate to one another (Cowan et al., 1994, 1998; see also Jarrold, Hewes, & Baddeley, 2000). Cowan and collaborators have argued that the duration of pauses provides an index of 'memory search' processes. To prepare a response item, an individual has to scan through all of the items held in short-term memory, as in memory scanning tasks (see Sternberg, 1966) in which individuals have to determine whether a target item occurred in a previously presented list. Alternatively, Jarrold et al. (2000) proposed that these pauses reflect speech planning processes required before the utterance of words, which is more directly related to Baddeley's view on the implication of language-based processes into verbal short-term storage.

Phonological coding of nonverbal information

Another important prediction from the phonological loop proposal made by Baddeley is that auditorily presented items have direct access to the phonological store while visually presented items (e.g. nameable pictures of animals) can enter the store indirectly after a phonological coding by the articulatory rehearsal process. This was evidenced in adults by the phonological similarity effect, that is the poor recall of similar-sounding letters/words compared to dissimilar sounding items (e.g. Baddeley, 1966; Conrad & Hull, 1964). This effect under visual presentation disappears when rehearsal is impeded at encoding (Baddeley, 2007). Baddeley (1986,

2007) suggested that this effect is attributable to confusion in the phonological store, but there may also be confusion at the recall or reconstruction/redintegration stage (Cowan, Saults, Winterowd, & Sherk, 1991; Hasselhorn & Grube, 2003). However, the rehearsal process is not thought to develop until about 7 years of age (Baddeley, Gathercole, & Papagno, 1998). This should thus introduce a qualitative change in short-term maintenance of nameable pictures.

Actually, it has been reported that children use speech coding by the age of 5 or 6 years and become sensitive to phonological similarity when maintaining nameable pictures (Conrad, 1971; see also Cowan et al., 1991; Hulme, 1987). However, noticing that there was some auditory input in these studies, Halliday, Hitch, Lennon, and Pettipher (1990) replicated Conrad's study using 'silent' presentation, and found phonological similarity effect in 10- but not 5-year-olds. In the preschool years, memory for visually presented stimuli appears to be primarily dependent on visuospatial working memory. As evidenced by Hitch, Halliday, Schaafstal, and Schraagen (1988; see also, Frick, 1988a, 1988b; Logie, Della Sala, Wynn, & Baddeley, 2000; Longoni & Scalisi, 1994; Palmer, 2000a), sequences of items of similar visual forms are recalled less accurately than visually distinct items. On the contrary, in a later stage in development, this visual similarity effect disappears (Brown, 1977; Hayes & Schulze, 1977; Hitch et al., 1988; Hitch, Halliday, Schaafstal, & Heffernan, 1991; Hitch, Woodin, & Baker, 1989; Longoni & Scalisi, 1994; Palmer, 2000), but children show susceptibility to the phonological similarity of visually presented items. The phonological similarity effect can also emerge in 5-year-olds when pictures are labelled during presentation (Ford & Silber, 1994; Hitch, et al., 1991), the overt speech priming the use of phonological representations in young children who would not otherwise use them with visual items. Some disagreement remains about the precise chronology of the shift to phonological recoding (Ford & Silber, 1994; Hulme, 1987; Palmer, 2000b). For example, Al-Namlah, Fernyhough, and Meins (2006) reported phonological similarity effect in children below 6 years of age using 'silent' presentation, but with spoken recall that requires planning and execution of speech (see also, Henry, Messer, Luger-Klein, & Crane, 2012, in 5-year-olds).

Following a similar line of reasoning, it was suggested that the word length effect (i.e. a poorer recall for long- than short-word lists) with items presented as pictures indicates the use of phonological coding. This effect in picture span tasks emerges at 7–9 years (Allik & Siegel, 1976; Halliday et al., 1990; Henry, Turner, Smith, & Leather, 2000; Hitch, Halliday, Dodd, & Littler, 1989; Hitch et al., 1991). There is still a debate about the precise cognitive processes responsible for this development in relation to verbal rehearsal and verbal output (Cowan et al., 1992; Dosher & Ma, 1998; Henry, 1991; Henry et al., 2000; Yuzawa, 2001). Some authors have even doubted that the word length effect is related to articulatory processes (Hulme et al., 2006; Romani et al., 2005).

The view that a shift in representation coding appears at age 7, with children under this age preferring visual code and older children favouring verbal code, has been called into question. Palmer (2000b) suggested that 3–4-year-olds use neither visual nor phonological coding but may rely on semantic representations that are automatically activated from long-term memory. She argued that children between the ages of 6 and 8 years use both visual and phonological coding strategies through a dual coding, before the predominant phonological coding at 10 years of age. The presence of dual phonological and visual coding as interim stage was evidenced by the absence of significant effects of picture type in 4-year-olds, while 5- and 6-year-olds showed evidence of using both phonological coding (with significant phonological similarity and word length effects) and visual coding (resulting in a visual similarity effect). By 7/8 years, visual similarity effect had disappeared, and children showed only phonological coding. However, and contrary to Palmer's (2000) proposal, younger children showed no semantic similarity effect, suggesting that semantic coding is not a key method by which young children recall lists of pictures. These results were replicated by Henry et al. (2012) who reported that 4/5-year-olds did not show any visual similarity, phonological similarity, semantic similarity, or word length effects in a picture span task, whereas 6–8-year-olds showed phonological similarity and word length effects (see also Al-Namlah et al., 2006; Ford & Silber, 1994; Tam, Jarrold, Baddeley, & Sabatos-DeVito, 2010; Winsler & Naglieri, 2003). Al-Namlah et al. (2006) suggested that this verbal mediation in older children may emerge from the gradual internalization of social speech as proposed by Vygotsky (1934/1962). Finally, it should be noted that evidence of a visual coding in older children and adults under articulatory suppression (Brandimonte, Hitch, & Bishop, 1992; Hitch et al., 1989) questions the fact that the dual coding may not be an interim stage in childhood. Thus, instead of characterizing development by a shifting (from visual to verbal) in representational code, the latest research shows that the two codes are available through the life span, with strategic use of one or the other depending on the constraints of the task.

Does development of verbal storage capacity depend on articulatory rehearsal?

Despite the current debate about the transition stages in representation coding of pictures, there is a consensus on the fact that older children tend to favour verbal coding of memory items. As a consequence, articulatory rehearsal is thought to become the dominant maintenance strategy across childhood and its efficiency of use, as measured through articulation rate, is thought to be a determinant of developmental change in verbal working memory (see section above on articulation rate and increase in the number of verbal items maintained in working memory). However, some recent studies reassessed the explanatory power of rehearsal in accounting for developmental change in verbal working memory (Jarrold, 2016, for a review). In the two previous sections, we have seen that two main arguments support the role of rehearsal in the developmental increase in memory span. The first evidence is the fact that young children tend not to show a strong association between measures of speech rate and span. However, such correlations may be particularly 'noisy' in young children. Second, young children tend not to show reliable effects of word length and phonological similarity for visually presented material. However, it was suggested that such effects in adults are scale proportionate (Beaman, Neath, & Surprenant, 2008; Logie, Della Sala, Laiacona, Chambers, & Wynn, 1996). As a consequence, they should be harder to detect in absolute terms among individuals who exhibit low recall performance as is the case for young children (Jarrold, Danielsson, & Wang, 2015; Wang, Logie, & Jarrold, 2016). Accordingly, when analysed in proportional terms, young children have comparable effects of phonological similarity than children older than 7 (Ford & Silber, 1994; Jarrold & Citroën, 2013; Tam et al., 2010).

Finally, the extent to which children appreciate the benefit of using rehearsal to maintain information may lead to variation in its use. Many studies in the 1980s have shown the importance of children's metamemory skills in the choice of strategy and overall memory performance (Schneider, 1985; Schneider & Pressley, 1997; and recently Bebko, McMorris, Metcalfe, Ricciuti, & Goldstein, 2014). It is thus possible that the implementation of articulatory rehearsal requires some top-down executive control (St Clair-Thompson, Stevens, Hunt, & Bolder, 2010), and would be sensitive to working memory load. For example, McGilly and Siegler (1989) found more evidence for rehearsal use when shorter (vs. long) lists were presented to young children. Thus, though phonological representations and articulatory processes have a predominant role in verbal short-term storage, many open questions remain to explore to have a full picture of the development of verbal maintenance.

The development of visuospatial maintenance

As we have seen, the maintenance of verbal information has received considerable attention in the study of short-term memory. However, in the last 20 years, visuospatial maintenance has become the object of greater interest (Kibbe, 2015; Vogel & Awh, 2008). Behavioural and neuroimaging studies in typically developing population as well as in special populations, such as neuropsychological patients and individuals with learning disabilities, brought converging evidence that the short-term maintenance of verbal and nonverbal material are independent from each other (for reviews, see Gathercole & Baddeley, 1993; Logie, 1995).

The independence of visuospatial maintenance in working memory

In children, there is some evidence that skills in verbal and nonverbal memory tasks are unrelated to each other. In 5-year-old children, Michas and Henry (1994) found no significant correlations between the performance in a spatial memory test and two measures of verbal short-term memory. A similar independence of children's verbal and visuospatial memory skills was also reported by Liberman, Mann, Shankweiler, and Werfelman (1982) in 8-year-olds. Pickering, Gathercole, and Peaker (1998) found that scores on verbal and spatial tasks were dissociable in 5- and 8-year-olds, although error patterns were similar (particularly for the 5-year-olds),

90 The development of working memory

which indicates that while different memory systems are involved in verbal and spatial memory, there may be a common mechanism underlying the reconstruction of serial order in both domains (see also Chuah & Maybery, 1999).

Recently, other phenomena favour the idea that, although verbal and visuospatial representations are stored in distinct subsystems, they are not entirely separated because they can be linked (Baddeley, 2000; Mate, Allen, & Baqués, 2012; Morey & Cowan, 2004, 2005). For example, when to-be-remembered digits were presented in a familiar visuospatial array such as the numeric keyboard of a mobile phone, recall performance was better compared to the presentation of digits in a single location like the centre of screen (Darling & Havelka, 2010). This phenomenon, named visuospatial bootstrapping by these authors, shows that participants were able to extract visuospatial information (irrelevant for the digits memorization) and to integrate it with the verbal material. It was subsequently shown that the availability of a compatible representation in long-term memory is necessary for observing bootstrapping (Darling, Allen, Havelka, Campbell, & Rattray, 2012). In children, although 9-year-olds exhibited similar visuospatial bootstrapping as adults, 6-year-olds did not (Darling, Parker, Goodall, Havelka, & Allen, 2014). Because the difficulty of the task was titrated to individual level, the absence of effect at age 6 cannot result from low performance in young children (as was argued for the absence of phonological similarity effect in young children, for example). Though a precise account to explain bootstrapping remains to be firmly established, these results show that the visuospatial bootstrapping ability matures earlier than other working memory processes, because the 9-year-olds show a similar effect to adults, while performance in complex span tasks are known to continue developing through adolescence (Gathercole, 1999; Siegel, 1994).

Age-related increase in visuospatial maintenance

Because visuospatial storage is independent from verbal maintenance, different paradigms are used to assess it. Three main tasks are used to study age-related changes across childhood: visual pattern span, Corsi block, and change detection tasks. The two latter tasks were already described in the first section about infant studies. The visual pattern span task is designed to measure visual short-term memory (Della Sala, Gray, Baddeley, Allamano, & Wilson, 1999). A matrix with some cells filled to make a pattern is presented to participants and then removed. The task is to reproduce this pattern by marking squares in a blank grid of the same dimensions as the presented one. The advantages of this task is that it is difficult to enlist the aid of verbalization to memorize the pattern and it reduces sequential spatial requirements, especially compared to the Corsi block task in which participants have to reproduce a motor sequence. The Corsi block task places also a strong requirement to recall the order of arbitrary elements, as in the digit span task in verbal domain.

Across childhood, memory for visual patterns increases with age (Orsini, 1994; Orsini et al., 1987; Wilson, Scott, & Power, 1987, see also Hamilton, Coates, &

Heffernan, 2003), as does performance in the Corsi block task (De Renzi & Nichelli, 1975; Isaacs & Vargha-Khadem, 1989; Kemps, De Rammelaere, & Desmet, 2000). This was also replicated by Logie and Pearson (1997) who administered recall and recognition versions of both tasks to children of 5/6, 8/9 and 11/12 years of age. They also observed that memory span for visual patterns develops more rapidly than memory for spatial sequences. What is not clear from all studies on visuospatial maintenance is the cause of these age-related improvements in performance. As previously discussed in the section on phonological coding of nonverbal information, the increasing use of a verbal coding for visually presented material may account (at least in part) for the developmental improvement in memory performance. In agreement with this proposal, Miles et al. (1996) have shown that the performance of 10-year-olds and adults in the visual pattern task was detrimentally affected by a concurrent articulation during presentation, maintenance, and output of the matrix patterns, which would prevent the phonological recoding of visuospatial information. However, the performance of 5- and 7-year-olds was not (see also Kemps et al., 2000, for similar findings in the 'Mr Peanut' task). This indicates that older children and adults can use phonological processes to carry out a relatively 'pure' visuospatial task, while younger children may have insufficient capacity to carry out phonological recoding operations and favour visual code because this is modality-dependent and probably automatically activated (Hitch et al., 1988; Longoni & Scalisi, 1994).

Younger children differ not only from older ones in the type of code they use in the visuospatial tasks, they also differ in the implication of executive or attentional processes. In a large latent-variables study including measures of verbal and visuospatial short-term and working memory in seven different age groups, Alloway et al. (2006) have shown that the link between the domain-specific visuospatial construct and the domain-general processing construct was higher in the 4–6-year-olds compared with the older (7- to 11-year-old) children. Indeed, when the correlation between these two variables was fixed to represent a perfect association, the fit of the model remained unchanged for the younger age groups, but decreased for the older groups. This suggests that young children draw more on executive resources than older children when performing visuospatial tasks (see also Cowan et al., 2005). Nevertheless, it should be noted that the visuospatial tasks used in this study included dynamic formats, such as the perceptuo-motor tracking of dots, and there is growing evidence that executive functions support the dynamic (but not the static) aspects of visuospatial tasks, such as tracking visual sequences and transforming visuospatial images (Duff & Logie, 1999; Logie, 1995). Nevertheless, in a structural equation modelling study involving 8–9-year-old children, Campos, Almeida, Ferreira, and Martinez (2013) reported a high correlation ($r = .91$) between the central executive and the visuospatial storage factors. Thus, they proposed a model with executive functioning and visuospatial tasks loading on the same factor, which was more parsimonious to account for children's performance than a three-factor model. In the same vein, Michalczyk, Malstadt, Worgt, Konen, and Hasselhorn (2013) found that a three-factor model fits their data for each age group (5–6,

92 The development of working memory

7–9, 10–12), but they reported also a high correlation between the visuospatial sketchpad and the central executive ($r = .81$), especially in the younger groups (see also Gray, Green, Alt, Hogan, Kuo, Brinkley, & Cowan, 2017, for a model combining focus of attention and visuospatial storage in 7-year-olds). To conclude, though studies in adults have been able to dissociate specific processes dedicated to the storage of visuospatial material, the picture in children, and especially for the younger, is not so clear, and a strong link exists between visuospatial storage and executive or attentional processes. Future developmental research should aim at analysing the kind of attentional processes involved in visuospatial storage and how they are less and less required through childhood.

A slot memory capacity or allocation of resources?

The renewal of research on visuospatial storage stems from the interest in the change detection task (Luck & Vogel, 1997) and its use to measure short-term memory capacity (Cowan et al., 2005, 2006; Cowan, Morey, AuBuchon, Zwilling, & Gilchrist, 2010; Riggs, McTaggart, Simpson, & Freeman, 2006; Shore, Burack, Miller, Joseph, & Enns, 2006). Most recent work aimed at adapting this task to children, and in the first part of this chapter, we have seen how this was possible for infants (Ross-Sheehy et al., 2003). In children, only minor modifications were made to assess developmental changes in 3- to 12-year-old children (Cowan et al., 2005; Cowan, Fristoe, et al., 2006; Riggs, et al., 2006; Riggs, Simpson, & Potts, 2011; Simmering, 2012). Based on this task, estimates of working memory capacity increase from about two items at 3 years, up to four or five items by 12 years.

The nature of this limitation has been a source of considerable and still unsolved debate. This debate focuses on whether slot-like, fixed-resolution representations (e.g. Zhang & Luck, 2008), or the allocation of a limited resource pool with decreasing resolution per item as the number of items increases (e.g. Bays & Husain, 2008), defines visuospatial working memory capacity. In development, authors like Cowan et al. (2005, 2011) and Riggs et al. (2006) attribute the developmental improvement to an increase in the discrete number of items that can be held simultaneously in visual working memory. Errors arise when an item is not stored in memory because the number of to-be-remembered items exceeds the number of available memory slots. By this account, working memory capacity should be the same across objects with different feature types. However, recent children studies using change detection task focused on memory for coloured squares (Cowan et al., 2005; Riggs et al., 2006; Simmering, 2012).[1] Thus, it is difficult to know whether capacity is comparable across feature types during childhood. Nevertheless, other studies using different paradigms shed light on this question. Abstract shape span (a pure visual recall) was found to be poorer than location memory across four different age groups (4-, 6-, 7- and 8-year-olds; Visu-Petra, Cheie, & Benga, 2008), and age-related changes in abstract object maintenance had a slower trajectory than in spatial maintenance (Hitch, 1990; Van Leijenhorst, Crone, & van der Molen, 2007). Using a probed memory task, Walker, Hitch, Doyle, and Porter (1994) compared short-term visual memory for an object's spatial location or colour, and showed a developmental enhancement (from 5 to 7 years of age) in memory for spatial location but no effect of age with regard to the recall of colour. The results go against Hasher and Zacks' (1979) proposal that spatial location in contrast to colour would not show developmental improvement because it is remembered automatically. Moreover, these results do fit with the idea that working memory capacity is defined by a limited number of slots that should not vary across different objects.

An alternative theoretical approach emerged in adult studies and proposed to investigate working memory precision, i.e. a continuous measure reflecting the resolution of items held in working memory. This perspective known as a resource perspective was put forward by Bays and Husain (2008), who argue that adults can hold an unlimited number of items in memory, but the resolution of representations decreases proportionally as their number increases. Two studies have shown that resolution improves developmentally during the same period during which capacity increases (Burnett Heyes, Zokaei, & Husain, 2016; Burnett Heyes, Zokaei, van der Staaij, Bays, & Husain, 2012; Simmering & Patterson, 2012). In Burnett Heyes et al.'s (2012) study, five age groups of 9- to 13-year-old children were presented with either one or three oriented bars in sequence, and after a brief delay they reported the orientation of one of those bars. The precision with which items could be recalled showed a linear increase across childhood (see Burnett Heyes et al., 2016, for similar findings from a longitudinal follow-up with the same participants). Moreover, the addition of a concurrent processing during maintenance reduced the quality of item representation as well as the likelihood of the target being represented in memory. Using a similar paradigm as Burnett Heyes et al. (2012), Sarigiannidis et al. (2016) observed that children were less precise in their memory for target while their probability of guessing increased when they had to perform a concurrent mental rotation task. Burnett Heyes and collaborators suggest that one possible mechanism for developmental improvements in visuospatial maintenance is the gradual improvement in maintenance accuracy, rather than an increase in the discrete number of items that can be maintained per se. They attribute this increase in resolution to 'sharpening' neural representation (see also Simmering, 2016).

A final mechanism that might drive age-related differences is the ability to bind multiple features of an object. This ability may improve with age (Brockmole & Logie, 2013; Cottini et al., 2015; Cowan, Naveh-Benjamin, Kilb, & Saults, 2006), and could account for the extent to which children confuse the order or location of the items stored in memory. Luck and Vogel (1997) suggested that encoding an object into working memory results in all features being entered into working memory. However, recent work has shown that the requirement in adults to maintain both shape and colour results in fewer colours (or shapes) being remembered than when only colour (or shapes) need to be remembered (Cowan et al., 2013; Hardman & Cowan, 2015; Oberauer & Eichenberger, 2013). Though additional work is needed in children to understand the role of feature binding, these accounts are not mutually exclusive, and the development of visuospatial maintenance could stem from a combination of these mechanisms.

Conclusion

The development of short-term storage has been studied extensively. Research has aimed at documenting age-related changes in the capacity of short-term storage and at understanding the mechanisms responsible for such changes. Concerning the age-related changes in capacity, and thanks to specific paradigms, it has been shown that the capacity to maintain information in the short term increases both in terms of duration and size during the first year of life. These increases continue across childhood. However, it remains difficult to perfectly fill the gap between infancy and childhood, or even to make comparisons between infants and young children, because the paradigms employed in the two age periods are so different that one cannot assume they actually assess the same processes. The most striking fact is that infants are able to maintain up to three or four items, knowing that this is the usual capacity limit observed in adults, and that children are not able to maintain so many representations. Some authors like Cowan (2007) discussed this discrepancy and saw in it evidence for the implications of different processes. To our view, this also questions the existence of genuine mental representations in infants who would rather rely on percepts to perform the looking or reaching tasks involved in paradigms used during infancy. Furthermore, increasing the research effort in the transitional age between 1 and 3 years, which is poorly examined, might provide decisive elements to better understand the age-related changes in the short-term storage.

Concerning the factors that could account for these age-related changes in storage capacity, brain maturation is very often mentioned, which is more specifically thought to underlie the capacity increase observed during infancy. Although this factor could also account for changes over childhood, authors favour other factors to explain the quantitative and qualitative changes occurring during this developmental period. The most frequently evoked factors are the changes in maintenance strategies, or in the nature of working memory representations as well as the use children can make of their growing long-term memory knowledge. The current chapter reviewed some evidence that these factors are involved in the increase in storage capacity. In the final chapter of this book, we shall re-examine them in the light of a particular model of working memory.

Note

1 There is one exception: Riggs et al. (2011) compared performance on orientation versus both orientation and colour of coloured oriented bars, but no cross-condition comparisons were provided.

6

THE DEVELOPMENT OF THE EXECUTIVE CONTROL

The role of executive functions in cognitive development has been emphasized for many years, and prominent models of cognitive development such as Case (1987) or Pascual-Leone (1970) considered them as a driving factor of cognitive development. As described in previous chapters, Pascual-Leone suggested that the development of executive functions helps children to inhibit salient but irrelevant information, which can interfere with the information relevant for problem solving. Case also proposed that the development of executive functions are linked with working memory development through the construction of executive control structures.

In the field of working memory, prominent models incorporate executive functions as part of working memory (cf. Chapter 4). The best example is Baddeley's model in which a central executive subsystem is a kind of supervisory attentional system in charge of the multitasking, the shifting between tasks, or the inhibition of irrelevant information (Baddeley, 1986). In Engle's model, working memory is often described as the ability to maintain selected information in the short term and to inhibit distractors and interfering material (Kane & Engle, 2000, 2002). Intriguingly, while these models integrate executive functions as part of working memory functioning, researchers in executive functions refer to working memory as a subcomponent of executive control, and they often mention working memory as one of the three main executive functions. Thus, such a state of affairs makes clear that, although the relationships between working memory and executive functions are far from being fully understood, they should be very tight.

After presenting the different ways to define executive control, we will focus on the development of what are often conceived as the three main executive functions, namely working memory updating, inhibition, and shifting (also named cognitive flexibility). Finally, we will present the four main approaches that frame the study of executive functions and their development.

96 The development of working memory

Definitions of executive functions

Executive control is not a unitary process but a construct composed of several related skills. This construct is notoriously ill-defined and a plethora of definitions has been proposed. However, these definitions share some commonalities. Under the umbrella of executive control fall the mental functions that are responsible for purposeful, goal-directed, problem-solving behaviour. This includes self-regulatory skills involved in goal-directed modulation of thought, emotion, and action (Barkley, 2012; Diamond, 2014; Zelazo, 2015). Executive control refers thus to a family of top-down mental processes needed when you have to concentrate and pay attention, when going on automatic or relying on instinct or intuition would be ill-advised, insufficient, or impossible (Diamond, 2012). They are also called executive control or cognitive control, and they have been referred as a 'conductor', which controls, organizes, and directs cognitive activity (Gioia, Isquith, & Guy, 2001). In the past decade, it has been proposed to dichotomize executive functions into 'cold' and 'hot' executive functions (Zelazo, Qu, & Müller, 2004). The cold executive functions are purely cognitive and process decontextualized abstract problems, while the hot executive functions are emotionally driven, and involve the regulation of affect and motivation.

Originally, the concept of executive functioning arose to define what the prefrontal cortex does (Pribram, 1973, 1976), and to understand the neurospsychological functions mediated by this brain region. But executive functions are not exclusively functions of the prefrontal cortex, because various networks of connections to other cortical and subcortical regions are involved in executive control (e.g. Denckla, 1996; Fuster, 1989, 1997; Luria, 1966; Nigg & Casey, 2005; Stuss & Benson, 1986). Moreover, the prefrontal cortex is also involved in other functions that do not fall under the umbrella of executive functions, such as automatic sensory-motor activities (Barkley, 2012). Thus, as Barkley (2012) noted, there is no consensual definition of executive functions nor an explicit operational definition of the term that would allow to determine which human mental functions can be considered executive in nature, and which ones cannot be so classified. As a consequence, the number of skills considered as executive functions as well as their nature can vary greatly from one author to another. Nevertheless, any definition of executive functions makes obvious that attention is essential to these skills or that attentional processes can be themselves considered as executive functions. For example, selective attention and shifting attention are often required during goal-oriented behaviours. Barkley (1996) suggests that the executive system could be a general form of attention (see also Zelazo, 2015, for whom executive skills are attentional skills or ways of using attention).

Among the plethora of definitions, three different approaches can be distinguished on how to define executive functions. First, executive control can be treated as a higher-order cognitive mechanism or ability, a unitary process. For example, Denckla and Reiss (1997) suggested that executive control 'refers to a cognitive module consisting of effect or output elements involving inhibition, working memory, and organisational strategies necessary to prepare a response' (p. 283). This approach conceives executive functions as a homunculus controlling behaviour, like the supervisory attentional system (Shallice, 1988) or the central executive in Baddeley (1986). This conception makes it difficult to understand how executive control is actually accomplished (Parkin, 1998; Zelazo & Müller, 2002). Furthermore, subsequent research has demonstrated that a modular unit is too simplistic and this has led to the decomposition of this unit into distinct but related components (like the fractionation of the central executive in Baddeley, 1996, 1998).

A second approach uses comprehensive neuropsychological batteries to reveal the underlying structure of executive functions (see Zelazo & Müller, 2002, for a review). However, results of factor-analytic studies are potentially misleading. Indeed, it should be noted that the same tasks are often clustered in different ways, and characterized by different labels. For example, the Wisconsin Card Sorting Test (WCST, Grant & Berg, 1948) is considered as part of a 'perseveration-disinhibition' factor in Levin et al. (1991), but is considered to assess 'set shifting or cognitive flexibility' by Pennington (1997). Thus, the absence of understanding of the underlying cognitive processes undermines the usefulness of this approach to reveal the structure of executive functions. Finally, following Luria (1973), executive control can be considered as a functional construct that makes reference to the psychological processes involved in goal-oriented problem solving (see Zelazo, Carter, Resnick, & Frye, 1997). The various processes involved in goal-oriented problem solving, from building the initial representation of the problem to the evaluation of the appropriateness of the answer with the possible correction of errors, can be included under the label of executive functions. Although this approach does not give us an explanation of what executive control is, it gives a promising perspective of research. For example, authors like Zelazo, Müller, Frye and Marcovitch (2003) use this approach to derive specific hypotheses regarding the role of some cognitive processes, such as attention, memory, or action monitoring, in executive functioning. Such an approach has framed their investigation and has produced enlightening findings.

The development of executive functions

As we mentioned above, though some authors favour a unitary approach to executive control, the dominant view is to conceive the existence of a diversity of executive functions, which share some common ground. Evidence for a fractionation of executive functions derives from different findings. Patients with dysexecutive symptoms rarely present global deficit (e.g. Pennington & Ozonoff, 1996), and lesion studies lead to localize distinct executive processes in the frontal lobe (e.g. Stuss et al., 2002). Moreover, the developmental trajectories of different executive functions vary (e.g. Anderson, 2002). But it is most probably the work of Mikaye and colleagues (Miyake, Friedman, Emerson, Witzki, Howerter, & Wager, 2000) that is considered as the strongest argument. While examining three executive functions in a latent variable analysis, Miyake et al. (2000) reported that updating

98 The development of working memory

and monitoring of working memory contents, inhibiting prepotent responses, and shifting between mental sets or tasks, share a significant part of variance, although they are clearly distinguishable, a three-factor model producing the best fit. This study, performed on young adults, has had a long-lasting impact on the field, because it installs the idea of unity and diversity among executive functions, but also because it enlightens these three functions, which are often considered now as the core executive functions.

Unity and diversity of executive functions across childhood

Some research with children has investigated the executive control construct and has found at least partial support for an integrative framework, as reported by Miyake et al. in young adults. Hughes (1998) extracted three distinct factors, attentional flexibility, inhibitory control, and working memory,[1] from preschoolers' performance on several executive tasks, suggesting that executive functions are differentiated even at a young age. Senn, Espy, and Kaufmann (2004) observed in preschoolers that performance in working memory and inhibition tasks was correlated, shifting performance being unrelated to the other measures. This provided evidence that the executive functions are dissociable in early childhood, but also that these functions are interrelated to some degree. Confirmatory factor analysis (CFA) with older children provide stronger support for the 'unity and diversity view'. First, Lehto, Juujärvi, Kooistra, and Pulkkinen (2003) found that the same three-factor model reported by Miyake et al. in adults provided the best fit of data from children aged 8 to 13. Second, while comparing 7-, 11-, 15-, and 21-year-old participants, Huizinga, Dolan, and van der Molen (2006) found partial support for the three-factor model because only the working memory and shifting measures loaded onto latent variables, whereas the inhibition measures did not load onto a common latent variable (see also Friedman et al., 2008, 2011, for similar results in adults). Importantly, this model was consistent across the different age groups, suggesting a stability of the executive functions from middle childhood to early adulthood. Reviewing different studies using CFA, Bardikoff and Sabbagh (2017) suggest that executive control is differentiated across childhood from a unitary construct in preschoolers, to a two-factor construct in middle childhood, and finally to a three-factor at adolescence. Together, these studies provide evidence that executive functions are interrelated, and yet dissociable. They also show that these three core functions provide a suitable framework to examine the development of executive control. In the following, we examine in turn the developmental trajectory of these three main executive functions (see also Diamond, 2006, for a review).

Updating or working memory

Miyake et al.'s (2000) analysis isolated an updating component, which refers to the ability to revise the content of working memory, replacing previously stored information by new and more relevant one. This focuses on a very specific aspect of working memory, keeping aside other important functions of working memory, like the storage and the processing of information. As we have seen in the previous chapter, many developmental studies in working memory restricted their investigation to the short-term maintenance, and reported an increasing capacity in time and quantity to store information from infancy to adulthood. This focus on maintenance function could be explained by two reasons, one methodological and one theoretical. First, working memory tasks that have been primarily developed for adults require the joint storage and processing of information. Paradigms like the complex span task and the Brown-Peterson task are among the most often used to assess working memory capacity. The complexity of these paradigms makes them very difficult to use in children, and especially with the younger. Thus, tasks requiring the mere storage of information are easier to implement in children, which gives rise to numerous developmental studies on age-related changes in maintenance capacity. From a theoretical point of view, a second reason could explain the focus on maintenance. For some working memory models, like the models of Cowan or Engle (Chapter 4), or the TBRS model (Chapter 7), the storage as well as the processing of information in working memory rely both on a limited attentional or executive resource. Within this conception, tasks that require only the maintenance of information without any processing would also depend, and thus inform us, on this attentional/executive resource.

Nevertheless, although they are less common than studies on short-term maintenance, some studies examined the development of the updating function in working memory using the self-ordered pointing task (Petrides & Milner, 1982). In this task, children have to point at an element they never pointed at before among a set of elements, the arrangement of which changes after each pointing act. Thus, children have to constantly update the mental list of elements at which they have already pointed. Performance in this task improves from age 3 to adulthood (Cragg & Nation, 2007; Hongwanishkul et al., 2005; Ward et al., 2005).

Inhibition

Inhibition refers to the ability to block or suppress information or responses. It is not a unified process and several types of inhibitions are distinguished. Among them, the resistance to interference allows the blocking of information before it enters working memory. It was suggested to be a major factor in cognitive development and aging, intimately associated with the operation of the frontal cortex (Dempster, 1992). This concept is very close to selective attention, which aims at selecting some information in the environment, avoiding attention to irrelevant information. It is also related to the idea of controlled or executive attention developed by Engle (2002; Engle et al., 1999; Kane & Engle, 2003). We have seen that in Engle's working memory model, individuals with high working memory capacity differ from individuals with low capacity especially on this ability to control their attention, i.e. to resist interfering material. Another type of inhibition is the inhibition of prepotent responses, which blocks automatic, well-learnt responses

100 The development of working memory

that could be directly activated by stimuli in the environment. For example, in one task of the NEPSY battery (i.e. the only specific battery to measure executive functions in children), children have to pose as a statue and to stay still when the experimenter makes various noises (Korkman, Kirk, & Kemp, 1998). Finally, the conceptual inhibition refers to the inhibition of representations. In other words, it suppresses irrelevant information from working memory to permit its updating.

Although these different types of inhibition are described in the literature, developmental studies have rarely distinguished them, and generally they have reported an overall improvement in inhibition. Since the very first months of life, inhibition improves, as can be seen in the A-not-B task already mentioned. Recall that, in this Piagetian task, infants are prompted to search for an object. This object is placed and retrieved in a location A on several occasions, and then placed in a different location B. While they have seen that the object was placed in B, 8-month-old children search for it in A, which is where they found it on several occasions before. This error disappears at 12 months, suggesting that the inhibition of motor responses can be achieved at this age. From 1 to 3 years, inhibitory capacity further increases, children being more and more able to delay a gratification (to have a bigger one later! Carlson, 2005). Their performance also improves in Stroop-like tasks, like the Day-Night task, or in Go/no-Go tasks (Best, Miller, & Jones, 2009). The Day-Night task assesses complex response inhibition by requiring the child to inhibit a prepotent verbal response (i.e. saying 'day' upon viewing a picture of a sun) and activate an alternative verbal response (i.e. saying 'night'; Gerstadt, Hong, & Diamond, 1994). On the contrary, the Go/no-Go tasks are simple response inhibition tasks in which children are instructed to perform the same task on most trials (go trials) but to withhold responding when a specific category of stimuli or a specific cue is displayed (no-go trials). For example, they have to press a key when any fish appears on screen but not for a shark. Although improved inhibition during the preschool years is striking, significant improvements also occur later until adolescence and young adulthood. Unlike the fundamental changes during preschool years (e.g. acquisition of the ability to inhibit a prepotent response consistently), changes during adolescence mainly consist of refinements in speed and accuracy. Complex cognitive inhibition tasks (e.g. the Eriksen Flankers task and the Stroop task) appear to be more sensitive to the subtle improvements in performance than simpler conflict tasks (e.g. the Day/Night task) or motor inhibition tasks (e.g. the Statue task in the NEPSY battery). Even in young adults, for whom inhibition capacity is mature, individual differences in controlled attention lead to differences in these complex inhibition tasks, low-span individuals being more error-prone and slower than high-span individuals in Stroop and Flanker tasks (Heitz & Engle, 2007; Kane & Engle, 2003).

Shifting or cognitive flexibility

As for the broad concept of executive control, the specific executive function of shifting benefits from various definitions, and is often called switching or cognitive flexibility. While the use of shifting or switching refers clearly to the ability to move efficiently from one task to another, the term flexibility is more broadly used when describing the ability to adapt adequately one's behaviour, which goes far beyond the mere alternation between tasks. This wide conception of this executive function leads some authors to suggest that cognitive flexibility relies in fact on the two previously examined executive functions. Indeed, to behave flexibly, one needs to inhibit the no-longer relevant information and to update the content of working memory with relevant information and new instructions. As we will see in the next section, some models of executive control account for the development of cognitive flexibility through age-related changes in working memory (Morton & Munakata, 2002a) or in inhibition (Kirkham, Cruess, & Diamond, 2003). However, other authors suggest that this function can be distinguished from working memory and inhibition (Best et al., 2009; Garon et al., 2008). For example, the inhibitory capacity improves faster in children from 4 to 13 years than the ability to flexibly alternate between rules (Davidson, Amso, Cruess Anderson, & Diamond, 2006).

Besides these differences in conceptions, cognitive flexibility can be conceived as the ability to adequately select the more adapted strategy or task-set and to modify it in accordance with the changes occurring in the environment (Deak, 2003). Accordingly, the tasks used to assess cognitive flexibility require the way to process a set of stimuli to be changed during a task. The main example of these tasks is the Dimensional Change Card Sort (DCCS, Zelazo, 2006), in which children have to sort a series of cards initially on one dimension (e.g. the colour), and after several cards and following instructions to change the sorting criterion (e.g. to sort cards by shape). While 3-year-old children can perform the initial sort, they fail at changing the criterion and persevere on using the first dimension. By contrast, 4- and 5-year-old children can change across the task the dimension used to sort the cards. Thus, an important developmental evolution in cognitive flexibility occurs between 3 and 4, but performance in tasks assessing cognitive flexibility improves also after 4. First, children will improve in their ability to make more than one change for a series of stimuli. For example, some cues can lead children to alternate between two sorting dimensions across the task or several sorting dimensions can be used one after another, as in the WCST in which cards have to be paired according to colour, shape, or number of stimuli on the cards. The second aspect that improves across childhood is the ability to self-initiate the change. For example, in the WCST, children have to infer the change on the relevant dimension based on the feedback given by the experimenter about the previous trial. Improvements in these two aspects are observed until the end of adolescence (e.g. Davidson et al., 2006; Somsen, 2007), which suggests that age-related changes in cognitive flexibility occur until late in development. Recent works propose that these changes are sustained by an increased capacity to determine the goal of the task in absence of any indications or instructions (Chevalier & Blaye, 2009; Chevalier, Dauvier, & Blaye, 2009).

To conclude, as in the case for short-term maintenance, executive control undergoes important improvements over the entire developmental period, from

102 The development of working memory

the very first months of life to the very end of adolescence, lending support to the hypothesis that it plays a major and motor role in cognitive development. However, this protracted development of executive functions raises the question of what produces the improvement in executive control itself. Not so surprisingly, different accounts have been advanced that are expounded in the next section.

Models of executive control

Among the different models accounting for the development of executive control, four leading theoretical conceptions can be distinguished. Each of these approaches emphasizes one specific aspect to understand the development of executive functions, favouring either age-related changes in complexity, proposing a prominent role to memory or to inhibitory control, or stressing the redescription of representations. We will describe each of these approaches in turn.

The complexity theories

The complexity theories find their roots in Piaget's and Vygotsky's theories. One influential developmental theory in this approach was proposed by Halford (Halford et al., 1998; Chapter 2). As we have seen, this theory suggests that children increasingly understand complex relations among objects. Halford defines complexity in terms of the number of relations that can be processed in parallel. Although this theory has focused on explaining age-related increases in understanding, and not on executive control, it has been extended to the study of prefrontal cortical functions (e.g. Robin & Holyoak, 1995), and complexity theories could thus be a useful framework to account for executive control.

Within this theoretical conception, probably the most influential theory that accounts for the development in executive control is the Control Complexity and Cognitive (CCC) theory proposed by Zelazo (Frye, Zelazo, & Burack, 1998; Zelazo & Frye, 1998; Zelazo et al., 2003). According to the CCC theory, the development of executive control (considered as a functional construct) can be understood in terms of age-related increase in the maximum complexity of the rules children can formulate and use when solving problems. Complexity is defined in terms of the hierarchical structure of children's rule systems (Figure 6.1). It is the level of embedding that provides the metric for measuring the degree of complexity of the entire rule system that needs to be kept in mind (i.e. in working memory) in order to perform particular tasks. These age-related changes in the maximum rule complexity are, in turn, made possible by age-related increases in the degree to which children can reflect on the rules they represent. For example, in the DCCS, rule A can be 'If it is red, put it here' and rule B 'If it is blue, put it there'. To sort by colour, a child needs to reflect on rule A, contrasting it with rule B (Figure 6.2). To sort by shape, another pair of rules is needed, such as rule C 'If it is a rabbit, put it here' and rule D 'If it is a boat, put it there'. At 2 years of age, children would only consider a single rule (e.g. rule A) at a time. As a consequence, they produce

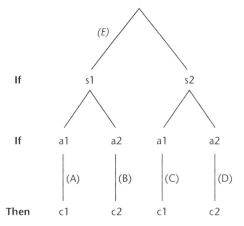

FIGURE 6.1 Hierarchical tree structure depicting formal relations among rules (A–E)

Source: Adapted from P. D. Zelazo, U. Müller, D. Frye, and S. Marcovitch (2003). The development of executive function in early childhood. *Monographs of the Society for Research in Child Development, 68*, p. 8, with permission from Wiley.

Note
s1 and s2 are setting conditions; a1 and a2 are antecedent conditions; c1 and c2 are consequences. The higher order rule (E) requires children to consider both a setting condition and an antecedent condition in order to determine the appropriate consequence.

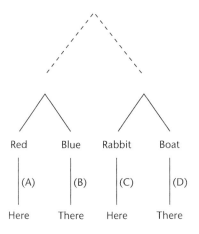

FIGURE 6.2 Unintegrated rule systems, in the absence of a high order rule, for the DCCS task

Source: Adapted from P. D. Zelazo, U. Müller, D. Frye, and S. Marcovitch (2003). The development of executive function in early childhood. *Monographs of the Society for Research in Child Development, 68*, p. 10, with permission from Wiley.

104 The development of working memory

some perseveration errors, even before the switch (i.e. some blue cards can be put in the red stack). At 3, they would consider one pair of rules (e.g. rules A and B) simultaneously, which allows them to succeed at the DCCS before the change in sorting dimension. Because each pair of rules can only be considered in separate context, this allows 3-year-old children to sort cards either by colour or by shape, but not to switch between sorting dimensions. At 4, children represent a higher rule system in which the two pairs of rules are integrated into a single rule system. This allows them to conceive that different pairs of rules apply to different contexts, and to deliberately switch between the pairs, flexibly selecting the pair adapted to the situational demand.

In this account, rules are formulated in an ad hoc fashion, potentially silent self-directed speech. As exemplified above, more complex rule systems permit the more flexible selection of certain rules for acting when multiple conflicting rules are possible. This leads to flexible responding as opposed to perseveration: It allows for cognitive control, as opposed to stimulus control. In other words, the control and choice of rules is deliberate and not determined associatively by the stimulus. According to CCC theory, several age-related changes in executive control occur during childhood, and for each developmental transition, a general process is recapitulated. Specifically, a rule system at a particular level of complexity is acquired, and this rule system permits children to exercise a new degree of control over their reasoning and their behaviour. It could be noticed that some characteristics of the CCC theory resonate with Piaget's theory. Especially, the children's actions, and the internal representations that support them, are described in rather formal, propositional terms. Furthermore, cognitive development occurs through stage-like changes in the complexity of possible mental transformations. This conception also echoes Case's (1985) proposals about the executive control structures and the process of hierarchical integration of subgoals and associated actions or operations of increasing complexity (see Chapter 2). However, in the CCC theory, the use of a rule system is subject to limitations that cannot be overcome until yet another level of complexity is achieved. In particular, the rule system cannot be selected when there is a salient, conflicting rule system. Consequently, according to the CCC theory, abulic dissociation, i.e. dissociations between having knowledge and actually using that knowledge (a reminiscence of the distinction between competence and performance), occurs until incompatible pieces of knowledge are integrated into a single, more complex rule system via their subordination to a new higher-order rule.

Although CCC theory is similar in many respects to Halford's relational complexity theory, Halford and collaborators (Halford et al., 2002) note that an increase in the number of dimensions processed simultaneously is not the same as the creation of a hierarchical *if-if-then* relation between dimensions as proposed by the CCC theory (Figure 6.1). The CCC theory and the relational complexity theory also postulate different mechanisms for the construction of increasingly complex knowledge structures (Zelazo & Müller, 2002). According to the relational complexity theory, age-related changes in complexity are related to increases in effective processing capacity brought about by experience in particular domains. In contrast, according to CCC theory, it is largely through age-related changes in reflection that cognitive development unfolds. This reflection is mediated by the reprocessing of information via neural circuits that coordinate hierarchically arranged regions of the prefrontal cortex (Bunge & Zelazo, 2006; Zelazo, 2015). Thus, that information is fed back into the system where it can be combined with other relevant information, yielding a more elaborate construal.

To account for this mechanism, Zelazo (2015) proposed the Iterative Reprocessing (IR) model, which was built in part on the Levels of Consciousness model (Zelazo, 2004), the CCC-revised theory (Zelazo et al., 2003), and other related theoretical models of executive control (Bunge & Zelazo, 2006; Marcovitch & Zelazo, 2009). The IR model characterizes deliberate self-regulation as the product of a dynamic interaction between more bottom-up (reactive) and more top-down (reflective) influences. Reflection allows for the ad hoc construction of more complex representations. As in the CCC theory, this is measured by the hierarchical complexity of the rule systems that can be formulated and maintained in working memory. More complex rule representations, maintained in working memory, allow for more flexibility and goal-directed control in a wider range of situations. On this view, cognitive flexibility, working memory (conceived here as both keeping information in mind and manipulating it in some way), and inhibitory control (i.e. deliberately suppressing attention or other responses to something, e.g. ignoring a distraction or stopping an impulsive utterance), all depend on the iterative reprocessing of information, which permits the formulation of more complex rules that can then be used to control behaviour (Cunningham & Zelazo, 2007).

In the IR model, reflection is the deliberate sustained consideration (and reconsideration) of something in the context of goal-oriented problem solving. Developmental improvements in reflection are necessary (but not sufficient) for the formulation of more complex rules or the use of language to facilitate the goal-oriented control of attention, flexibly (i.e. cognitive flexibility), over time (i.e. working memory), and selectively (i.e. inhibitory control). These reflective, verbally mediated executive skills vary across hot and cold contexts, and become more efficient and effective as they are exercised in the context of goal-oriented problem solving. With more reprocessing of information, more details are perceived and integrated into one's representation of one's experience, allowing for the construal of a stimulus within a larger context, leading to a richer qualitative experience, and importantly to the opportunity to select and amplify attention to different aspects of a stimulus.

Within Zelazo's view, the goal-directed construals of a stimulus are typically verbally mediated, and when formulated in the context of goal-directed problem solving, they are often formulated as rules that vary in complexity and flexibility (see the seminal ideas of Vygotsky and Luria concerning the importance of verbal processes in the exercise and development of self-regulation). For example, with age, children increasingly use verbalization to maintain task information in mind (Karbach & Kray, 2007), and blocking the use of inner speech disrupts cognitive control in

106 The development of working memory

children and adults (Kray, Eber, & Karbach, 2008; Emerson & Miyake, 2003). Reflection is inherently metacognitive, and is a source of first-person information regarding developing ideas of cognition (i.e. metacognitive knowledge).

The memory accounts

An alternative perspective emphasizes the importance of memory, especially working memory. Several theoretical accounts have suggested that the development of executive functions and more generally cognitive development is made possible by the growth of short-term or working memory (Case, 1985; 1992; Demetriou et al., 2002; Gordon & Olson, 1998; Olson, 1993; Pascual-Leone, 1970).

In this particular perspective, an influential account of the development of executive function has been suggested by Morton and Munakata (2002a), who have presented a connectionist model of children's performance on the DCCS. These authors suggest a distinction between active memory representations and latent memory traces. While the active memory representations are sustained by activity in the prefrontal cortex, latent memory traces are implicitly instantiated as changes in the strength of connections between units in more posterior cortex. The active–latent distinction accounts for perseveration error as perseveration occurs when an active trace for currently relevant information is insufficiently strong to compete against a latent trace for previously relevant information. In such a conception, flexible behaviour is understood in terms of the relative strengths of latent and active memory traces. Thus, according to this model, age-related changes in performance on the DCCS, and by extension in cognitive control, are attributable to increases in the strength of active memory.

In addition to perseveration, the model of Morton and Munakata can also account for two important phenomena observed in tasks assessing executive functions: the dissociation between knowledge and action, and the occurrence of *décalage* (i.e. success in some tasks and failure in others though they have similar formal structure). The dissociation between knowledge and action is observed in tasks, such as the DCCS, in which children who persist in using the old rule after a rule switch can nevertheless verbally report the rule to use. The simulation of the model demonstrates how apparent dissociation between knowledge and action may reflect differences in the amount of conflict between active and latent memories. The test of knowledge (i.e. the question asked at the end about the rules to follow) and the action (the sorting behaviour) involve different amount of conflict and thus depend differentially on the two types of memory representations. When knowledge and action measures are equated on the conflict dimension (e.g. by asking 'Where do red trucks go in the shape game?' instead of the standard question 'Where do trucks go in the shape game?'), children show worse performance on such conflict question than on the standard question, and no systematic difference in their sorting behaviour and their answers to the conflict questions appears (Munakata & Yerys, 2001). Concerning *décalage*, Morton and Munakata (2002a) noted that the reflection mechanism proposed by Zelazo has difficulty in accounting for such a phenomenon. Indeed, if reflection allows children to subordinate lower-order perspectives to a higher-order representation, it is unclear why reflection should emerge earlier in some task than in another, especially when tasks are formally similar. To exemplify this *décalage*, Morton and Munakata contrasted two tasks that both rely on the switch between rules, e.g. the DCCS and the speech-interpretation task (Morton & Munakata, 2002b). In the latter task, children have to judge a speaker's feeling. In the first part of the task, they have to base their judgement on the content of the speech, and in the second part, new instructions ask children to listen to the speaker's voice and not to what it says. Half of the sentences present a mismatch between the content and the tone of voice. For example, some sentences with a sad content are spoken in a happy tone of voice (e.g. 'My dog ran away from home' said happily). While perseveration errors (i.e. persisting using the old rule after a switch in instructions) in the DCCS are observed in most 3-year-old children, children as old as 6 years of age produce perseveration in the speech-interpretation task (Morton & Munakata, 2002b). In Morton and Munakata's (2002a) model, *décalage* results from differences in the strength of children's initial biases, i.e. the latent memory. Tasks that involve strong pre-existing biases may place greater demands on active memory representations than tasks with weak biases. For the DCCS, children have probably no particular bias for either shape or colour. By contrast, children have a strong initial bias for the content of speech, which would place more demand on active memory in the speech-interpretation task.

Recently, Chatham, Yerys and Munakata (2012) proposed a revised version of the Morton and Munakata's model to account for another phenomenon, i.e. the impact of feedbacks. While feedbacks do not seem to strongly influence perseverative behaviour in some tasks like the A-not-B task (Smith et al., 1999), they substantially reduce them in other tasks, such as the DCCS (Bohlmann & Fenson, 2005). To account for this effect, Chatham et al. (2012) introduced an updating process that should be subserved by striatal regions. Morton and Munakata's model focused on the maintenance function of working memory (active memory representations), keeping aside another important function of working memory, which is updating. The inclusion of an updating mechanism that may fail to flexibly update actively maintained representations in the prefrontal cortex provides one mechanistic basis for the attentional inertia account of perseveration (Kirkham et al., 2003). The 'attentional inertia' labels the behaviour of children when they are literally 'stuck' on the pre-switch features of a task (this conception is developed in the next section). In the revised model of Munakata and collaborators, this attentional inertia could, at least in part, reflect a failure in updating working memory with the current rule. In a similar vein, Chatham et al. (2012) also suggest that the failure to sufficiently represent superordinate rule in the CCC theory (see previous section), which leads to perseveration, could also rely on updating failure.

Among active memory representations, one type of representations could have a particular role in executive control and its development. Indeed, developmental transitions in cognitive control can be understood in terms of the development of

108 The development of working memory

increasingly active and abstract goal representations in the prefrontal cortex (Munakata, Snyder, & Chatham, 2012; Snyder & Munakata, 2010; see also Marcovitch, Boseovski, & Knapp, 2007; Towse, Lewis, & Knowles, 2007). As development progresses, goal representations can have increasing robustness and abstractness. Children's goal representations shift from concrete objects towards increasingly abstract goals, and become more robust in face of distraction and delay. Increasingly robust representations thus support the active maintenance of goals in working memory, which provides top-down support for goal-relevant representations. These increasingly robust and abstract goal representations should support three key developmental transitions. First, they support increasingly flexible goal-appropriate behaviours over habitual ones in response to signals in the environment. Second, they allow cognitive control to become less externally driven and more self-directed. Munakata et al. (2012) suggested that the abstractness of representations could be viewed as most critical for self-directed behaviour. As children's capacity for active maintenance increases across development, it increasingly becomes sufficient to support proactive control. Such developments may support additional aspects of future-oriented thinking, such as monitoring for goal-relevant cues rather than relying on such cues to serve as reminders (as seen in prospective memory tasks, e.g. Einstein et al., 2005). Third, they allow such cognitive control to become less reactive and more proactive, the robustness of representations being seen as most critical for proactive control. The transition from exogenous to endogenous control can be understood partly in terms of the development of increasingly active, abstract goal representations (Chatham et al., 2009).

Finally, the development of executive control could result in part in the increasing capacity of children to process environmental cues, which allows them to identify the goal to reach. This increasing capacity probably relies on a more and more efficient inner speech (Chevalier, Blaye, & Maintenant, 2014). As a consequence, it is possible that the growth of (working) memory, and particularly of the phonological loop, which would be required for rehearsing verbal rules, would thus constrain the maintenance of the goal, and also the number of rules that children can use.

Accounts emphasizing inhibitory control

In the previous section about the development of executive functions, we mentioned that inhibition is considered as one of the main executive functions. Starting perhaps with Luria (1961) and White (1965), numerous authors (e.g. Dempster, 1993, 1995; Harnishfeger & Bjorklund, 1993) have indeed suggested that the growth of an inhibition mechanism occurs in parallel with the growth of prefrontal cortex. One class of models stresses the role of inhibition in accounting for the development of executive control. Following Luria, these accounts have emphasized the lack of response control and hold that children frequently fail to suppress overlearned, or otherwise prepotent, response tendencies, despite representing an appropriate plan or rule (Diamond & Gilbert, 1989; Luria, 1959, 1961; Perner et al., 1999).

Development of the executive control **109**

The work of Kirkham et al. (2003) that we mentioned briefly in the previous section developed specifically this conception to account for children's behaviour in executive control. The main proposal of these authors is to interpret perseverations in the DCCS as an example of representational inflexibility caused by an immature inhibition mechanism. In this task, when asked to sort by the second criterion (e.g. shape), 3-year-old children experience difficulty inhibiting their focus on an aspect of a stimulus (e.g. its 'blueness') that was relevant based on the first sorting dimension (e.g. the colour). Hence, children do not switch the focus of their attention to the currently relevant aspect (e.g. its 'boatness'). Children's difficulty lies in disengaging from a mind-set that is no longer relevant. Kirkham et al. (2003) proposed describing this behaviour as the already mentioned 'attentional inertia': because attention had been focused on a particular dimension, it gets stuck there, and children have extreme difficulty redirecting it. As a consequence, the poor performance observed in 3-year-old children in DCCS can be accounted for by a failure to inhibit what had been relevant (the pre-switch dimension) and to redirect attention to what is newly relevant (the post-switch dimension), children behaving as if they were cognitively rigid.[2] Kirkham et al. (2003) suggest that attentional inertia is eventually overcome by the maturation of dorsolateral prefrontal cortex. It should be noted that Diamond had long before developed an account of executive control based on inhibition. In Gerstadt et al.'s (1994) study that introduced the famous Day-Night task, a similar account was already put forward. Recall that in the Day-Night task, children have to say 'day' when cards with a moon are presented, and 'night' for cards with a sun. Children younger than 5 years of age experience difficulty in performing this Stroop-like task, with lower accuracy (less than 70 per cent compared with 90 per cent at 6) and long response times (around 2000 ms vs. 1000 ms in older children). Because a control condition showed that children could maintain two rules, the authors proposed that the Day-Night task requires the exercise of inhibitory control. The tendency to inhibit what the picture represents is probably very difficult for young children, especially to keep this up for several trials.

Based on the assumption of attentional inertia, Kirkham et al. (2003) derived a series of predictions. They predicted that children should be able to succeed if the pre-switch dimension is absent on the stimuli presented after the switch of sorting dimension. In accordance with this prediction, Zelazo et al. (1995) observed that 3-year-old children who sort rabbits and boats by their colour (red and blue) are capable of switching to another dimension (shape) when sorting yellow flowers and green cars. Similarly, a beneficial effect should be observed when the pre-switch dimension is not present on the target cards (i.e. cards placed on the sorting boxes as model). To confirm this prediction, Kirkham et al. (2003) mentioned that children succeed when target cards are not presented, making reference to two previous studies (Perner & Lang, 2002; Towse et al., 2000). In fact, the target cards were not absent in Perner and Lang (2002), but replaced by cards with a picture of famous characters (Mickey Mouse and Donald Duck), and the post-switch instructions stated that the character changed his preference (e.g. 'Donald now wants the suns'). Under such a condition, 3- and 4-year-old children did not differ in the

110 The development of working memory

post-switch trials (see the next section, for an alternative account of this result). Towse et al. (2000) did contrast a condition with target cards to a condition without target cards. They found no difference in success in the post-switch trials between the two conditions. However, they observed in both conditions a very high rate of success, as nearly all the children sorted cards correctly by two arbitrary and conflicting rule sets, even the younger children. Such a pattern contrasted with the regularly observed failure in 3-year-old children.

A third prediction based on the attention inertia assumption states that children should succeed in switching if this does not require changing their attentional focus, i.e. if the switch does not change the dimension to take into account for sorting cards. For example, children in the pre-switch phase have to sort the cars to the car target and the suns to the sun target, and in the post-switch phase they have to put the cars to the sun-box and the suns to the car-box. Perner and Lang (2002) have shown that, in such conditions, named reversal shift, 3-year-old children perform as well as 4-year-olds, and achieve a better performance than in the standard DCCS. Finally, children should find it easier to switch if the second dimension is more salient, i.e. if the correct aspect is highlighted. This was previously suggested by Towse et al. (2000). These authors proposed that the cognitive salience of test card features could modulate performance in DCCS, as it was shown in other paradigms (Carlson, Moses, & Hix, 1998; Flavell, Flavell, & Green, 1983; Russell, Mauthner, Sharpe, & Tidswell, 1991). Towse et al. (2000) thus proposed asking children to label the pre-switch feature, which should increase the cognitive salience of the relevant dimension. This manipulation was successful, and 3-year-old children, who mostly failed the standard DCCS, succeeded (78 per cent of the children vs. 42 per cent in the standard task) when they were required to label stimuli (Kirkham et al., 2003). Conversely, 4-year-old children tended to fail when the cards were left face up in the box (Kirkham et al., 2003). Indeed, more of them (43 per cent) failed in such a condition than in the standard face-down procedure (8 per cent), although they still do better than the 3-year-old children for whom 75 per cent failed in the face-up condition (a trend that just failed to reach significance, $p = .078$). According to Kirkham et al. (2003), leaving the card face up, instead of face down as in the standard procedure, increased the salience of the previously correct dimension (i.e. the pre-switch dimension). In a similar vein but for another task, the Day-Night task, it should be expected that reducing the inhibitory requirement of the task should improve performance in young children. Diamond, Kirkham, and Amso (2002) modified the Day-Night task to test this prediction. Instead of saying 'day' to the moon and 'night' to the sun, children were instructed to say 'pig' to the moon and 'dog' to the sun. This reduced the demand on inhibitory control because the correct responses ('dog' and 'pig') were not semantically related to the responses to be inhibited ('day' and 'night'). In agreement with the prediction, 4-year-old children performed significantly better in the dog–pig condition than in the standard condition (94 per cent vs. 65 per cent of correct responses).

Despite the fact that the predictions based on Diamond and collaborators' inhibition account received empirical support, several aspects of this account have been criticized. As noted by Happaney and Zelazo (2003), the inhibition account makes the same predictions as the CCC theory, because both accounts rely on children's ability to redirect attention and to inhibit inappropriate responding. However, while Kirkham et al. (2003) claim that inhibition and refocusing suffice as an explanation of children's behaviour, the CCC theory treats inhibition and refocusing as behaviours to be explained, not as explanations in themselves. The idea underlying the CCC theory is that these two mechanisms are made possible by reflection on rules and formulation of a higher-order rule for selecting the appropriate perspective from which to consider a stimulus. In a similar vein, Munakata, Morton, and Yerys (2003) wondered if the inhibition account goes beyond a mere description by proposing that children are stuck in what they attend to and have difficulty overcoming this (see Kirkham & Diamond, 2003, for reply). More substantially, Cepeda and Munakata (2007) contrasted the inhibition account to their memory account, which was proposed to explain children's difficulty in switching from one task to another despite demonstrating awareness of current task demands. This behaviour could reflect problems in either directly inhibiting previously relevant information (as suggested by Diamond and collaborators) or sufficiently activating working memory representations for the current task (as proposed by Munakata in her memory account of executive control). Under conflict conditions, memory and inhibition accounts are difficult to distinguish, because correct sorting could be attributed to either inhibition of the old task or the maintenance of the new task. Thus, Cepeda and Munakata (2007) suggested testing children in non-conflict conditions (e.g. answering questions like 'In the shape game, where do cats go?'). In such conditions, the memory account predicts that children who are able to switch tasks (i.e. the switchers) should show faster responses to non-conflict questions. The switchers should have stronger working memory representations of the current rule, compared to those who perseverate (i.e. the perseverators), leading to faster performance when answering non-conflict questions about that rule. By contrast, the inhibition account predicts no correlation between the ability to switch and the response time to non-conflict questions, because there is nothing to inhibit. In accordance with the memory account, switchers were faster than perseverators at answering non-conflict questions, even after factoring out processing speed and age (Cepeda & Munakata, 2007). Finally, it should be noted that, for other authors like Perner et al. (1999), such a difficulty in switching between rules is overcome by the emergence of 'executive inhibition', which depends on children's conceptual understanding of the unintended consequences of action schemata. In the next section, we will examine a further theoretical elaboration of Perner based on the redescription of representations.

Accounts emphasizing the redescription of representations

Perner, Stummer, Sprung, and Doherty (2002) developed an account of the development of executive functions influenced by precursor works by Flavell (1988) and Inhelder and Piaget (1964). This account suggests that representational inflexibility

112 The development of working memory

is due to lack of a concept of perspectives, and hence children cannot understand that a single stimulus can be redescribed in a different, incompatible way from two different perspectives. Although the seminal notion of 'representational redescription' was first developed by Karmiloff-Smith (1979, 1992), Perner's redescription account can be distinguished from Karmiloff-Smith's (1992) Representational Redescription model. In this latter model, knowledge is initially implicit and procedural, thus modular and inflexible: procedures are data-driven, and must run off in their entirety. With sufficient practice, behavioural mastery of these procedures is achieved and the knowledge is automatically redescribed into a more abstract, explicit format that reveals the structure of the procedures. This newly redescribed knowledge is explicit but not yet conscious. Consciousness comes with yet additional levels of redescription or explicitation that occurs spontaneously as part of an internal drive toward the creation of intra-domain and inter-domain relationships.

Whereas the redescription in Karmiloff-Smith' theory involves a change in representational levels related with an increased consciousness, Perner refers to redescription as the capacity to produce alternative representations of the same object (e.g. a duck is also an animal), an idea akin to the coordination of points of view in Piaget's theory. The particularity of Perner's conception is to envisage a functional dependency between the development of executive control and theory of mind. For example, Perner (1991, 1998) suggested that improved understanding of one's mind leads to greater self-control as the child develops; that is, theory of mind is seen as a prerequisite for executive functions. For the famous DCCS task, Perner proposes that DCCS points to a specific difficulty with redescribing the cards to be sorted (e.g. this card shows a red object, which is also a boat; Kloo & Perner, 2003; but also Kirkham et al., 2003; Perner & Lang, 2002; Towse et al., 2000). As evoked above, Perner and Lang (2002) found that children had no serious problems in the DCCS if the switch in dimension (and consequently the need to redescribe the cards) was avoided by using a reversal shift instead of an extradimensional shift (switching from one dimension to another as in the standard DCCS) or if the visual clash was avoided by replacing the target cards by target characters. Therefore, the combination of an extradimensional shift and a visual clash between target and test cards seems to be critical for the difficulty of the DCCS task. Moreover, it is well known that young children, before 4 years of age, have difficulty understanding that objects can be redescribed. Although children acquire different names for things fairly early (Clark, 1997), they are reluctant to use both terms at the same time (see the mutual exclusivity bias, Carey & Bartlett, 1978; Markman & Wachtel, 1988). For example, Doherty and Perner (1998) asked children to acknowledge explicitly that something can be a rabbit and a bunny, or a rabbit and an animal. They found that this ability emerges with the ability to understand false belief (which requires understanding that someone else can have a description of the real world that differs from one's own description). Thus, Kloo and Perner (2003) suggested that children's inability to understand redescription is the common denominator underlying difficulty with the standard DCCS and failure to understand false belief. This explains why performance on the DCCS tends to be strongly correlated with performance in the false-belief task (Carlson & Moses, 2001; Frye et al., 1995; Perner et al., 2002). Moreover, and in accordance with this suggestion, Kloo and Perner (2003) showed that a card sorting training had some effect on children's ability to pass a false-belief test. Conversely, training on the false-belief problem had some beneficial effect on their ability to sort cards correctly. Thus, children's difficulties with the standard DCCS task can be effectively remedied by giving them feedback and explanations about the need to redescribe the cards to be sorted.

Conclusion

As Garon et al. (2008) mentioned, whether the development of executive control is framed as a difficulty in integrating conflicting rules (Zelazo et al., 2003), overcoming latent representations (Munakata, 2001), overcoming a prepotent thought or behaviour (Diamond et al., 2002), or redescribing mental representations (Perner & Lang, 2002), the effortful control of attention and conflict resolution are the common threads that link these competing theories. Because attention is relevant to conflict resolution in most of these theories, exploring attentional mechanisms in executive functions would be one way to assess how well these theories explain early changes in executive control.

More generally, this rapid overview of the literature shows that the development of working memory cannot be restricted to an age-related increase in the amount of information that can be maintained available for treatment, but that the functions united within the central executive in Baddeley's theory exhibit themselves a strong development with age. However, the modern dissociation of the developmental study of executive functions from the study of working memory seems to have introduced some circularity in the theoretical accounts. As we have seen, several theories explain the development of executive functions by some age-related improvement in the quality, strength, or complexity of the representations held in working memory. For example, Zelazo (2015) explains the construction of more complex rules by a process of iterative reprocessing of the representations held in working memory that leads to the integration of more characteristics of the situation. We have seen that Munakata associates success in executive control to the increase in strength of active memory that becomes able to overcome latent representations. Similarly, Diamond assumes that executive control requires the inhibition of associative responses, but also the activation of the correct representation. Thus, development of executive functions is often implicitly or explicitly explained as resulting from working memory development. Moreover, the development of representations in working memory is usually associated with the reprocessing or redescription of these representations (e.g. the iterative reprocessing in Zelazo's account or Perner's redescription). Such mechanisms have some commonalities with the former notions of reflective abstraction in Piaget's theory. Barrouillet (2015) noted that the recourse of redescription or reprocessing was already present in information processing theories by Klahr and Wallace (1976) who hypothesized some review or replay of previous mental activities, a mechanism in turn akin to the metacognitive processes postulated and simulated by Shrager and Siegler (1998). Barrouillet (2015) concluded that the resurgence of the concept of reflection on existing cognitive processes is striking and probably indicative of the enduring difficulty of developmental psychology to renew its theoretical tool-box when accounting for developmental changes.

Notes

1 We need to clarify here how working memory is conceived in the field of executive functions, because such a conception differs from the view generally shared by working memory researchers. Working memory is conceived in the field of executive functions as a short-term memory, and even restricted to the updating function of working memory.

2 Conversely, it has been suggested that the values of the irrelevant dimension (e.g. shape) have to be inhibited in the pre-switch (e.g. colour) phase to sort correctly. In the post-switch phase, this inhibition has to be cancelled, the formerly irrelevant dimension (i.e. shape) suffering thus from a negative priming effect (Chevalier & Blaye, 2008; Müller, Dick, Gela, Overton, & Zelazo, 2006).

7

THE SOURCES OF WORKING MEMORY DEVELOPMENT

Based on the fractionation of working memory into a central executive control system and some short-term storage systems, the two previous chapters have presented working memory development in its two distinct aspects. The present chapter evokes the general factors that have been suggested as underpinning working memory development. It is still unknown what the determinants of the age-related changes observed in working memory capacity are. Among the variety of factors cited in the literature, we will focus on those that are the most often invoked, but also those that are considered as the basic processes underlying working memory development. Nevertheless, it should be clear that no theory claims that a single source accounts for working memory development. On the contrary, several concomitant factors would sustain the age-related increase in performance observed in working memory tasks. Indeed, it is difficult to ensure that a single source is the determinant of working memory development, because many factors experience simultaneously some age-related improvements. This is the fundamental difficulty of cognitive developmental research, because brain growth is organic and thus multiple processes improve with age. Thus, it is difficult to isolate the effect of a specific factor. In this chapter, we examine in turn the role and impact on working memory development of age-related changes in speed of decay, cognitive resources, processing speed and efficiency, size of the focus of attention, strategy use, and long-term memory knowledge.

Speed of decay

Change in the speed of decay during childhood is probably the most straight-forward idea one can have to account for the increase in working memory capacity. If memory traces vanish faster in young children, they would have poorer recall performance. However, there is a persistent and hot debate on the existence of

116 The development of working memory

decay, that is, the loss of working memory information as a function of elapsed time between its encoding and its recall (Barrouillet & Camos, 2009; Brown, 1958; Keppel & Underwood, 1962; Lewandowsky, Oberauer, & Brown, 2009). If decay exists, then age-related increase in working memory capacity could rely, at least in part, on a reduced speed of decay in older children. To examine decay, maintenance mechanisms should be prevented, and several studies either used memory items that cannot be rehearsed (e.g. pitch tones; Keller & Cowan, 1994) or examined memory for unattended stimuli (Saults & Cowan, 1996). These studies provided evidence of developmental change in duration of passive maintenance of information in working memory.

In a pitch tone memory task, Keller and Cowan (1994) asked participants to compare two tones very close in frequency. A silent period elapsed between the tones and varied from two to 20 seconds. To compare the memory loss in children of different age groups and adults, the frequency difference was adjusted to each individual level in such a way that participants had the same proportion of correct responses at two-second retention intervals. When the silent retention interval was increased to eight seconds, 7-year-old children had a reduction in correct responses to a performance level reached by 12-year-olds after a ten-second delay and by adults after 12 seconds. This age difference could result from a longer preservation of the memory traces, but also from the fact that older children could better use their attention to maintain information active. In other words, older children would have a better attentional control and maintain their attention focused on memory traces for a longer period of time. To test this alternative hypothesis, the memory for ignored sounds was assessed in 7- and 12-year-old children and adults (Saults & Cowan, 1996). While participants were playing a silent video-game, some words they had to ignore were presented through headphones. Unexpectedly, the video-game stopped and was replaced by some pictures, participants having to choose the one corresponding to the last heard word. When the unexpected test occurred one second after the last word was heard, all age groups performed equally well. After a five-second delay, the younger children suffered from severe memory loss, which occurred only after ten seconds in older children. At this long delay, adults exhibited little forgetting. The fact that an age-related change in forgetting occurs also under dual-task conditions for ignored stimuli is considered by Saults and Cowan (1996) as evidence for a developmental change in the rate of decay, because attention was distracted away from the sounds and mnemonic strategies prevented by the game play.

However, a follow-up study led to a rather different developmental pattern. Using a similar paradigm, Cowan, Nugent, Elliott, and Saults (2000) assessed recall for unattended lists of spoken digits in 8- and 11-year-old children and adults who were playing a picture-name-rhyming game. While Saults and Cowan (1996) were assessing memory for a single item (the last heard word), Cowan et al. (2000) tested developmental differences in memory of series of items, the length of which was individually adapted. Although the increase in retention intervals resulted in substantial forgetting in the three age groups, there was no age difference in the overall rate of forgetting, contrary to Saults and Cowan's (1996) study. Nevertheless, an important age difference appeared in the decay of the last list digit. The authors suggested that the memory traces of this last item is likely to be stored not in working memory, but in an auditory sensory memory, in which each presented item overwrites the previous ones. As a consequence, they concluded that no age-related change in decay can account for the development of working memory. A recent study by Cowan, Ricker, Clark, Hinrichs, and Glass (2015) confirmed the absence of developmental change in the speed of decay. Using spatial arrays of letters or unfamiliar characters followed by a mask to reduce the use of sensory memory, 7-, 9- and 12-year-old children and adults had to judge if a probe item was presented in a particular location after a retention interval of one, five or ten seconds. Following Cowan's (2001) model, the authors estimated the number of items k stored in working memory. As expected, k values increased through age, indicating a developmental improvement in working memory capacity, but were reduced by longer retention intervals, revealing a time-based forgetting, both findings commonly reported in the literature. However, there was no age-related difference in the rate of decay of memory.

To conclude, although age-related changes in the speed of decay is an obvious factor to account for the development of working memory, few studies examined this issue, probably because studying decay requires particular experimental conditions to be examined (i.e. blocking maintenance strategies). These studies revealed that there is no age-related change in childhood in the speed of decay in working memory, contrary to what is observed in sensory memory. Nevertheless, this does not definitively exclude any change in the speed of decay throughout life, as infant studies report an increase in duration of memory traces, but mostly during the first year of life (Chapter 5). Further evidence for a constant rate of decay through age will be discussed in Part III.

Global increase in cognitive resources

It is frequently assumed that working memory development results from some undifferentiated increase in mental resource or energy. The first neo-Piagetian theories invoked this factor for accounting for cognitive and working memory development, a hypothesis that is commonly used in contemporary theories of executive development.

As explained in Chapter 2, Pascual-Leone (1970) suggested that cognitive development was sustained by an increase in the number of schemes that could be kept active at once (called 'M space'). These schemes are used both for storage and processing of information. Any given problem could be solved only if the number of available schemes allows holding the necessary information while carrying out the necessary processing of this information. The growth of the M space through childhood would then explain the increasing ability of children to perform more and more complex tasks requiring the coordination of an increasing number of schemes, but also store and recall more memory items.

118 The development of working memory

However, although memory performance increases with age, it does not necessarily mean that the M space grows. Indeed, the amount of space taken by processing for a given problem could also reduce with age, resulting in more space for storage. As we have seen in Chapter 2, this is exactly the rationale followed by Case (1985) and tested by Case et al. (1982). Recall that, in this study, using a counting span task in which participants counted several arrays of dots and memorized the different counts, Case and collaborators showed a correlation between processing speed assumed to reflect the efficiency of counting and the number of counts correctly stored and recalled. Moreover, when Case and collaborators asked adults to use new words to count, they observed that adults' recall performance fell at the level of performance of 7-year-old children when using the regular number sequence. Thus, Case et al. proposed that developmental improvement is based on an increased efficiency in processing (see the following section), rather than in age-related increase in M space.

Recently, Gilchrist, Cowan, and Naveh-Benjamin (2009) reassessed this question. They asked 7- and 12-year-old children and adults to memorize lists of sentences from which they derived two measures of performance. One measure assessed the number of clauses for which at least one word was recalled. This was assumed to evaluate the storage capacity of working memory, i.e. how many clauses were somehow encoded in working memory. The other measure reported the proportion of words recalled from clauses from which at least one word was recalled, a measure that would reflect the chunking or grouping capacity. Although there was no developmental increase in this latter measure, suggesting that chunking was comparable across age groups, the number of clauses for which one word was recalled increased with age, indicating that the capacity of working memory has increased. However, as noted by the authors, the efficiency of processing that was not measured might have improved across age groups, possibly accounting for the observed difference or part of it. It nevertheless remains that the capacity has increased with age.

A striking and contradicting observation is the fact that infants' capacity in visual array procedures seems already similar to adults (Ross-Sheehy et al., 2003; Chapter 5). As we have already noted, it might be that the use of different paradigms between infancy and adulthood and the inferred relationship between looking time measures used in infant studies and capacity could lead to this apparent absence of change in working memory capacity. Across childhood, studies of visual arrays reported developmental increases in working memory capacity (e.g. Riggs et al., 2006), even when the task relies on the recognition of unfamiliar stimuli, which excludes the role of increased long-term memory knowledge (Cowan et al., 2015).

To conclude, though of particular importance, the issue of a developmental increase in cognitive resources and its explanatory power in the age-related increase in working memory capacity remains a rather unsolved question. It is indeed difficult to assess cognitive resources, because of the vagueness of this concept (Halford, 1993; Navon, 1984). As a consequence, measures of memory performance are often used as a proxy to evaluate changes in cognitive resources, resulting in rather circular reasoning. In the final part of this book, we will present further studies examining the hypothetical role of an increase in general cognitive resource on working memory development.

The size of the focus of attention

Prominent theories of working memory assume that its main limitation is due to the limited size of the focus of attention (Cowan, 2001). Development of working memory could result from an age-related increase in this size, a conception that echoes neo-Piagetian proposals, especially Halford's theory (Halford, 1993; Halford et al., 2014).

To assess the size of the focus of attention and its changes across childhood, Cowan and collaborators used three main tasks. The first is the array comparison task developed by Luck and Vogel (1997), which asks the subject to compare two arrays briefly presented one after the other and to detect any change. The briefness of presentation minimizes the possibility to group or chunk information, as well as preventing use of strategies like articulatory rehearsal, which would require time to recode information into verbal inputs. The running memory span is another task used to measure the size of the focus of attention. Lists of digits of various and unpredictable lengths are auditorily presented at a fast pace. Participants had to recall as many digits as possible from the end of the list. Because such presentation makes rehearsal difficult, participants can only passively store information and retrieve as many items as possible at the end of list presentation. Finally, memory for unattended stimuli, as in Saults and Cowan (1996) previously described, allows also the measurement of the size of the focus of attention. Based on these different tasks, Cowan and collaborators suggested that the capacity of the focus of attention increases from two items at 6–7 years of age to about four items in adulthood. An increase in the size of the focus of attention permits a person to attend to a larger amount of information. Moreover, in theories like Cowan (2001), in which the maintenance of information in working memory is achieved by the focalization of attention on memory traces, attending to a higher number of items in a larger focus of attention results in greater efficiency of maintenance in working memory.

Though coming from a different epistemological tradition, Halford's (1993; Chapter 2) theory sees also in the increase in the number of elements on which attention can focus a major source of cognitive development. An age-related increase in the number of elements that can be interconnected would allow the construction of more complex mental models and account for the development of reasoning capacity that would depend on the maximum number of dimensions individuals are able to take simultaneously into account (Halford et al., 1998). This number of dimensions echoes nicely what some authors such as Cowan define as the scope of attention or the size of the focus of attention. Moreover, when Halford et al. (2005) estimated the maximum number of dimensions that adults can simultaneously hold, they showed that four variables or dimensions are the limits of human processing capacity, because performance was at chance level when five dimensions were involved in the task. This estimate fits the measure of adults' scope of attention. Accordingly, Halford et al. (2007) explicitly acknowledged the commonality between limits in the focus of attention and in reasoning capacity, and they proposed that it is contingent on the common demand for attention when binding elements into slots. We will comment later on this commonality (see Chapter 9).

Beyond a developmental evolution in the size of the focus of attention, age-related evolution in the efficiency of keeping attention focused on relevant information could also determine developmental changes in working memory, as well as the ability to inhibit the activation of irrelevant information. Maccoby and Hagen (1965) have shown that children improve their ability to focus attention on the relevant information. They showed a series of pictures of animals or objects to first- to seventh-graders and asked them to memorize only their colours for further recall. However, in a surprise test, children were prompted to recognize the picture presented with a given colour. Though the recall of colours increased regularly with age, performance in the surprise recognition task decreased from fifth to seventh grades. Commenting on this surprising result, Cowan (1997) suggested that the intrusion of irrelevant information in the focus of attention due to attention wandering in children could account for their reduced colour span score.

However, Maccoby and Hagen's (1965) findings can also be accounted for by an increasing ability to inhibit irrelevant information (animals and objects) in older children. As discussed in Chapter 6, infants have increased ability to inhibit the inappropriate behaviour in the A-not-B task (Diamond, 1985), and Bjorklund and Harnishfeger (1990) have shown that the use of inhibition continues to improve through childhood. A nice illustration of this developmental change is given by Tipper et al. (1989) who studied negative priming in a Stroop task in which participants have to inhibit the printed word to name the colour of the ink in incongruent trials (e.g. they have to say 'red' for the word *blue* printed in red). As a consequence, when in the following trial, the previously inhibited name ('blue') is the correct response (i.e. it matches the ink colour), adults' responses are slowed down, revealing a negative priming effect. However, this effect does not appear in second-graders, as if children did not carry out as much inhibition as adults, and therefore did not suffer from negative priming.

Despite the attractiveness of these hypotheses, Maccoby and Hagen (1965) reported that scores on the main and incidental tasks were independent, which is rather difficult to reconcile with both Cowan's proposal and the inhibition hypothesis that would lead to expect some trade-off relationship. In our view, this independence is more in line with the involvement of two different memory systems sustaining the tasks. The main colour task could reflect the active maintenance of information in working memory, while the incidental task of recognizing animals and objects would be supported by retrieval from episodic long-term memory.

To conclude, the age-related increase in the size of the focus of attention would be a determinant factor of working memory development for theories in which attention is implicated in maintenance. Moreover, the control of attention, which

Sources of working memory development **121**

improves across childhood, is another source of development. To our knowledge, only one study examined across different age groups the relationships between the scope and the control of attention (Cowan, Fristoe et al., 2006). Cowan and collaborators (2006) derived measures from different span tasks to assess the control of attention and from the Luck and Vogel's (1997) visual array task to evaluate the size of the focus of attention in 11-year-old children and young adults. Though measures of size and control of attention were significantly correlated in adults, they were not in children, suggesting a possible independence between the two constructs. However, extended investigations are needed before any firm conclusion can be drawn.

Processing speed and efficiency

Age-related increase in processing speed and efficiency is among the most spectacular developmental changes, and most probably a direct consequence of brain maturation (Kail & Salthouse, 1994; Rabinowicz, 1980). Some authors like Case (1985, 1992), Kail (1991), and Towse and Houston-Price (2001) have assumed that these factors are at the origin of working memory development.

Age-related change in processing speed and efficiency would have two consequences that affect the development of working memory. First, it induces that any task is performed faster across childhood, which reduces the time during which information has to be maintained. This is especially important if information is lost over time through time-based decay. It also means that the cognitive cost to achieve a task would diminish. As described in Chapter 2, Case's (1985) theory assumes that the overall processing capacity has to be shared between storage and processing. Because older children can achieve processing more efficiently, it leaves more processing capacity available to store information. For example, in the counting span task in which participants have to count dots presented in cards and recall the different counts, older children being more efficient in counting benefit from more remaining capacity to store the counts, hence their better recall performance (Case et al., 1982). Towse and Hitch (1995) proposed an alternative hypothesis to account for this age-related difference in counting span. They suggested that older children are faster at counting, resulting in shorter retention intervals compared to young children who take longer to count the same number of dots. Thus, the processing demand of counting is confounded with its duration that impacts the retention duration of memory items. If memory traces decay with increased delay of retention, as these authors supposed, better recall in older children could result from shorter retention interval and not from processing efficiency. This proposal differs largely from Case's theory, which proposes that the age-related increase in working memory span results from increased efficiency in processing. In accordance with their view, Towse and Hitch (1995) reported that when children enumerated arrays that differed in processing difficulty and in counting time, the easier condition led to better working memory span. However, when the arrays differed in difficulty but not in counting time, spans no longer differed. Conversely, when the material

122 The development of working memory

to be processed in a counting, reading, or operation span task was the same across conditions, but that retention interval differed, spans were larger for the shorter retention conditions (Towse, Hitch, & Hutton, 1998). These findings lend strong support to the hypothesis that processing speed accounts, at least in part, for the developmental increase in working memory performance.

There is considerable evidence that processing speed increases throughout childhood (Kail, 2000; Kail & Park, 1994), and such an age-related change has been often evoked to account for cognitive development. Towse and Hitch's work clearly emphasizes the importance of processing speed to account for the increase in working memory span. Because older children achieve processing faster than younger children, they benefit from shorter retention interval before recall, which gives them a considerable advantage in memory performance. However, this is not the only way developmental change in processing speed could impact working memory capacity.

A second consequence of increased processing speed is the faster implementation of maintenance strategies. For example, Baddeley (1986) suggested that verbal items are maintained through articulatory rehearsal. Being able to rehearse faster permits older children to reactivate more items in a fixed amount of time, and to recall more items than young children. We have already discussed in Chapter 5 the role of articulation speed in working memory development. It should be noted that increase in processing speed could potentially improve the efficiency of any maintenance strategy. For example, a faster retrieval of information from long-term memory can help to elaborate or to semantically categorize memory items, both strategies being known for improving memory performance.

Strategy use

Beyond a pure increase in capacity, either of some cognitive resource or of the size of the focus of attention, or an increase in speed or efficiency of processing, it has been assumed that strategies (e.g. rehearsal, chunking, grouping, categorizing) have a strong impact on the amount of information that can be maintained in the short term. Geary (1995) proposed to classify cognitive processes into two categories: the biologically primary abilities and the biologically secondary abilities. The former are those that have been selected through evolution, and are found in similar forms across cultures. The previously evoked factors can be considered pertaining to these processes. In contrast, the biologically secondary abilities are shaped by one's particular culture and can be acquired through practice. The discovery or learning by children of some maintenance strategies can participate in this second category of processes. For some maintenance strategies, one would not expect that children use them spontaneously without instruction or acquisition of appropriate knowledge (for example, strategies of categorization that require acquisition of knowledge about objects – screwdriver and hammer are tools – hence the impact of long-term memory knowledge on maintenance, see the following section). Moreover, contrary to the previously evoked factors, the age-related change in strategy use is often

Sources of working memory development **123**

described as qualitative, with the appearance of new maintenance strategies being the source of development.

A large part of the working memory literature dedicated to the emergence of strategies focuses on the developmental changes in verbal rehearsal to account for working memory development. Rehearsal is subdivided into two types: rote rehearsal, also named articulatory rehearsal, and elaborative rehearsal. While rote rehearsal is a recirculation of information to preserve its phonological form, elaborative rehearsal uses long-term memory knowledge to enrich the to-be-maintained items or to create connexions between them (e.g. creating a sentence with the words of a memory list). The elaborative rehearsal is then strongly dependent on the acquisition of long-term knowledge, and also on the individual ability to use it to create connexions.

As mentioned in Chapter 5, it has been shown that the use of articulatory rehearsal increases through childhood (e.g. McGilly & Siegler, 1989) and is often considered as the main developmental source of improvement in verbal working memory. Accordingly, the seminal study by Flavell et al. (1966) reported that older children exhibit more lip movements than younger children and they are also those who have better recall performance. However, the difference between age groups does not rely on a metacognitive deficit in younger children (i.e. the lack of knowledge that rehearsal is a good strategy), because when young children of about 5 years of age are instructed to use rehearsal, this does not improve their recall performance, and they do not continue to rehearse when not explicitly instructed to do so (Naus et al., 1977; Ornstein et al., 1975). Most probably, this is due to the fact that rehearsing takes more effort in young children. As shown by Guttentag (1984), younger children have difficulties performing a secondary task concurrently with rehearsal. For example, second- and third-graders slow down their tapping on a plastic pad when they have to rehearse rather than being silent, whereas the speed of tapping in sixth-graders remains rather similar. Moreover, older children have a greater tendency to use rehearsal in a cumulative way, that is, starting from the first item of the list and following the order of presentation of items, a strategy that is more efficient to maintain more items in correct order (Lehmann & Hasselhorn, 2007; Ornstein & Naus, 1978). When young children are trained to use cumulative rehearsal, their recall performance improves, especially for the first items in the list (Naus et al., 1977). Thus, a critical developmental difference concerns the inclination to implement a strategy rather than its efficiency.

The increasing use of articulatory rehearsal through childhood also has an impact on the maintenance strategies children and adults might use to store information requiring verbal-spatial associations. Cowan, Saults, and Morey (2006) examined how 9- and 12-year-old children and adults are able to store series of names in specific locations. They pretended that arrays of three to seven boxes were houses and sequentially presented an equal number of names, each name being shown in a box (the house where the character is living). At least two strategies can allow maintaining the verbal–spatial association between names and houses. Participants can either bind the two types of information and maintain these associations as

124 The development of working memory

chunks, or reactivate the visual path from house to house while rehearsing the name list in parallel. This latter strategy is particularly adapted when each box is associated with one name only, i.e. under one-to-one associations. To examine the used strategy, the authors built two versions of the verbal–visual mapping task: a one-to-one condition and an uneven condition in which one box is left empty while another was associated with two names. In the uneven condition, the visual path is confusing and its maintenance probably error-prone. Findings revealed an interesting developmental change. While third-graders' recall benefited from the uneven condition, adults were better in the one-to-one condition, sixth-graders showing no difference between conditions. The emergence of rehearsal allows older participants to use the parallel method and to benefit from the one-to-one condition. In contrast, younger children who could not use rehearsal must use the verbal–spatial associations. In such a case, the uneven condition which involved fewer houses to memorize is less demanding than the one-to-one condition. This developmental change depends on the use of rehearsal, because when adults were asked to repeat 'the' in the verbal–spatial mapping task to impede rehearsal use, their performance was akin to that of third-graders.

The elaborative rehearsal is another type of rehearsal which uses long-term memory knowledge. It can be used either to create some associations between memory items (e.g. an image or a sentence) or to sort items by category based on meaning or visual appearance (Schneider, Kron, Hünnerkopf, & Krajewski, 2004). For example, adults, and not second-graders, try to group digits together when they have to memorize lists of digits (Cowan, Elliott et al., 2006). Until the middle of elementary school, children do not take advantage of pauses between subsets of memory items to group them (Towse, Hitch, & Skeates, 1999).

To summarize, through childhood, there is an increasing knowledge of what strategies are useful, a better implementation of the strategies with a reduction of effort in doing so, and a better control in the selection and use of different versions of each strategy.

Long-term memory knowledge

Working memory is in close relationship with long-term memory, several theories even assuming that working memory is nothing more than its activated part (see Cowan's and Engle's theories). It is rather obvious that the amount of acquired knowledge increases during childhood. This acquisition of new knowledge has an impact on how much can be maintained and processed in working memory. For example, asking children to maintain lists of either words or non-words, Roodenrys et al. (1993) have shown that older children benefited from knowing the words and had better recall performance for the word lists than the non-word lists. In contrast, younger children did not show any difference between lists. Chi (1978), in an attempt to dissociate the role of knowledge acquisition from other age-related changes (as in speed of processing or capacity), compared children who were expert chess players to novice adults. Although children had poorer performance in short-term memory tasks, they outperformed adults when memorizing chessboard setups (see also, Schneider, Gruber, Gold, & Opwis, 1993). This evidenced the role of long-term memory knowledge in working memory development, as new acquisitions would help to chunk memory items (e.g. in a larger configuration of chess pieces), resulting in a reduction of memory load and easier maintenance in working memory. Conversely, when adults performed a counting span task using a newly learned number sequence, their recall performance did not differ from that observed in 7-year-old children (Case et al., 1982). Thus, long-term knowledge has a major impact on working memory performance.

As previously mentioned, it is difficult to disentangle the impact of the different factors put forward for accounting for working memory development. Using computational simulations, Jones, Gobet, and Pine (2008) proposed a means to disentangle the effects of a developmental increase in working memory capacity from those of the age-related changes in long-term knowledge in accounting for the improvement observed through childhood in non-word recall (as, for example, reported by Gathercole and Adams, 1993). Within Baddeley's multi-component model, such an improvement is considered as evidence for an increased capacity of the phonological loop. However, because non-word recall is better for word-like items or for non-words containing a high frequency phonemes (e.g. Gathercole, 1995), the role of long-term memory knowledge cannot be excluded. In varying independently long-term knowledge and working memory capacity in a computational simulation of vocabulary learning, Jones et al. (2008) revealed that long-term knowledge alone may be sufficient to match the developmental data from Jones, Gobet, and Pine's (2007) study in 2- to 5-year-old children.

Although long-term knowledge may explain age-related differences in recall performance, there is still the possibility of developmental differences in working memory capacity itself. Recently, Cowan et al. (2015) examined the impact of knowledge by contrasting the retention of letters compared to the retention of unfamiliar characters. Congruently with previous studies, they observed that after a 1-second delay of retention, participants had better recall for letters than for unfamiliar items. Moreover, the advantage for letters grew with age from 7-year-old children to adults. However, when participants were selected to filter out children with insufficient letter knowledge, the same developmental increase in the k score, which estimates the number of items in working memory, was observed for both letters and unfamiliar characters. This finding indicates that capacity, and not only knowledge or use of strategies, increases with age.

Conclusion

This chapter has shown that many different factors have been evoked to account for the development of working memory. The picture is even more complex if we consider that these different factors do not necessarily exclude the other and that a body of factors could jointly underpin working memory development. Interestingly, these factors reflect the different metaphors used by psychologists to understand and describe working memory limitations. Indeed, three main metaphors coexist in the working memory literature concerning the nature of its limits: time, space, and energy (Cowan & Alloway, 2009; Kail & Salthouse, 1994). Among the factors we described, both speed of decay and speed of processing are examples of temporal factors that constrain working memory functioning. Size of the focus of attention is evidently related with a kind of space limit, whereas cognitive resources concern energy limitation. However, we have seen that other factors such as strategy use and long-term knowledge have also been assumed to affect the efficiency of working memory.

These metaphors refer in turn to the different definitions of working memory that have been proposed. As we discussed in Chapter 4 (see also Cowan, 2017b), research in working memory field is made difficult by the large variety in definitions adopted by different authors that lead to favour some factors over others to account for working memory development. In a definition of working memory as a multi-component system as Baddeley (1986) proposed, age-related variation in speed of decay would play a crucial role, as well as the emergence and efficiency of maintenance strategies like articulatory rehearsal. If, contrary to Baddeley, some trade-off is assumed between processing and storage, development depends, at least in part, on processing efficiency (Case, 1992) or processing speed also (Barrouillet & Camos, 2015). These factors could in turn depend on the development of strategies to process information faster and more efficiently (Siegler, 1996). Within the generic definition proposed by Cowan (2017; i.e. to conceive working memory as the assembly of components holding a limited amount of information temporarily in a heightened state of availability), increase in the size of the focus of attention, but also some increase in cognitive resources for activation, can become the main factors of development. However, the control of the focus of attention would be more important than its size when favouring an attention-controlled view of working memory (Engle, 2002). Finally, Ericsson and Kintsch's (1995) long-term working memory model would favour a development of knowledge to explain increase in working memory capacity.

As we previously mentioned, studying working memory development is an arduous endeavour because the different evoked factors are not totally independent from each other and, in many cases, the age-related evolution of one of them affects the development of the others. For example, an increase in cognitive resources could lead to the emergence of a new strategy that speeds up processing, which could in turn alleviate difficulties resulting from decay. The coexistence of these different explanatory factors in the literature is probably due to the fact that working memory remains a fuzzy concept, as its various definitions testify.

PART III

Development in the Time-Based Resource-Sharing model

Parts I and II of this book have recounted the emergence of the notion of working memory as an explanatory factor of cognitive development, the way the concept of working memory has evolved itself from the first theoretical description by Baddeley and Hitch (1974), what is known about working memory development from infancy to adulthood regarding the maintenance of information and the control of attention, and what are the main factors that have been assumed to underpin these age-related developmental changes. These previous pages have illustrated how the concept of working memory, despite its seeming clearness – a system able to temporarily maintain, from the continuous flow of information entering the cognitive system, that part needed by ongoing cognition in a state appropriate for its treatment – revealed itself as more complex than expected.

This part of the book addresses the same questions, but from the perspective of a single theory of working memory, the Time-Based Resource-Sharing (TBRS) model, that we have developed during the last 15 years (Barrouillet & Camos, 2001, 2015; Barrouillet, Portrat, & Camos, 2011). Chapter 8, after a brief overview of the model and its main tenets, reviews the main developmental studies that have been conducted within the TBRS model framework. This will allow us to draw from these studies what are the main determinants of working memory development from the specific view of the TBRS model. Chapter 9 will discuss how a working memory conceived as a time-based resource-sharing system could impact general cognitive development.

8

SOURCES OF DEVELOPMENT IN THE TBRS MODEL

The previous chapter of this book illustrated how it is difficult to identify the factors responsible for the development of working memory capacity. This capacity certainly increases with age, but why and how? A popular answer to these questions, at least among developmental psychologists, was the trade-off hypothesis advanced by Case (1992) that we presented in Chapter 2. Recall that Case et al. (1982) established that counting span increases with age with the efficiency of the counting procedure. They interpreted this correlation in a causal way: as counting becomes more and more automatic, it occupies less mental space (the so-called total processing space), leaving more space available for storing the to-be-remembered totals. It went unnoticed for a long time that it was possible to account for this correlation in a far simpler way. This is what Towse and Hitch (1995) did. Case and colleagues assessed counting efficiency through counting speed, observing that this speed strongly increases with age. Would it be possible that the higher counting spans in older children are simply due to the fact they count faster, hence benefiting from shorter delays of retention? As we briefly mentioned in the previous chapter, to test this hypothesis, Towse and Hitch created arrays that elicited either different attentional demands for counting (targets differed from non-targets by either a single feature or a conjunction of features) or different counting times. In children aged 6 to 11, they observed that spans were lower when counting took longer, whereas the difficulty of counting had no effect per se. They interpreted this finding as evidence against a resource trade-off as originally proposed by Case, a mere temporal decay of memory traces during counting being able to account for their results. Subsequent studies confirmed that the duration of the intervening task was the main determinant of working memory performance (Hitch, Towse, & Hutton, 2001; Towse, Hitch, & Hutton, 1998, 2000, 2002). Towse and Houston-Price (2001) concluded that the notion of resources was then superfluous, a switching of attention between storage and processing phases being sufficient.

130 Development in the TBRS model

The time-based resource-sharing model (TBRS) was developed as an attempt to integrate and synthesize the findings issued from a series of studies inspired by the thought-provoking ideas of Towse and Hitch. We reasoned that if the duration of the processing component was the unique determinant of recall performance, replacing the counting task by a non-demanding activity of the same duration (e.g. simply repeating the syllable *ba*) in a complex span task in which children had to maintain and recall series of letters should leave working memory spans unaffected (Barrouillet & Camos, 2001). In line with Towse and Hitch's (1995) predictions, this is what we observed. However, further experiments revealed that complex spans were affected by the nature of the processing component, even when its duration was kept constant. For example, while maintaining letters, solving arithmetic problems led to lower recall performance than repeating *ba*, even when durations were strictly equated. Nonetheless, the difference was smaller than we would have expected. As Baddeley (1986) said, the cognitive system proved to be much more robust than anticipated. A possible explanation of this robustness was to imagine that while performing complex tasks like arithmetic problem solving, individuals take advantage of short pauses to surreptitiously switch their attention to the decaying memory traces, thus reactivating them and avoiding their complete loss. This would mean that a task occupying attention almost continuously would have a strong detrimental effect on concurrent maintenance, whereas a task allowing for frequent attentional switches should have only a slight effect. This is not that resources are not shared in working memory between processing and storage, but they are shared on a temporal basis – hence, a time-based resource sharing.

We have already provided elsewhere integrative descriptions of the TBRS model (see Barrouillet & Camos, 2007, 2010, 2012, 2015). In the following we will just give an overview of the model before addressing its developmental implications.

Overview of the TBRS model

The basic notion of the TBRS model is *distraction*, with the idea that we cannot think of two things at the same time. A central bottleneck would constrain cognitive activities to take place one at a time (Pashler, 1998), only one item at a time being taken as an object for cognitive operations (McElree, 2001; Oberauer, 2002). Items from which attention has shifted away, attracted by other thoughts or activities, are at risk of being rapidly lost as they suffer from temporal decay and interference. Avoiding their complete loss requires abandoning these other thoughts and activities for refocusing attention on the decaying memory traces in order to refresh them. This implies that the multiple demands that working memory faces in its everyday functioning (e.g. selecting words and formulating sentences for taking notes while listening to an orator and trying to understand what she is saying) are completed through a constant and rapid switching of attention.

TBRS and cognitive load

These hypotheses led to a new conception of cognitive load (*CL*) understood as the effect that a given task has on the concurrent maintenance of information. Within the TBRS model, the *CL* of a task corresponds to the proportion of time during which it occupies attention, preventing refreshing of working memory traces to take place. Thus, the amount of information maintained in working memory should be an inverse function of the *CL* of the task concurrently performed. Barrouillet, Bernardin, and Camos (2004) tested this hypothesis in the context of a complex span task in which participants had to maintain letters for further recall, each letter being followed by a series of digits that appeared successively on screen at a constant pace and that adult participants had to read aloud. Both the duration of the inter-letter intervals and the number of digits to be read during these intervals were varied. It appeared that increasing the number of digits to be read within a fixed interval, or reducing the time available for reading an unchanged number of digits, resulted in poorer recall performance. Working memory spans, the maximum number of letters that could be recalled in correct order, linearly decreased as the *CL* of the reading digit task, expressed as the number of digits presented per second, increased. Reading digits could seem to be a fairly simple activity, but as the TBRS model predicts, it has a dramatic effect on concurrent maintenance when performed at a sufficiently fast pace and proves more disruptive than reading sentences for comprehension (Lépine, Bernardin, & Barrouillet, 2005).

The *CL* hypothesis was strengthened by the fact that the detrimental effect that concurrent tasks have on the amount of information that can be concurrently maintained depends more on the temporal parameters of these tasks than on their nature. Barrouillet, Bernardin, Portrat, Vergauwe, and Camos (2007) had adult participants maintaining letters for further recall while processing digits that appeared either in the upper or lower part of the screen. While one group performed a spatial location task (deciding whether each digit was up or down), another group performed a parity task on the same digits. Not surprisingly, the more difficult parity task elicited lower spans, but it also took longer. When memory performance was regressed onto a proxy of *CL* (i.e. the ratio between the total time taken to process the digits during the inter-letter intervals and the duration of these intervals), it appeared that working memory spans fell on the same regression line for both tasks (Figure 8.1).

The span–*CL* function was further explored and received a mathematical expression in Barrouillet et al. (2011), who observed that manipulating the duration of processing tasks involving inhibition, updating, response selection, or long-term memory retrieval resulted in variations in working memory spans that almost perfectly reflected the proportion of time devoted to perform these tasks, whatever their nature. Mean spans appeared to follow a linear function of the form

$$\text{Span} = k(1 - CL) \qquad\qquad 8.1$$

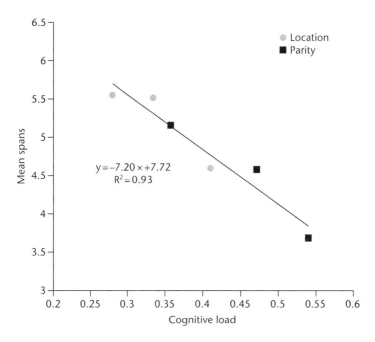

FIGURE 8.1 Mean working memory span as a function of the cognitive load in adults when the processing component was either parity or location judgement task in the study by Barrouillet et al. (2007)

Source: Adapted from P. Barrouillet and V. Camos (2009). Interference: Unique source of forgetting in working memory? *Trends in Cognitive Sciences, 13*, p. 145, with permission from Cell Press.

in which the intercept k (when $CL=0$) corresponds to working memory spans when there is no concurrent task at all (i.e. a situation of simple span). In Barrouillet et al. (2011), the value of k was close to 8, compatible with Miller's (1956) estimate. In line with the TBRS model, Equation 1 also reflects the fact that recall performance would be virtually null when CL is maximal (i.e. $CL=1$), that is when attention is continuously occupied by distracting tasks without any possibility to refresh memory traces.

The linear relationship between spans and CL was observed not only for verbal but also for visuospatial working memory (Vergauwe, Barrouillet, & Camos, 2009). Interestingly, and contrary to Baddeley's multi-component model that assumes an independence between verbal and visuospatial working memory, visuospatial working memory (maintaining spatial locations) proved to be disrupted to the same extent by variations in the CL of verbal and visuospatial concurrent tasks (semantic categorization and spatial judgement, respectively). However, verbal working memory proved more affected by verbal than visuospatial concurrent tasks (Vergauwe, Barrouillet, & Camos, 2010). This discrepancy suggests some asymmetry in the mechanisms by which verbal and visuospatial information is maintained in working memory.

Maintenance mechanisms

The trade-off observed by Vergauwe et al. (2010) reveals that visuospatial maintenance and verbal processing share a domain-general pool of resource assumed to be attention, which is necessary for both refreshing decaying memory traces and implementing and controlling the operations necessary for verbal processing such as semantic categorization. Moreover, the similar disruption of visuospatial memory by either a verbal or a visuospatial concurrent task suggests that there is no mechanism specifically dedicated to visuospatial maintenance (see Morey & Bieler, 2013; Morey, Morey, van der Reijden, & Holweg, 2013, for a similar conclusion). This does not seem to be the case for verbal maintenance, that was more affected by verbal than visuospatial processing. Camos, Lagner, and Barrouillet (2009) argued that there are two maintenance mechanisms for verbal information in working memory, one corresponding to the attentional system also responsible for the maintenance of visuospatial information, and another one corresponding to the articulatory rehearsal hypothesized by Baddeley (1986) in his multi-component model. The additive effects on verbal maintenance of a concurrent capture of attention, which impedes attentional refreshing, and a concurrent articulation, which blocks verbal rehearsal, suggest that the two systems are independent and operate jointly for maintaining verbal information.

This independence is buttressed by three important findings (see Camos, 2015, 2017, for reviews). First, each mechanism is characterized by specific constraints related to the nature of the information it preferentially processes. Accordingly, Camos, Mora, and Barrouillet (2013; see also Mora & Camos, 2013) observed that recall performance in complex span tasks is affected by phonological properties of the material (phonological similarity or word length) when information is maintained through articulatory rehearsal, but not through attentional refreshing. By contrast, maintaining information through refreshing improves long-term retention whereas rehearsal has no long-term effects (Camos & Portrat, 2015; Loaiza & McCabe, 2012). Second, adults are able to adaptively use one or the other of these mechanisms depending on the specific demands of the task or under instruction (Camos, Mora, & Oberauer, 2011). Finally, refreshing and rehearsal are sustained by distinct brain structures, with rehearsal involving brain areas associated with language production while refreshing engages the anterior prefrontal cortex and the inferior parietal cortex (Gruber, 2001; Trost & Gruber, 2012). This diversity in the systems of maintenance and the trade-off between processing and storage observed in all our studies led us to design a cognitive architecture for working memory.

A cognitive architecture

The TBRS model is implemented in a working memory cognitive architecture in which a central system is in charge of both the maintenance and the transformation of working memory representations (Barrouillet & Camos, 2015; Figure 8.2). These representations can be described as transient mental models that integrate

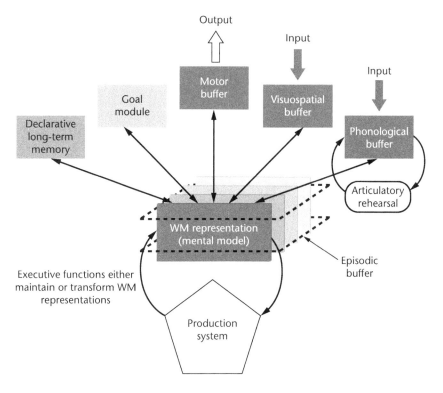

FIGURE 8.2 The working memory architecture according to the TBRS model

Source: P. Barrouillet and V. Camos (2015). *Working memory: Loss and reconstruction*, p. 118. Hove, UK: Psychology Press, adapted with permission.

Note
The episodic buffer maintains working memory representations integrating information from peripheral buffers. These representations are read by a production system and either modified or reconstructed depending on the goal at hand (i.e. processing or storage). This continuous interaction between the episodic buffer and the procedural system creates an executive loop. Among the peripheral buffers, an articulatory rehearsal system can maintain a limited number of phonological representations, whereas the visuospatial buffer is devoid of such a maintenance mechanism.

incoming information available in a series of peripheral sensory stores and elements retrieved from declarative long-term memory. The transient, heterogeneous and composite nature of these representations make them akin to the mental models hypothesized by Halford (1993) or to the representations stored in the episodic buffer hypothesized by Baddeley (2000). This episodic buffer, which corresponds to the focus of attention in Cowan's (1995) model or to the region of direct access in Oberauer's (2002) theory, is assumed to hold about four representations, but only one of these representations could be processed at a time (as in the one-item focus of attention of Oberauer, 2002). This representation in the focus of attention corresponds to the current content of consciousness. Those representations that have left the focus of attention suffer from a temporal decay and are at risk of being lost if they are not refreshed. As in the ACT-R model (Anderson, 1993; Anderson et al., 2004), a production system that stores conditions–actions rules (productions) continuously reads the active representation. The production the condition part of which matches the content of this representation fires and its action part is executed to either modify or reinstate the representation. More precisely, the productions operate on representations by triggering executive functions that can update the content of these representations, switch from one representation to another, or reconstruct a representation for its maintenance. Thus, this central structure made of the episodic buffer and the production system acts as a self-regulated *executive loop* that constitutes the seat of controlled cognitive activities and thinking, taking in charge both processing and temporary storage in working memory. Because only one representation can be treated at a time, the functioning of this executive loop is sequential, hence the alternation between processing and storage activities.

In the TBRS model, the peripheral sensory stores are conceived as passive in nature. They hold information for only a short period of time without the support of on going sensory stimulation, with the exception of the phonological buffer, the content of which can be maintained by articulatory rehearsal, constituting a phonological loop as in Baddeley's (1986) model. The content of these stores can become part of the central representations through attentional focusing directed by the central system. Thus, according to the TBRS model, verbal information can be maintained in both the executive and the phonological loop (though in a purely phonological form in the latter system), whereas the visuospatial information can only be held in the executive loop. Figure 8.2 shows also a goal module inspired from Anderson et al. (2004). Whether goals are or are not represented in working memory is a complex problem. It could be imagined that there is some buffer that stores goals and subgoals in an ordered stack, as in the executive control structures hypothesized by Case (1985). Another way to conceive goals and their effect on cognitive processes would be to imagine that they constitute transient representations in working memory that preactivate a restricted set of productions suited for their achievement, these representations being no longer useful as soon as this pre-activation is effective.

In the remainder of this chapter, we review the studies that we have conducted in order to explore the factors of development of a working memory in which resources are shared on a temporal basis. However, before evoking these factors, we report studies that examined the existence of a time-based resource-sharing mechanism in children.

A Time-Based Resource-Sharing mechanism in children

As described above, assuming a time-based resource-sharing mechanism in working memory leads one to expect that the amount of maintained information should be an inverse function of the *CL* of the concurrent task, which is conceived as the proportion of time during which this concurrent task prevents refreshing of memory

136 Development in the TBRS model

traces. Although such a relationship between recall performance and concurrent *CL* have been often reported in young adults (see Barrouillet & Camos, 2015, for a review), only a few studies have examined this phenomenon in children (Corbin, Moissenet, & Camos, 2012; Gavens & Barrouillet, 2004; Portrat, Camos, & Barrouillet, 2009; see also Camos & Barrouillet, 2011a, for a review).

Using a complex span task similar to the one used by Barrouillet et al. (2007) in adults, Portrat et al. (2009) asked 10-year-old children to maintain a series of consonants while judging the location (up or down) of squares appearing successively on screen. To vary the *CL* of this location judgement task, the squares could appear on two different locations that were either distant or close from each other. In the latter condition, the greater difficulty in discriminating between locations was assumed to increase the attentional demand of the task, thus resulting in a higher *CL* and poorer recall performance. Accordingly, the 'close' condition elicited slower responses, which reflected an increased *CL*, and poorer recall performance than the 'distant' condition (mean spans of 2.86 and 3.39, respectively). In a second experiment, the authors implemented another manipulation to increase the *CL* of the location judgement task by varying the visual discriminability of the squares. High- and low-contrast conditions were created by displaying black and dark grey squares on a light grey background. As in the previous experiment, rendering the location judgement task more difficult led to longer response time as well as poorer recall performance with a mean span of 3.30 in the low-contrast condition compared to 3.58 in the high-contrast condition. Thus, as has been observed in adults, variations in the *CL* of the location judgement task impacts the maintenance of information in children's working memory.

However, in these complex span tasks, one can remark that children could have used articulatory rehearsal because the material to be maintained was verbal (letters) while the concurrent task involved silent responses (i.e. by pressing keys) to visuospatial stimuli. Indeed, in the TBRS model, the maintenance of verbal information can be achieved through attentional refreshing, and thus reflects the time-based resource-sharing mechanism, but also through articulatory rehearsal. Thus, to prevent any implication of rehearsal and examine the unique contribution of the time-based resource-sharing mechanism, Gavens and Barrouillet (2004) asked children to perform a verbal concurrent task aloud. In a complex span task, 8- and 10-year-old children had to maintain series of letters while they read aloud series of digits appearing successively on screen after each letter (Gavens & Barrouillet, 2004). The *CL* of this reading digit task was manipulated by presenting the same series of digits either in a random or in canonical order (e.g. 5 3 2 4 1 vs. 1 2 3 4 5). Reading digits in an unpredictable random order would require more attention because children can not anticipate the nature of the forthcoming digit while they have to inhibit the utterance of the very automatized numerical verbal sequence. Interestingly, because children read exactly the same digits in the two contrasted conditions, such a manipulation of *CL* allows for a strict control of the amount of representation-based interference induced by the task, as well as of the amount of concurrent articulation preventing rehearsal. As expected, children in the two age groups had poorer recall performance in the random order condition. Thus, this experiment provided clear evidence of the effect of *CL* in children's working memory, supporting the assumption of a time-based resource-sharing mechanism in children. It should be noted that such an effect of *CL* in children's working memory is not restricted to typically developing children. In a very similar complex span task, atypically developing children with learning difficulties and presenting lower working memory capacities than their age-matched peers proved sensitive to variations in *CL* when they had to maintain letters while reading series of digits (Corbin et al., 2012).

Finally, a more extensive study examined the *CL* effect in children aged 8 to 14 (Barrouillet et al., 2009, Exp. 1). In a reading digit span task, children had to memorize letters while reading digits presented at four different paces (i.e. at a rate of 0.4, 0.8, 1.2, or 2 digits per second). According to the TBRS model, a distracting digit reading task performed at a faster pace involves higher *CL* because attention is more often captured and less available for maintenance activity. The results of this experiment revealed two main phenomena. First, in each age group, recall performance declined as the pace of the digit reading task increased. This replicated and extended previous results, confirming the existence of a time-based resource-sharing mechanism in children, at least from age 8. Second, the effect of the pace of presentation was more important in older children's recall performance. In other words, the slope between *CL* and memory span was increasingly steeper with age. This suggested that older children were more able to divert their attention from the processing to the storage activities, while the young children were probably more passive or less efficient in doing so.

To conclude, developmental studies brought evidence that a time-based resource-sharing mechanism is at the heart of children's working memory functioning as it is in young adults. Such a result leads to a reconsideration of the role of temporal parameters in accounting for working memory development. For example, in the last described study, results suggested that the age-related increase in working memory depends on the ability to shift one's attention from processing to storage. If older children are faster in switching their attention, they would be able to maintain more information and have better recall performance. However, it is also possible that part of the developmental differences observed could result from the fact that older children are probably faster in reading digits, benefiting from longer pauses to refresh memory traces. Consequently, the *CL* induced by the distracting task was probably lower in older children. Thus, to understand the development of working memory, the dynamic of working memory functioning should be carefully considered. The speed at which memory traces decay, the speed to process distracting information, as well as the efficiency to switch attention and refresh memory traces might vary with age across childhood and result in working memory improvement. In a way, these dynamic aspects of working memory contrast with more static parameters, such as the size of the focus of attention. In the following section, we present studies framed within the TBRS model that examined these different sources of working memory development.

Developmental factors in the TBRS model

The previous chapter presented the different sources of working memory development that have been evoked in the literature. Some of these sources are particularly important for the TBRS model and the way it conceives working memory functioning. In the following, we present developmental studies that were framed within the TBRS model and that aimed at examining the role of these potential sources of working memory development. We will address in turn the developmental impact of age-related changes in the rate of memory decay, in processing speed, in attentional refreshing efficiency, as well as the emergence and use of maintenance strategies.

Decay of working memory traces

In the TBRS model, a major source of forgetting lies in the temporal decay of memory traces. When attention is switched away from the to-be-maintained memory traces because of a concurrent processing, they are fading away. This phenomenon is time-dependent, the longer attention is switched away from memory traces, the stronger their forgetting. In a developmental perspective, it could thus be conceived that the better working memory performance exhibited by older children results from a slower rate of memory decay. Declining more slowly in older children, memory traces would remain more accessible after equivalent delays of distraction. As we noted earlier, this hypothesis of more resistant memory traces in older children is probably the most straightforward way to account for the age-related increase in working memory capacity. However, the number of studies examining developmental change in the rate of forgetting is few. We described these studies in infants and children in Chapters 5 and 7, and their divergent findings did not lead to any firm conclusions.

Within the TBRS model, as in most working memory models, the challenge in examining the rate of forgetting is to prevent attention from reactivating memory traces. Thus, many previous studies in children had to test memory either for ignored material in order to deter active maintenance, or when maintenance strategies are prevented through concurrent distracting tasks. However, these research designs have pitfalls, as one can not assure that ignored material has been properly encoded and that distracting tasks do not introduce representation-based interference, which both can affect recall performance and the measure of forgetting rate. As a consequence, Camos and Bertrand (2017a) developed an alternative research strategy and examined the rate of forgetting in young children aged between 4 and 6 who are known for not spontaneously using maintenance strategies (see section below on developmental changes in maintenance strategies). In working memory span tasks, these children were presented with series of items to memorize. Because they do not implement maintenance strategies, their recall performance was assumed to be affected by the mere passage of time and to depend on the delay of retention between the presentation of memory items and recall.

To give a stimulating context to such a young population, Camos and Bertrand (2017a) designed two new game-like span tasks. One mimicked grocery shopping. After the experimenter placed some plastic fruits in a bag, children had to reproduce the series of fruits by introducing the same fruits into their own bag. In the other task, a series of dolls were engaged in a ski race, and children had to reproduce the race choosing the same dolls in the same order of arrival. In both tasks, the delay between presentation and recall of series of fruits or dolls was varied. Children were asked to reproduce these series either immediately, or after a delay of 2, 4, or 6 seconds in the shopping span task, or after 4, 8, or 12 seconds in the ski racing span task. Because of the absence of use of maintenance mechanisms, poorer recall performance was expected with increased delays of retention. Accordingly, recall performance in 4-, 5- and 6-year-old children was affected by the delay of retention in both span tasks. Importantly, and although older children exhibited better recall performance, the effect of the retention delay did not interact with age.

This suggests that although working memory capacity increases from 4 to 6 years of age, this developmental improvement does not rely on a slower rate of forgetting in older children. On the contrary, this rate seems to remain constant across this age range. It should be noted that the same authors evaluated the rate of forgetting in younger children, aged between 2.5 and 3.5 years. Using the previously described shopping span task, Camos and Bertrand (2017b) reported that recall performance increased with age, but the rate of forgetting as estimated by the effect on recall of increased delays of retention remained constant between 2;6 and 3;6 years. This last study supports the conclusion that developmental improvement in working memory capacity is not a direct consequence of some age-related change in the rate of forgetting, at least in childhood.

Processing speed

If the development of working memory capacity is not due to an age-related change in forgetting rate, this does not discard the possibility that other temporal parameters are at the root of working memory improvement with age. We described in Chapter 2 Case's (1985) theory, which assumed that working memory development depends on an increase in processing efficiency, and the study by Case et al. (1982) who demonstrated that when processing efficiency is equated between adults and children, age-related differences in working memory spans vanish. As we noted above, Towse and Hitch (1995) proposed a different theoretical perspective according to which older children, being faster to process information, would benefit from shorter retention intervals in paradigms traditionally used to assess working memory capacity such as complex span tasks. Concerning the TBRS model, we have seen that it postulates a time-based decay of memory traces when attention is occupied by concurrent processing. As a consequence, any age-related increase in processing speed would reduce the critical time during which attention is distracted from maintenance activities and memory traces degrade. Following the rationale of the Case et al. (1982) study, the hypothesis of a working memory development underpinned by an

140 Development in the TBRS model

age-related increase in processing speed would lead to predict that controlling for processing time across age should make developmental differences disappear. Several studies aimed at testing this hypothesis (Barrouillet et al., 2009; Gaillard et al., 2011; Gavens & Barrouillet, 2004). To this end, children of different age groups were compared in working memory span tasks in which the duration and the difficulty of the concurrent task were equalized across age groups.

In a first attempt, Gavens and Barrouillet (2004, Exp. 3) compared the performance of 9- and 11-year-old children in a complex span task named the continuous operation span task, which requires children to maintain letters while solving series of simple arithmetic operations. After the presentation of each letter, children saw a one-digit number (the root of the operation), followed by a series of sign-operand pairs (+1 or −1) displayed successively on screen at a fixed rate. Children had to read aloud the root, each sign-operand pair, and to utter the successive answers. For example, for the '6 + 1 + 1' series, children had to say 'Six, plus one, seven, plus one, eight'. In order to equalize the difficulty of the arithmetic task across age, the continuous operations contained three sign-operand pairs for 9-year-old children, but four pairs for 11-year-olds within the same inter-letter intervals of nine seconds. Indeed, we had verified in a pre-test that these conditions led to the same percentage of correct responses to the solving-operation task in the two age groups. The results revealed that equating the duration and the difficulty of the concurrent task significantly reduced, but did not abolish, the developmental difference in span between the two groups. The residual difference in spans, which was at odds with the predictions issued from Case's (1985) model, was interpreted by Gavens and Barrouillet (2004) as reflecting an increase in some total amount of resources.

Similarly, Barrouillet et al. (2009; Exp. 2) controlled for the duration and difficulty of the concurrent task in a complex span task administered to 8- and 14-year-old children. We have already evoked the first experiment of this study (Barrouillet et al., 2009; Exp. 1; see section above on a TBRS mechanism in children) in which children performed a reading digit span task (i.e. memorizing letters while reading digits). Increasing the *CL* of the reading task by increasing the pace of presentation of the digits resulted in poorer recall of the letters, the *CL* effect being even stronger in older children. In this follow-up experiment, children had to perform the same reading digit span task, but the time available to read each digit was adapted to the reading efficiency in each age. Average reading times of the digits were evaluated in a preliminary test on two independent groups. As might be expected, older children were faster than younger children (mean reading time: 489 ms and 622 ms, respectively). Three levels of *CL* were created by presenting each digit for a duration equivalent to one, two, or four times these average reading times (for example, for a reading time of 622 ms per digit in the pre-test, each digit was presented 622 ms, 1244 ms, or 2488 ms for a high, medium, and low level of *CL*, respectively). It should be noted that the rhythm or pace of the concurrent task (i.e. the number of digits presented per second) varied between age groups because the time available to read the same number of digits was longer in young than in older children. However, the reading digit task involved the same distraction of attention (i.e. the same *CLs*) between age groups as reading occupied the same proportion of the inter-letter interval (100, 50, and 25 per cent for a high, medium, and low level of *CL*, respectively). In line with the existence of a time-based resource-sharing mechanism in children, *CL* had a significant effect on spans in both age groups with higher *CL* resulting in lower spans. However, and more importantly, as in Gavens and Barrouillet (2004), controlling for developmental differences in processing speed reduced the developmental difference in working memory spans, but a residual difference remained, 14-year-old children still largely outperforming their younger peers (mean spans of 2.88 and 1.80, respectively).

Finally, in a more recent attempt, Gaillard et al. (2011) examined the reduction of the developmental difference in spans between 9- and 12-year-old children. In a series of experiments, these authors used a complex span task in which children maintained letters while doing simple additions on digits appearing successively on screen. To establish the initial developmental difference, children of the two age groups were subjected to the same complex span task involving the same operations that consisted in adding one to each digit. As expected, older children outperformed their younger peers when performing the same task (mean span of 3.05 and 1.79, respectively). In a second experiment, the difficulty of the distracting addition task was equalized across ages. A pre-test revealed that the time taken by 12-year-olds to add two to the digits was similar to the one needed by 9-year-olds to add one. Thus, two other groups of children performed a similar complex span task but the older children were asked to add two to each digit, while the young children still added one. As such, the duration of processing was equalized between age groups. This manipulation strongly affected the pattern of results. A sharp reduction in developmental differences was observed, 12-year-olds' mean span falling from 3.05 in the previous experiment to 2.31. Nevertheless, older still surpassed younger children (mean span of 1.72).

To conclude, when age-related differences in processing speed are taken into account and controlled for in comparing different age groups, developmental differences in span are strongly reduced. However, contrary to the predictions issued from Case's (1985) theory, a residual developmental difference still remains. Thus, the duration of processing is partly responsible for the age-related differences in working memory performance, but it cannot alone account for all the developmental differences observed.

Refreshing efficiency

Where does the residual developmental difference systematically observed in the studies reported above come from? An important source of developmental improvement could rely on the use and efficiency of maintenance strategies. New strategies emerge and become more and more efficient during childhood in a variety of domains (Siegler, 1996). Strategies for maintaining information in working memory could develop during childhood, leading to a better and better maintenance of memory traces. In the TBRS model, such a strategy is at the heart of working

142 Development in the TBRS model

memory functioning. Attentional refreshing permits the restoration and maintenance of memory traces through the refocalization of attention on the working
memory representations temporally stored in an episodic buffer. Could working
memory development be related to the development of attentional refreshing
efficiency?

To evaluate this efficiency, Barrouillet and colleagues (2009; Exp. 2) took
advantage of one of their experiments in which 8- and 14-year-old children performed a complex span task in which the distracting task (reading digits) induced
the same *CLs* in the two age groups (see the previous section for a description of
this experiment). In this experiment, it was possible to estimate for each age group
and each *CL* condition the time available for refreshing memory traces. Linear
regression analyses linking spans to this available time revealed a quasi-linear function in each age group, with a more pronounced slope in young children. While,
at 14 years of age, adolescents saw their recall performance increased by approximately one item (letter) per additional second of available time after reading a digit,
the benefit was only of 0.5 item in 8-year-olds. This difference in slope confirmed
that older children were far more efficient at refreshing memory traces.

Consequently, Gaillard et al. (2011) proposed to give to young children more
time for refreshing in order to reduce the residual developmental difference they
observed after having equalized processing duration (see previous section). The
authors assumed that the amount of information that refreshing can reactivate is
dependent on its speed, a faster refreshing allowing the maintenance of a greater
number of items. Thus, to compensate for a slower maintenance process in young
children, the available time for reactivation should be longer, and proportionate to
the processing speed of these children. Thanks to the data collected during the pre-
test, the authors were able to evaluate the difference in processing speed between
9- and 12-year-old children, and thus to determine the amount of time that young
children need to reach the same level of refreshing as older children. In the third
experiment of this study, two new groups of children performed the same complex
span task as in the previous experiment (i.e. which required adding two or one to
digits for old and young children, respectively), but young children benefited also
from more free time after each addition. This increase in free time available for
refreshing led to an increase in recall performance for these children, which rose
from 1.79 to 2.28 of span and abolished the residual developmental difference (the
initial difference in span of 1.26, between 3.05 and 1.79, was reduced to 0.03,
between 2.31 and 2.28). In summary, the large difference in span observed between
children of 9 and 12 years who performed the same complex span task was reduced
when processing efficiency was equalized across ages, and it disappeared when the
time available to refresh memory traces was tailored to children's processing speed,
that is when younger children had longer available refreshing times (Figure 8.3).

Although the vanishing of developmental differences in working memory span
resulting from mere manipulations of temporal factors might seem remarkable, it
remained possible that such a surprising phenomenon is limited to small differences
in age, children aged 9 and 12 pertaining to the same developmental stage in most

Sources of development in the TBRS model **143**

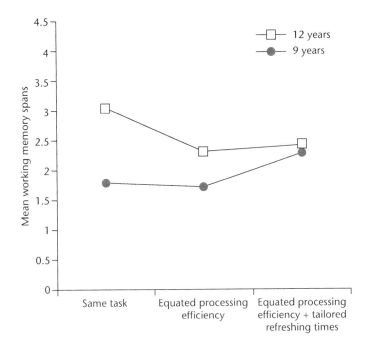

FIGURE 8.3 Evolution of the mean working memory spans in 9- and 12-year-old children when performing the same complex span task, when processing efficiency was equated, and when processing efficiency is equated and free time available for refreshing memory traces is tailored to processing speed

Source: Adapted from V. Gaillard, P. Barrouillet, C. Jarrold, and V. Camos (2011). Developmental differences in working memory: Where do they come from? *Journal of Experimental Child Psychology, 110*, p. 477, with permission from Elsevier.

of the theories of cognitive development (Case, 1985, 1992; Halford, 1993; Piaget & Inhelder, 1966). A more stringent test would be to compare age groups pertaining to clearly different developmental periods such as childhood and adolescence. Thus, Barrouillet, Dagry, and Gauffroy (2017) used the same research rationale and design as Gaillard et al. (2011) for comparing children aged 9 and 15. As in all our previous studies, equalizing processing time (younger children added one to each digit whereas adolescents added four) reduced, but did not abolish developmental difference. When, additionally, the time available for refreshing was tailored to the capacities of each group, the huge initial difference in spans, which was of 1.99 items, was reduced to 0.38 and no longer reached significance.

Temporal factors are of particular importance in the TBRS model, which assumes that working memory performance is a function of the balance between the time during which attention is occupied by concurrent processing and memory traces decay, and the time available for refreshing degraded memory traces. Although putative age-related variations in the rate of decay might seem an obvious source of working memory development, we have seen that evidence for such variations is scarce. By contrast, processing speed, which determines the time during which attention is switched away from memoranda, and refreshing efficiency, which determines the number of items that can be refreshed per unit of time, proved to be key factors of development. Cowan (2016) suggested that a stringent test in identifying factors of development consists in verifying if controlling for these factors makes developmental differences disappear. He reviewed an impressive series of factors that failed to pass the critical test. Developmental differences always remain. We have provided evidence that controlling for temporal factors makes developmental differences almost disappear. Older children have higher spans because they are faster in processing information and refreshing memory traces. Deprive them of their higher speed or, reciprocally, provide young children with the time they need, and differences in spans vanish. This illustrates the importance of dynamic aspects of cognition. A greater capacity does not necessarily reflect a difference in size. What we call working memory capacity is measured through the output of complex, temporally extended processes. Our results suggest that this temporal dimension is of paramount importance in understanding developmental differences.

Use of maintenance strategies

The TBRS model makes clear that temporal factors are particularly important to account for working memory development. However, our model also acknowledges the role of maintenance strategies. As explained in the overview of the model, the TBRS model considers two main maintenance strategies: attentional refreshing, which is a domain-general process relying on the use of attention to maintain working memory representations, and articulatory rehearsal, which is a strategy specialized in the maintenance of verbal information through language-based processes. Thus, the emergence of these strategies as well as the strategic choice among them or their joint use are additional sources of development.

Emergence of maintenance strategies

Mostly motivated by Baddeley's multi-component model, the emergence of articulatory rehearsal during childhood has been widely examined. Although the age at which this strategy emerges in childhood and the kind of index that should be used to detect its appearance remain a matter of debate (see Chapter 5), many people consider that children use rehearsal after the age of 7, which results in an improvement in verbal working memory capacity. Research framed within the TBRS model was mainly dedicated to the other maintenance mechanism, attentional refreshing, which is a central process in working memory as depicted by the TBRS model.

Due to the pivotal role of refreshing in working memory maintenance as conceived in the TBRS model, recall performance should be low in the absence of use of this maintenance mechanism. Moreover, if young children do not voluntarily shift their attention from processing to storage, their recall performance should remain unaffected by variations in CL of a secondary task. Barrouillet et al. (2009; Exp. 3) tested this hypothesis in two groups of 5- and 7-year-old children performing an adapted complex span task. Children saw drawings of animals whose names they had to memorize (the experimenter named the animal aloud for each drawing). In the inter-animal intervals, they had to name the colour of heads ('smileys') successively displayed on screen. The duration of the inter-animal intervals was kept constant, but the number of colours appearing in each of these intervals varied from one condition to another (zero, two, or four colours). Although we expected that the colour naming task would impair recall by turning attention away from the memory trace of the last animal presented, we also predicted that younger children would not take advantage of the free time available between successive coloured heads to refresh memory traces, and as a consequence, the two- and four-colour conditions that had the same duration (inter-animal intervals were kept constant) would lead to comparable recall performance. On the contrary, if the attentional refreshing is effective at the age of 7, recall in older children should depend on the CL of the colour naming task. Thus, the four-colour condition should result in poorer recall performance than the two-colour condition. The results revealed two things. First, they replicated the effect of CL on recall performance in 7-year-olds. Second, they showed that before 7 years of age, the maintenance of elements in working memory was weakened by the presence of a secondary task, but the CL induced by this task had no impact on recall performance. This suggested that, unlike older children, 5-year-olds do not attempt, or are not able, to divert their attention from the distracting task to refresh memory traces. If this is the case, the main determinant of working memory in very young children should be the raw duration of the secondary task (i.e. the duration of the retention delay) rather than the CL it induces.

A follow-up study was specifically designed to test this proposal (Camos & Barrouillet, 2011b). We modified the colour naming span task to manipulate orthogonally the duration and the CL of the distracting task by presenting either one or two colours within intervals of two seconds, or two colours in four-second intervals. We reasoned that if young children do not use refreshing, the duration of the secondary task alone must determine recall performance. Thus, performance should not differ between the two conditions with two-second intervals whatever the number of colours presented, but should be better than in the condition with four-second intervals. On the contrary, if children can flexibly divert their attention from the colour task to reactivate the memory traces of the animals, their spans should depend on the CL of the processing component, and not on its raw duration. Consequently, performance should be lower when two colours were presented in two seconds (i.e. at a rate of a colour per second) than when one colour was presented in two seconds or two colours in four seconds. The results revealed that 7-year-olds' recall performance depended on the CL of the processing component and not on its duration, while the opposite trend was observed in the

146 Development in the TBRS model

5-year-olds. This change in the nature of the factor determining recall provides strong support for the assumption that a qualitative change takes place between 5 and 7 years of age in the strategies responsible for maintaining information in working memory. It should nevertheless be noted that some particularly meaningful context (such as a game) could favour the use of refreshing. In the shopping span task, Bertrand and Camos (2015) observed that very young children, aged between 4 and 6, could be sensitive to an increase in concurrent attentional demand, which usually indicates the involvement of attentional refreshing in the maintenance of information. However, further studies are in progress to determine exactly what are the characteristics of a working memory span task that could stimulate the use of refreshing in young children.

Coordinating different maintenance strategies

In young adults, evidence has been collected on the joint use of refreshing and rehearsal for maintaining verbal information in working memory (see Camos, 2015, 2017, for review). Moreover, as we reported above, adults have shown to be able to adaptively choose one of the two strategies depending on task constraints, i.e. whether the secondary task is attention demanding and impairs refreshing, or requires language processes and thus impedes rehearsal (Camos et al., 2011). We have also seen that this choice is not without consequences as adults' recall performance is affected by phonological characteristics of the memory items under the use of rehearsal, effects that disappear under refreshing use. However, few studies framed within the TBRS model have examined the same phenomena in children to assess the possible joint use of the two maintenance strategies, the ability to select strategies, and their impact on recall performance.

To examine the joint implication of rehearsal and refreshing in children's verbal working memory, Oftinger and Camos (2016) asked children aged 6 to 9 to perform a complex span task in which they maintained letters or words while performing a concurrent task on series of pictures sequentially presented in the inter-item intervals. To vary the opportunity to refresh memory items, the attentional demand of the concurrent task was manipulated. Children performed either a low-demanding colour-discrimination task (Is the picture in colour or in black and white?) or a high-demanding categorization task (Does the picture represent an animal or not?). Moreover, the concurrent task was performed either silently by pressing keys or aloud, the latter inducing a concurrent articulation that impaired rehearsal. As expected, recall performance increased strongly with age. More interestingly for the purpose of this study, the induction of a concurrent articulation by responding aloud had a detrimental effect on recall, even in the younger age group aged 6. In the same way, the increase in concurrent attentional demand reduced recall performance at all ages. Finally, and as previously observed in adults, the effects of the availability of rehearsal and of attentional refreshing never interacted in any age group. The same pattern of results was replicated in a second experiment in which the attentional demand of the concurrent task was differently manipulated. Children performed either a low-demanding serial reaction time task or the colour discrimination task that induced a higher CL. Similar findings were also observed when children performed a Brown-Peterson task, another paradigm to test working memory in which the distracting task is performed after the sequential presentation of all the memory items (Oftinger & Camos, 2017). This suggests that children from 6 to 9 use both refreshing and rehearsal, but the two mechanisms are independent in the maintenance of verbal information in children as well as in adults.

Because children can jointly use rehearsal and refreshing, are they able to make some strategic choice between the two, as was reported in young adults? In a series of two experiments using the Brown-Peterson paradigm, Oftinger and Camos (2017) examined the correlation between CL as defined by the TBRS model and recall performance when children aged 6 to 8 years of age had or had not the possibility of using rehearsal, depending on the production of a concurrent articulation. The pattern of correlations between CL and memory span showed a clear change around the age of 7 years. In 6-year-olds, the CL of the concurrent task was never correlated with span, whenever children performed or not a concurrent articulation. However, as previously reported for children older than 7, recall in 8-year-olds was negatively related to CL. This was observed whether children could or could not use rehearsal. This contrasted pattern echoes previous conclusions from Barrouillet et al. (2009) and Camos and Barrouillet (2011b) suggesting that refreshing is available in children older than 7, but not in younger children. Concerning the possibility of strategic choice, a novel phenomenon occurred in the 7-year-old group. At this age, children's recall was impaired by an increased CL but only under concurrent articulation. Although this brought evidence in favour of the existence of two maintenance strategies in this age group, this also points to the ability for 7-year-old children to adaptively choose between these strategies. This suggests that articulatory rehearsal is the default strategy for these children who can adaptively switch to refreshing when articulatory processes are unavailable.

We previously saw that the use by adults of verbal rehearsal involves effects related with the phonological characteristics of the memoranda, such as a poorer recall performance when memory items are phonologically similar than when they are dissimilar. Such an effect does not emerge when adults are instructed to use refreshing (Camos et al., 2011). In children, things are quite different as Mora and Camos (2015) reported. In this study, 8-year-old children had to memorize series of phonologically similar or dissimilar words in different complex span tasks. As in the previously described studies, these span tasks differed in the attentional demand of the concurrent task and in the involvement of language processes to produce responses, the two factors being orthogonally manipulated. Although Mora and Camos (2015) provided further evidence of the use of the two mechanisms of maintenance in children as well as their independence in maintaining verbal information, the impact of refreshing and rehearsal on the emergence of the phonological similarity effect was rather different from what is known in adults. Actually, the authors were able to dissociate two distinct patterns presented by different children. For about half of the children, the phonological similarity effect did not

148 Development in the TBRS model

affect recall in any complex span task in which a concurrent task or concurrent articulation was performed in the retention interval. On the contrary, when the delay of retention was unfilled, phonologically dissimilar word lists were better recalled than similar lists. For the other half of the children, the pattern was different, as the phonological similarity effect appeared in complex span tasks in which children performed a concurrent task, but it disappeared in its absence. The authors proposed that the difference in recall pattern resulted from differences in strategy choice, with each group having a systematic bias for one of the two processes. Further studies are needed to determine what triggers this bias for one of the processes, and what could be the consequences of such bias on the development of working memory for these children.

To summarize, the studies we conducted within the theoretical framework provided by the TBRS model revealed that the emergence of strategies for maintaining information in working memory is among the factors that underpin working memory development. As we saw in the previous section, the efficiency of these strategies increases with age, but the studies reported in the present section revealed that there is an age at which maintenance strategies are not yet available, or are not evoked outside of some facilitating contexts. Considering that adults are able to adaptively choose between strategies depending on task constraints, it can be surmised that the development involves an increase not only in the availability and efficiency of strategies, but also in the capacity to select between strategies. More generally, the changes that can be expected to characterize the development of maintenance strategies in working memory are most probably those that Siegler (1996) identified in cognitive development: acquisition of new strategies, variations in the frequency of use of the available strategies, increase in their speed of execution and efficiency, and more and more adaptive choice between strategies.

Conclusion

The theoretical framework provided by the TBRS model proved heuristic in investigating the sources of the development of working memory. The predominant role of temporal factors in determining the amount of information that working memory can hold naturally suggests that this development should result from age-related changes susceptible to having an impact on the dynamics of working memory functioning. Our findings indicate that working memory development, at least during childhood and adolescence, results from more efficient and faster processing that preserve memory traces from decay, and more efficient maintenance mechanisms able to restore degraded memory traces. Cowan (2016, 2017) established that working memory development is not entirely based on factors such as processing efficiency, use of rehearsal as a mnemonic strategy, encoding efficiency, learning or efficiency of attentional allocation. Indeed, controlling for these factors sometimes reduces, but does not make disappear, developmental differences. We reached the same conclusion for processing efficiency when considered in isolation. However, if the other side of the decay-and-refresh hypothesis that underlies the TBRS model is taken into account and refreshing time is also controlled for, developmental differences do vanish.

Cowan (2016) suggested that because the control of putative factors does not abolish developmental differences, we are left with the hypothesis of a global increase in capacity. The results of our studies temper this conclusion. Developmental differences over large age spans (from 9 to 15) almost disappear when the factors underpinning the basic mechanisms of working memory functioning are controlled. Does this mean that there is no global increase in capacity? We do not think so, but these capacities might not be specific to working memory, such as some mental space specifically dedicated to storage, or the size of a focus of attention that would increase with age. The age-related evolution of the factors that we identified as the basis of working memory development, i.e. processing speed and refreshing efficiency, is probably driven by developmental changes that are more general than the increase in efficiency of a specific system, as central as it may be, as working memory is. Instead, this evolution most probably results from a global change affecting all the mental processes. For example, the increase in processing speed affects in the same way a large range of processes spanning from visual search to lexical access and arithmetic problem solving (Kail, 1991). Such global change that goes beyond the development of specific modules or systems is most probably due to exercise and automation, but also to brain maturation, which does not end before at least the late adolescence (Lebel & Beaulieu, 2011; Thompson et al., 2000). More precisely, white matter maturation through axons myelination in working memory-related fronto-parietal networks seems to play a critical role, allowing for faster information transfer and a better timing in the communication between different cortical areas (Darki & Klingberg, 2015; Nagy, Westerberg, & Klingberg, 2004). The better and faster functioning of neuronal systems that results from this maturation could be considered as a mental resource or capacity that increases with age. Importantly, our studies revealed that an adaptation of the temporal factors of the task is sufficient, at least from childhood to adolescence, to compensate developmental differences in working memory, bringing strong evidence that these differences are not due to some structural change in the working memory system.

9

HOW A DEVELOPING TBRS WORKING MEMORY CAN FRAME OUR UNDERSTANDING OF COGNITIVE DEVELOPMENT

Part I of this book made clear that the development of working memory was not sufficient to satisfactorily account for the entire cognitive development. The neo-Piagetian attempts we reviewed encountered insuperable obstacles in determining the maximum capacity working memory reaches at the end of its development, the nature of its content (Does working memory store a mixture of figurative and operative schemes, representations of the problem at hand, stack of goals and sub-goals, strategies, mental models?), the grain at which tasks must be analysed in order to assess their working memory demand, and even what develops in working memory that could explain cognitive development. Endeavours within the information processing approach encountered the same difficulties, and it does not seem that 'cognitive development can, in fact, be reduced to memory development' as Brainerd (1983, p. 168) claimed. However, this is not to say that analysing working memory development does not shed any light on cognitive development. In this chapter, we will show how a developing working memory as hypothesized by the TBRS model could impact and frame cognitive development, demonstrating that the scope of our model is not restricted to working memory, but can provide an adequate framework to understand cognitive development.

The overview of the TBRS model in the previous chapter and the central role of the executive loop within this cognitive architecture means that working memory in the TBRS model can be seen as *an operation centre* bringing together the functions of both the central executive and the episodic buffer in the latest version of Baddeley's (2000) model. The increase in efficiency of this executive system has necessarily an impact on cognitive processes and their development. One of the main hypotheses of the TBRS model is that there are no representations in the cognitive system outside working memory. Thus, the TBRS working memory can also be described as *a representational medium* establishing a link between the organism and its environment through the construction of mental representations of the past, present, and putative future of this environment. The evolution in number, nature, and persistence of the representations constructed in working memory might also have a strong impact on cognitive development. However, beyond the executive and representational functions of working memory and following Cowan's proposal, the TBRS working memory is also *a learning device* that creates representational units deposited in long-term memory that can be subsequently retrieved and used for reaching current goals. We will see that this learning process strongly influences cognitive development. Finally, the central role of the TBRS working memory, which is in charge of creating representations of the world in order to achieve adaptation through goal achievement and learning, means that this TBRS working memory can be seen as *the seat of thought and intelligence*. We will discuss in turn these four aspects of the TBRS model, beginning with the last aspect evoked.

Working memory as the seat of thought and intelligence

La Pointe and Engle (1990, p. 1130) suggested that working memory provides 'the texture and context to our cognitive life at any given moment'. Indeed, it has been assumed from the very inception of the concept of working memory that its content has a special access to consciousness (Miller et al., 1960), a conception that has been regularly reaffirmed (see Baddeley, 1986, who suggested that the central executive has the function of consciousness). Accordingly, we have assumed that the representations stored by the episodic buffer in the executive loop of the TBRS working memory constitute the current content of consciousness (Barrouillet & Camos, 2015). This amounts to saying that working memory is the seat of thought and intelligence. In other words, working memory is the cognitive system in which are constructed the representations that occur in our mind, their rapid manipulation or substitution creating the mental stream that we experience as thought. We have seen that the determinant dimension characterizing the TBRS working memory is temporal in nature. As a consequence, the speed at which the different operations of the executive loop can be carried out is a determinant of paramount importance for our mental life. Intuitively, everybody surmises that a rapid mental stream, if adequately controlled, is a condition for higher intellectual achievements. Thinking faster is certainly better, but why? The fact that processing speed dramatically increases during childhood and adolescence (and decreases with aging) has been abundantly documented (Kail, 1991, 1992; Kail & Salthouse, 1994; Salthouse, 1996) and probably plays a crucial role in cognitive development. The TBRS model makes possible to understand how and why an increase in processing speed could have a strong impact on cognitive development.

Processing speed as a major source of development in a TBRS cognitive system

We reviewed in Chapter 8 the studies demonstrating that age-related differences in working memory capacity were abolished when temporal factors are controlled

152 Development in the TBRS model

across age, that is when older children no longer benefit from shorter processing times and when younger children are allowed more free time. We explained these phenomena by assuming that memory traces decay during processing, shorter processing episodes resulting in weaker decay but can be refreshed during free time, longer free time allowing for the refreshing of a greater number of memory traces. This interplay between decay of working memory representations when attention is diverted and their possible restoration when attention is available anew does not only concern performance in complex working memory span tasks, but has implications for a large range of cognitive processes.

Processing speed, within the TBRS theoretical framework, refers to the time needed to construct a representation in working memory by retrieving appropriate information from long-term memory[1] and organizing this information with external input in a coherent and meaningful way, to select the production appropriate for its treatment according to the current goal, and to implement the actions operating on this representation. The faster these operations, the shorter the time during which other representations previously constructed that must be maintained in an accessible state will suffer from decay and interference. In other words, faster processing allows for a higher number of memory traces that can be simultaneously maintained in a state of privileged accessibility. This could result in an enrichment of the representation that children can construct of a given situation problem and a better understanding of this situation. This benefit of an increased processing speed was already envisioned by Case (1985) who assumed that a higher processing efficiency resulted in more representations that could be simultaneously stored and allowed longer lists of hierarchically organized goals and subgoals. However, what Case overlooked is that maintenance in working memory is not a passive, but an active process that involves cognitive attentional mechanisms that suffer from temporal constraints, as any other cognitive operation. Processing speed not only determines the time during which concurrently held representations decay, but also the rate at which these representations can be restored. Accordingly, we have seen that Barrouillet et al. (2009) observed that children aged 14 were able to restore twice as many memory items per unit of free time as children aged 8. Thus, whereas equalizing processing time across age does not abolish developmental differences in working memory capacity, equalizing processing times *and* tailoring refreshing times to children's processing speed do. As a consequence, a higher processing speed not only protects working memory representations from the damages of temporal decay and interference, but it allows for their more efficient restoration when needed, resulting in more and more representations available for processing. Thus, the developmental increase in processing speed allows for the construction and simultaneous maintenance of an increasing number of working memory representations allowing in turn for more complex processes.

It is worth noting that, for a temporally constrained system like the human mind, speed is not just a modern obsession of computer users, it is a *sine qua non* condition for an efficient cognitive functioning. Piaget (1945) already noted that one of the conditions of the transition between sensorimotor to conceptual intelligence was an acceleration of movements, in such a way that successive actions merge into a moving contraction of the whole action, the rapid progress of the film constituting the internal representation. In the same way, all the high-level cognitive activities usually assumed to involve working memory such as reasoning, problem solving, or comprehension require some minimal processing speed to avoid the complete loss of premises, intermediary results, and relevant pieces of information needed for success. The higher the number of premises, intermediary results, and relevant pieces of information readily available in mind, the more complex the situations the subject can deal with, and the better the performance. It can be noted that cognitive development in the tasks analysed in the three first chapters of this book (the problem of the balance beam, the Latin square task, the transitive reasoning task or probability judgements) is always characterized by an increase in the number of elements children are able to take into account. This increase has often been explained by some augmentation of a space available for storage (Case, 1985) or of the number of slots in a storage device (Cowan, 2001; Pascual-Leone, 1970). Instead, the TBRS model and our developmental studies suggest that this increase is due to the age-related increase in processing speed.

Although the role of working memory in the development of high-level cognitive activities is indisputable, several recent theories assume that there are types of thinking that govern most of our behaviours and that do not require working memory. Thus, the development of this type of thinking outside working memory should not strongly depend on working memory. We address this question in the following subsection.

Thinking outside working memory

The last decades have seen the emergence of a host of theories, known as dual-process theories, mainly in the domain of social psychology (see Gawronski & Creighton, 2013, for a review), but also in cognitive psychology, and particularly in the domain of reasoning and decision making (see Evans, 2012, for a review). Although all dual-process theories are not the same, they share as a core principle the idea that there are two kinds of thinking, one fast and intuitive, the other slow and reflective (Evans & Stanovich, 2013; Kahneman, 2013). The former kind, often referred as a heuristic, System 1 or Type 1 process, has been described as parallel, automatic, associative, high capacity, whereas the latter kind, known as analytic, System 2 or Type 2 process, is serial, controlled, rule-based, and capacity limited. Type 1, which is considered as the default type of thinking by several theories (Evans, 2007, 2011; Kahneman & Frederick, 2002; Stanovich, 1999, 2010), is assumed to underpin the frequent fallacies and biases that characterize human reasoning and decision making (Kahneman, 2013). Type 2 processing may or may not intervene to override Type 1 intuitive responses. What is of interest for our purpose is that the main distinction between the two types of thinking is that Type 2 processing requires working memory, usually understood as controlled attention as in Engle's perspective (Feldman Barrett, Tugade, & Engle, 2004), whereas Type 1

154 Development in the TBRS model

processing does not, thus explaining the main characteristics of the two types of processing.

Because the Type 1 process, which is the default mode of thinking in human beings, does not require working memory, it could be argued that the development of a large, and maybe the major, part of cognitive processes does not depend on working memory development. However, things are more complex, and the development of Type 1 thinking might be more influenced by working memory than the dichotomy outlined above would lead one to expect. Indeed, as Stanovich, West, and Toplak (2011) noted, Type 1 processing does not refer to a single system, but is a grab-bag encompassing innate processing modules, unconscious implicit learning and conditioning, but also experiential associations, rules, procedures, and principles that have been learned to automaticity. In other words, Type 1 processing retrieves encapsulated knowledge bases, but also information that has been compiled through learning and practice, including normative rules of rational behaviour initially pertaining to Type 2 processing (Stanovich et al., 2011). This is why it is particularly difficult to draw developmental predictions from dual-process theories (Barrouillet, 2011a; Evans, 2011; Stanovich et al., 2011), because both types of processing have their own developmental course, as well as each of the varieties of Type 1 processing. For example, several studies have reported the surprising result that some reasoning biases exhibit a U-shaped developmental curve, with young children producing *more* normative responses than older children and young adolescents (Jacobs & Potenza, 1991; Morsanyi & Handley, 2008). However, as argued by Stanovich et al. (2011; see also De Neys & Vanderputte, 2011), this is due to the fact that young children have not yet learned the social stereotypes that usually underpin reasoning biases and heuristics in decision making. Thus, even if Type 1 processing is autonomous and the execution of these processes mandatory when their triggering stimuli are encountered, the information that these processes retrieve is not independent from working memory in its acquisition. The learning processes that lead to the construction of knowledge accessed by Type 1 processing through associative learning and compilation are constrained by working memory capacities, and consequently evolves with age, explaining that some reasoning biases are more frequent as children develop. Beyond the U-shape developmental curves, this also explains why Reyna and Brainerd (2011) in their Fuzzy-Trace Theory assume that adult behaviour is most often characterized by sophisticated intuitions that capture the gist of situations rather than by deliberate, step-by-step, and costly computations. Nonetheless, these sophisticated intuitions have very little to do with the intuitions that govern children's thinking as they result from long and complex learning processes and often involve compiled rules of rational responding. Thus, if the development of Type 2 processing is obviously constrained by working memory development, Type 1 processing most probably does not develop independently from working memory.

In summary, thinking development, even in its most autonomous and intuitive aspects, is not independent from working memory and its development. Beyond a possible increase in working memory capacity conceived as the number of items that can be held simultaneously (Cowan, 2001; Halford, 1993), the TBRS model provides a way to understand how working memory development can impact cognitive development by making possible the processing of more and more complex sets of information. From the key hypotheses that the main cognitive constraints are temporal in nature and development is accompanied by a release of these constraints, it can be understood that some processing sequences that are most frequently implemented reach automaticity through the age-related increase in processing speed, enriching the stock of autonomous processes known as a System 1 or Type 1 process.

Working memory as an operation centre

Historically, the concept of working memory was developed when it was shown that a short-term memory was not sufficient to account for cognitive functioning in a human cognitive system conceived as an information processing system (see Baddeley & Hitch, 1974). At the time, this new concept departed from short-term memory as it emphasized the 'works' or operations this memory is in charge of. In this section, we will discuss how a TBRS working memory integrates the operative aspects of cognition that are often neglected by other working memory models. This allows us to re-examine the role of operative and figurative aspects of cognitive functions in cognitive development. Finally, the TBRS model suggests an alternative view on executive functions accounting for their unity and diversity.

A working memory that works

Although working memory should depart from short-term memory because this concept adds processing to the storage function, most models of working memory actually focus on the maintenance of information in the short term. Among the prominent models described in Chapter 4, Cowan's and Engle's models conceive working memory as the activated part of long-term memory and propose that attention is necessary to keep information active, without any emphasis on how this information can be processed. In Baddeley's multi-component model, processing is clearly stated as one of the two functions of working memory beside storage. However, the processing side has been less studied and is theoretically less described than the storage function. It is assumed that each working memory function is taken in charge by distinct components, the processing by the central executive and the storage by different slave systems. However, the structure and functions of the central executive remains rather underspecified, and it is often described as a ragbag. At best, Baddeley (1986, 1996) proposed that this component is akin to a Supervisory Attentional System, as in Norman and Shallice's model (1986), which is involved in executive control.

As in the multi-component model, the TBRS model gives to working memory the functions of processing and storing information. However, contrasting with the aforementioned models, it describes the relationships between processing and storage (Barrouillet et al., 2011; Barrouillet & Camos, 2015). According to this model, working memory includes a procedural system responsible for the processing of the representations stored in the episodic buffer. This procedural system that forms with the episodic buffer an executive loop operates on the mental representations the episodic buffer contains. Depending on the goal of the task at hand, different operations would affect these representations, such as modifying their content, replacing one representation by another, or consolidating and keeping active a representation for maintenance purpose. Thus, within this framework, maintenance is only one type of processing among others that is performed by the procedural system. As a direct consequence, any other types of processing rely on the same executive loop, which is then occupied and unavailable for the maintenance of memory traces. The TBRS model thus provides some insight about the integration of the declarative and procedural aspects of cognition, the former referring to the representations and the latter to the procedures operating on these representations.

It is worth noting that the development of the procedural aspects of cognition has often been mentioned as a driving force underlying cognitive development. The most prominent example is the Piagetian theory that distinguished between what Piaget called the *operative* and the *figurative* aspects of cognitive functions. The development of the operative aspects, which subsumed schemes and operations, was assumed to underlie cognitive development, whereas the development of the figurative aspects (i.e. any type of representations exemplified by perception, language, imitation, or mental imagery) was under the dependence of the age-related development and structuring of the operative aspects. It should be noted that schemes and operations in Piaget's model are akin to the procedures described by information processing theories such as ACT-R model, which inspires the procedural system embedded in the TBRS model. In the same way as procedures are small abstract action plans, schemes were conceived as the structure of any perceptive, motor, symbolic, or operational action, what is transferred and generalized through the repetitions of this action in similar or analogous circumstances.

Contrary to Piaget's view and as summarized in Chapter 5, most working memory models do not account for cognitive development by some evolution of the procedural aspects, but by an increase in the number of representations that can be held active and available for processing, that is by an age-related increase in span (Cowan, 2016, 2017a; Gathercole et al., 2004). This is also what Case (1985) proposed in his model in which cognitive development is characterized by an increase in the number of representations integrated in executive control structures, with their maximum complexity being constrained by working memory capacity. Similarly, in Halford's (1993) model, structure mappings (i.e. the mapping of an internal structure onto the structure of a segment of environment) are more and more complex across childhood. However, contrary to the Piagetian structures that integrate schemes and operations, the structures hypothesized by Halford are representational in nature and changes in their complexity (named dimensionality by Halford) are mainly responsible for cognitive development. Thus, as Cowan (2017) notes, some commonalities seem to emerge between working memory models and neo-Piagetian theories in suggesting an important role of an increase in the amount of representations actively maintained (see next section for further discussion of this topic). However, neo-Piagetian theories do not ignore the impact on cognitive development of procedural aspects. For example, Case (1985) relates the increase in working memory span to changes in processing. In his theory, increased efficiency in processing leads to a reduction of the space needed by operating aspects and, consequently, to an increased space available for storage. Although Case recognized that age-related changes in figurative aspects are important in accounting for cognitive development, these changes are mediated or resulting from a development of the operative aspects. The impact of the operative aspects in cognitive development is more strongly exemplified by Siegler's theories (1978, 1996), in which development emerges from changes in rules or strategies children can implement. We have argued elsewhere (Barrouillet & Camos, 2017) that, although the information processing background of the rule-based approach favoured by Siegler seems to be totally different from the Piagetian structural and logic-based constructivism, the mechanisms by which development is explained in both approaches are the same. As Piagetian schemes and operations, rules are another variety of what is called 'procedure' in current psychology. As we will discuss later, the TBRS model also proposes that the emergence of new procedures and evolutions in their use have a determinant impact on cognitive development, allowing this model to account for the same developmental changes as in Siegler's theories.

Because the executive loop in the TBRS model is involved in both the operative and figurative aspects of cognition, this model shares also some commonalities with Pascual-Leone's (1970) hypothesis of a maturationally based increase in some total mental space, which encompasses operative and figurative schemes. It remains possible that with development, more procedures can be simultaneously activated and readily available for processing. It should be noted that Oberauer (2009) has suggested in a non-developmental theory to distinguish a procedural working memory from a declarative working memory. The declarative working memory is in charge of maintaining mental representations, while the procedural working memory aims at maintaining task-sets. The two working memories are thought to have symmetric structures. As the TBRS model, this conception includes both operative and figurative aspects in working memory. However, it also departs from the TBRS model, because it proposes that procedural knowledge is actively maintained while performing a task. On the contrary and more in line with ACT-R model, the TBRS model puts forward that mental representations stored in the episodic buffer would be the triggering conditions for procedures that do not have to be actively maintained in working memory.

As we will explain below, the action part of the procedures operates on working memory representations by triggering the appropriate executive functions (Barrouillet & Camos, 2015). Thus, the development of these executive functions, which are at the heart of working memory functioning, contribute to working memory development and more generally to cognitive development.

158 Development in the TBRS model

Executive functions

As explained in Chapter 6, working memory is either considered as one executive function (more specifically, working memory updating) or as the central structure of executive control. The TBRS model, as well as Baddeley's multi-component model, pertains to the latter theoretical tradition. As a consequence, the development of executive functions is subsumed under the development of working memory.

Within the TBRS model, executive functions are triggered by the action part of the production rules. When a production rule has its condition part matched by the current goal and content of the episodic buffer, it fires and the appropriate executive function operates. This would modify the content of the episodic buffer, resulting in new representations, which match the conditions of activation of another production rule that fires, and so on. This leads to a cyclic functioning in which the content of the episodic buffer is successively modified (see Barrouillet & Camos, 2010, 2015, for a more complete description). The production rules can either update the content of the episodic buffer by modifying working memory representations, select relevant information within the environment, retrieve an item of knowledge from declarative long-term memory, or even trigger the appropriate motor program for overt behaviour if necessary. Let us examine more specifically the three functions considered as core functions in executive control: updating, inhibition, and shifting. In the TBRS framework, all these functions can be subsumed under the modifications of working memory representations. For example, updating is modifying the content of the episodic buffer by transforming the currently stored representations. Inhibition refers to the action of blocking the construction of a mental representation or deleting an already constructed representation. The separation between the declarative and procedural aspects in the TBRS model could account for the difference the literature makes between this type of inhibition that blocks information (declarative aspect) and the inhibition of a prepotent response, which is related to the blocking of an action (procedural aspect). Finally, shifting refers to the ability to move from one task to another. Some authors have suggested that the development of this particular executive function actually depends on the two others (Kirkham et al., 2003; Morton & Munakata, 2002a). This is quite understandable within the TBRS framework, as moving efficiently from one task to another requires modifying the content of the episodic buffer because the mental representations are the triggering conditions of the production rules. Thus, shifting requires modifying representations (updating), and blocking the construction of some representation (inhibition). Hence, executive functions are diverse because they have different impacts on the content of the episodic buffer, but they are also unitary because they are involved in the same executive loop and have the same overall common function to shape working memory representations (see Barrouillet et al., 2011, for evidence in adults that diverse executive functions involve the same working memory structure and have the same impact on working memory storage when involved in concurrent tasks).

The TBRS model thus considers executive skills as ways of using attention to modify mental representations stored in the episodic buffer, as also proposed by Barkley (1996) or Zelazo (2015). Within this architecture, executive functions no longer play the role of a homunculus taking important decisions, but are subordinate processes involved in goal-directed cognition. As such, this model is closely related to Luria's (1973) functional conception of the executive functions that are the psychological processes involved in goal-oriented problem solving (from building the initial representation to the evaluation of the answer). Contrary to other working memory models, executive control in the TBRS results from 'unintelligent' processes monitored by goals, and not from an assembly of smart executive functions supervising the cognitive system. An important consequence of such a conception is that executive control would rely on working memory representations and thus part of the development of executive control should depend on the types of representations a child can create.

Working memory as a representational medium

Following Dulany (1991, 1997) and the self-organizing consciousness theory of Perruchet and Vinter (2002), the TBRS model assumes that the only representations people create are built in working memory, forming the momentary phenomenal experience. Contrary to some prominent models of working memory, representations in the TBRS model would not be mere long-term memory representations activated above threshold, but are rather constructed with tokens of information retrieved from long-term memory. This is why mental representations are transient and evanescent in nature, hence the need for mechanisms of their active maintenance and reconstruction. This makes working memory the representational medium through which human beings represent the past, present, and future of their environment and themselves. As such, a developing working memory might have a direct impact on the representations infants, children, and adolescents can construct and manipulate for supporting comprehension and directing action, and consequently on cognitive development. Age-related changes can affect working memory representations in many ways. First, there can be qualitative changes as representations can evolve with age in content (the type of things that can be represented). However, representations can also be affected by quantitative changes and evolve in complexity (the amount of information a single representation can integrate), and number (how many representations can be present and ready for quick access in working memory). We will comment in turn on these two aspects.

Qualitative changes in representational content

Several theories have assumed that cognitive development is, at least in part, characterized by an age-related evolution in the nature of the representations children are able to construct, which are also the units of thought. This is, for example, what

160 Development in the TBRS model

differentiates the successive developmental stages in Case's theory discussed in Chapter 2. Whereas infants are assumed to represent only sensory objects and physical actions, young children would be able to represent relations between objects, which constitute a first level of abstraction, and older children can represent dimensions such as length, weight, areas, or volumes. Similar ideas were proposed by Halford (1993) who suggested that infants are only able to represent isolated elements, uni-dimensional concepts such as associating a mental image or a word to an object, whereas young children can represent bi-dimensional concepts such as relations (higher than, longer than), while older children can represent and understand tri-dimensional concepts that can be conceived as systems (e.g. the additive relations between the numbers 3, 6, and 9, or the inclusive relations that cows and pigs entertain with animals). A last level would allow adolescents to represent complex four-dimensional concepts such as proportions.

It is worth noting that the hypothesis, in both theories, of an integrative development by which structures at level $n-1$ are integrated within structures at level n means that these changes in representational contents could be accounted for by quantitative developmental changes in the number of elements that representations can integrate. For example, in Case's theory, representations of relations emerge from the elaborated coordination of sensorimotor representations in the same way as dimensional representations result from the elaborated coordination of representations of relations. In Halford's theory, we have seen that developmental changes in the complexity of the representations that can be constructed (and the concepts that can be understood) result from an increase in the number of independent dimensions that can be integrated. Thus, developmental changes in the content of working memory representations might be accounted for by changes in the amount of information that these representations can coordinate and integrate at different developmental levels.

However, this is not to say that any age-related change in representational contents could be accounted for by such quantitative evolution. Consider, for example, the developmental evolution hypothesized by Perner (1991) in the representations constructed by children. A first level characterizing the first year of life would allow infants to represent only real situations through primary representations that constitute simple mental models. Complex models involving multiple (typically two) representations would allow infants, during their second year of life, to represent contrasts between past and present. They would also allow children to engage in pretend play with one model representing reality (e.g. representing as a fruit the banana held in hand and moved closer to the ear) and the other representing what this object is intended to represent in the play (a telephone). Although this level results from a change that can be seen as quantitative (i.e. an increase in the number of representations of a same reality that can be simultaneously constructed), the next change, characterized by the construction of what Perner calls meta-representations, is qualitative in nature. These meta-representations, which open the door to a genuine theory of mind according to Perner (1991), would consist of a representation of representation (e.g. being able to form a representation of the representation that somebody else has in mind, as in the false-belief task of Maxi and the chocolate imagined by Wimmer and Perner, 1983). In the same way, the changes in children's representations of animals and human bodies with the acquisition of a vitalist naive theory of biology around age 6 or 7 (Carey et al., 2015) can probably not be accounted for by a mere quantitative development.

However, Carey et al. (2015) argued that the construction of a vitalist biology draws upon the development of executive functions, which are assumed by these authors as including working memory, Carey and colleagues pertaining to that tradition of developmental psychology that conceives working memory as an executive function along with inhibition and set shifting, as has been explained in Chapter 6. It has also been argued that executive functions development is also involved in the construction of a theory of mind by children (Benson, Sabbagh, Carlson, & Zelazo, 2013; Sabbagh, Xu, Carlson, Moses, & Lee, 2006). Although Carey et al. (2015) noted that it is debatable whether the development of executive functions is needed for the *expression* of already existing theories early in childhood or for their *construction* (or learning), it seems that there is a consensus on the role of the development of executive functions on conceptual development. As we have argued above, the executive functions that Baddeley (1996) regrouped within the central executive component of his multi-component model and that the TBRS model conceives as triggered by the action part of production rules are part of the working memory architecture from which they cannot be dissociated. Thus, the development of conceptual representations, which at first glance could have little to do with working memory development, could actually closely depend on it. Whether working memory development is in its executive aspects needed for any conceptual development, such as, for example, the subtle progression of awareness and the emergence of human consciousness during childhood (Rochat, 2015), remains an open question.

Quantitative changes

At a first glance, it seems rather trivial that there must be quantitative changes in working memory representations when considering the strong age-related increase in span during childhood and adolescence (Dempster, 1985; Gathercole et al., 2004). However, the question is more complex than expected and, as we will see, there is some uncertainty about the kind of quantitative change occurring during development: do the number of representations, or the amount of information they capture, or both factors evolve with age? This question was already present in the neo-Piagetian theories we presented in the first chapters of this book. Pascual-Leone (1970), for example, assumed that cognitive development was underpinned by an increase in the number of schemes that can be simultaneously activated, something that corresponds, at least for figurative schemes, to an increase in the number of representations that can be maintained. By contrast, the transition from one developmental stage to another in Cases' theory does not proceed from an increase in the number of representations that working memory can hold. The

162 Development in the TBRS model

culminating substage of each stage is characterized by the same number of four representations that can be simultaneously maintained. What is changing is the type of information these representations convey (i.e. sensorimotor, relational, dimensional, etc.). The same is true in Halford's (1993; Andrews & Halford, 2002, 2011) approach. The main change in development concerns more the complexity of the representations that children can construct than their number, these representations involving successively single elements, binary relations, ternary, and then quaternary relations.

This question of the number and complexity of representations is, in the working memory literature, and keeping with the seminal work of Miller (1956), formulated in terms of chunk span and chunk size (e.g. Gilchrist et al., 2009; Ottem, Arild, & Karlsen, 2007). In short-term and working memory development, does the number of chunks or their size evolve with age? In line with the hypothesis of an increase in complexity, but not in number, Ottem et al. (2007) showed that the strong association between age and word span in children aged from 3 to 16 disappeared when language performance was controlled for. They assumed that the age-related increase in word span was underlain by two factors: a capacity-limited holding mechanism, responsible for a limited chunk span that remains constant across a wide range of ages, and a crystallized factor reflecting chunking capacity, a by-product of language abilities. In other words, chunk size would evolve with age, but not chunk span.

In order to investigate a possible increase in chunk span with age, Cowan and colleagues have suggested using procedures that limit the possibility of chunking in such a way that each presented item is assumed to comprise a separate chunk, for example by presenting items at a sufficiently fast rate to prevent chunking or rehearsal, as in the running span, or by testing memory for unattended stimuli (see Chapter 5). These methods revealed that while adults exhibit a chunk span between 3 and 4, young children are limited to a span about 2.5 (Cowan et al., 2005, 2006; Cowan, Nugent, Elliott, Ponomarev, & Saults, 1999). This chunk span in Cowan's theory is assumed to reflect the number of chunks or objects that can be held simultaneously in the focus of attention, as we saw in Chapter 4. However, is this age-related increase in chunk span accompanied by an increase in chunk size? This does not seem to be the case according to Gilchrist et al. (2009), a study already described in Chapter 7. Recall that the authors asked children aged 7, 12, as well as adults, to memorize and recall either four short spoken sentences made of a single clause, four long sentences made of two clauses, eight short sentences made of a single clause, or four pseudo-sentences made of random words. Clause access, the number of clauses from which at least one content word was recalled, was taken as a measure of chunk span, whereas clause completion, the proportion of words recalled in the accessed clauses, was taken as a measure of chunk size. The results revealed a moderate but significant increase in the number of clauses accessed (approximately two and a half in 7-year-old children and slightly more than three in 12-year-olds and adults), reflecting a developmental increase in chunk span, but no age effect on chunk size, the clause completion remaining constant across age.

At this point, it might be concluded that what evolves with age is the size of the focus of attention, the number of chunks that working memory can hold, whereas chunk size remains constant across age. However, other theoretical developments are blurring this straightforward picture. The striking commonality between the maximum number of chunks that the focus of attention can hold in Cowan's working memory theory, and the maximum number of independent dimensions that mental models in Halford's developmental theory can integrate (four in both cases), did not go unnoticed. Halford et al. (2007) suggested that working memory and reasoning share related capacity limits based on the limited ability to bind elements together and maintain these bindings. However, there is a difference between the two limits. Indeed, the limit to four elements in Halford's relational complexity theory (Halford et al., 1998) concerns the number of independent variables that can be related to each other in a *single* representation (Halford et al., 2007, p. 239), whereas the limit of the focus of attention advocated by Cowan concerns the number of different representations (objects) simultaneously held in this focus. In order to circumvent this problem, Halford et al. (2007) suggested that the similarity in the number of chunks, on the one hand, and their size, on the other, might be more than a coincidence. The formation of new chunks (i.e. new mental models or new representations) could be related to attention and might be possible only if the elements to be integrated in the new representation are simultaneously present in the focus. Thus, the maximum complexity of a single representation or chunk would correspond to the largest number of items that can be simultaneously held in the focus of attention for their association, hence the same limit for working memory capacity and relational complexity. This later explanation is tempting, but difficult to reconcile with the results we previously mentioned. For example, if chunk size and chunk span are under the dependence of the size of the same focus of attention, it becomes difficult to understand how chunk span could increase with age while chunk size remains constant across age, as Gilchrist et al. (2009) observed.

Facing such a dilemma, the TBRS model could provide some insight about a differentiation between chunk span and chunk size, and their development. Recall that this model assumes that working memory representations are stored in an episodic buffer where they suffer temporal decay and interference, with one representation at a time being in the focus of attention and the object of treatments. Thus, in this approach, the size of the focus of attention constrains the complexity of working memory representations by limiting the number of elements they can bind. This maximum number, that would result from a structural constraint, seems to be four as Cowan (2001) assumes. It remains difficult to know whether this maximum number strongly evolves with age, as infant studies have reported for a long time that three or four seems to be the limit in the number of elements that infants can apprehend and individuate in a scene (Feigenson et al., 2002; Kahneman, Treisman, & Gibbs, 1992; Zosh & Feigenson, 2015), even if these representations strongly evolve with age in accuracy and distinctiveness and can be more and more adequately controlled and used (Cowan, 2017a). By contrast, the number of

164 Development in the TBRS model

representations that can be held in the episodic buffer would not be limited by the size of the focus of attention, but by functional constraints resulting from the interplay between the loss (due to temporal decay and interference) and the reconstruction of mental representations (Barrouillet & Camos, 2015). Note that the effect of these processes on working memory representations depend in turn on processing speed as we previously explained in the first section of this chapter. The maximum number of representations that can be maintained would evolve with age and underlie the age-related increase in short-term and working memory spans so often reported, even if it is not excluded that at least a part of this increase is attributable to chunking activities and the intervention of the phonological loop when verbal information is to be maintained. Although it is possible that the number of representations that can be held in the executive loop of the TBRS model usually approaches four in adults as suggested by Vergauwe, Camos, and Barrouillet (2014), the similarity between this limit and that of the size of the focus of attention might be purely coincidental.

Working memory as a learning device

Many studies have shown the importance of working memory in learning, for example by examining the correlation between working memory capacity and school achievement (e.g. Gathercole, Pickering, Knight, & Stegmann, 2004; Pickering, 2006). It is also known that working memory is involved in the acquisition of numerous skills and a variety of knowledge (Anderson, 1993; Anderson & Lebière, 1998; Cowan, 2014; Gathercole & Baddeley, 1993; Geary, 1990, 2013). In this last section, we will discuss how a cognitive architecture like the TBRS model makes it possible to understand learning, and especially how new procedures can be acquired during childhood and how new declarative knowledge can be stored in a long-term memory.

Cognitive development supported by the creation of new procedures

One major characteristic of cognitive development is the increasing efficiency to implement procedures, resulting in lower attentional demand of an activity with improved performance (i.e. lower error rates and shorter response times). As previously discussed, this improvement could result either from an age-related increased in attentional resource (Pascual-Leone, 1970) or a reduction in processing demand (Case, 1985), due to brain maturation and experience. However, besides this increased efficiency, a major change occurring throughout childhood results from the creation of new procedures, allowing children to widen the range of their skills. In order to describe the creation of the new procedures, and in line with the ACT-R model (Anderson, 1993; Anderson et al., 2004), the TBRS model assumes that all knowledge starts out in declarative form on which analogy process applies. Thus, procedures result from compiling this analogy process through the creation of variables that would replace specific tokens. According to Anderson (1993), this compiling process occurs in learning by discovery, but also in systematic tuition. The academic environment provides the most suitable examples from which analogies can be mapped and thus facilitates learning. More advanced procedures could also be constructed by coordinating already existing procedures.

The ADAPT model – A Developmental Asemantic Procedural Transcoding model (Barrouillet, Camos, Perruchet, & Seron, 2004) – is a spin-off of the TBRS model with which it shares the same cognitive architecture. While the TBRS model primarily accounts for the functioning of working memory and its interaction with attention and long-term memory, ADAPT is specifically dedicated to number transcoding from a verbal form (e.g. *two hundred and thirty-six*) to an Arabic number chain (*236*). Although transcoding is a very specific and rather limited activity, it is advantageous to study such a simple task because it helps to clarify the role of some learning mechanisms, without being overwhelmed by the inherent complexity of cognitive development. For example, within the ADAPT model, the analogy and concatenation processes are easily exemplified. For the analogy process, knowing that *five* is transcribed 5 and *twenty-five* is transcribed 25 allows transcribing *twenty-six* as 26 when knowing that *six* is 6. The concatenation of rules is made possible because all transcoding rules in the ADAPT model share the same condition-action structure, and more advanced procedures would be constructed by coordinating already existing procedures. For example, procedures dealing with the transcoding of *thousand* are simple rewritings of the procedures for *hundred* with the programming of a three-slot instead of a two-slot frame, these slots being subsequently filled with digits.[2] As they are described, these processes allowing the creation of the new procedures are, at first sight, rather independent from working memory capacity, and should mostly depend on reasoning and abstraction capacity as well as on experience. However, the examination of transcoding errors in children differing in working memory capacity offers a different perspective. Camos (2008) has shown that the errors produced by 7-year-old children with low working memory span came either from the inappropriate use of correct rules firing in the wrong situation or from the use of incomplete rules. For example, low-span children set a smaller number of slots as prescribed in rules dedicated to smaller numbers than the dictated ones (e.g. setting a two-slot frame for *thousand*). This results from the fact that the current information stored in working memory (precisely, in the episodic buffer) partially matches the conditions of activation of some previously acquired rules, and these rules fire in the wrong situation following a process of partial matching (Anderson, 1993). This shows that low-span children are late in the acquisition of transcoding rules compared with high-span children. More specifically, in Camos (2008), low-span children exhibited difficulties in the process of generating advanced rules for transcoding four-digit numbers, whereas the rules for the three-digit numbers were already learned. By contrast, high-span children have acquired all of the transcoding rules (even for the four-digit numbers), but their difficulties came from the load induced by recently acquired and demanding rules. Thus, Camos (2008) suggested that the coordination of procedural knowledge is less efficient in children with low working memory capacity.

166 Development in the TBRS model

The TBRS model accounts for the fact that working memory capacity plays a determinant role in the emergence of procedural rules. A higher working memory capacity would permit maintaining simultaneously active a greater amount of representations that would ease the implementation of the analogies on which the creation of new procedures is based. Indeed, analogy relies strongly on the simultaneous maintenance of different pieces of information to make the commonalities between the different elements appearing.

The acquisition of declarative knowledge

To explain the creation of new declarative knowledge, let us keep the same example of number transcoding. The first step in the learning process to achieve accurate transcoding is the acquisition of the mapping between verbal forms and digital forms (e.g. learning that '*six*' should be written '*6*') for the lexical primitives.[3] This would rely on an associative learning process that builds up the associations between each verbal form and its related digital form, both forms being provided by the environment (e.g, parents, siblings, educators). To create such associations, the two forms should be in temporal proximity or, in other words, they have to be maintained simultaneously in working memory to allow the establishment of a link between them. The efficiency of working memory at maintaining these forms would thus impact the acquisition of these associations. In a similar way, when children are transcoding the first numbers that are DU forms (i.e. Decade-Unit, like '*twenty-one*') using the transcoding rules we described in the previous section, they can also learn to associate verbal to digital forms. The main difference in this process compared to what happens for the primitives is that children themselves are producing the digital forms using the transcoding rules and the previously learned associations for the primitives. The impact of working memory efficiency would be even more determinant in such a learning process. Indeed, according to the TBRS model, the transcoding process relies on the executive loop because the transcoding rules in the procedural system construct the digital form, which is temporarily stored in the episodic buffer. As we just explained, the necessity to have the verbal and digital forms in close proximity to allow their association makes it particularly important that the transcoding should be done quite rapidly before the verbal form vanishes, or that the maintenance of the verbal form should last long enough. In both cases, this requires an efficient working memory.

Through a computational simulation of the ADAPT model, we have shown that a large part of the development in number transcoding is due to the increase in size of the pool of numbers for which the digital form is stored and directly retrieved from long-term memory without the need to transcode them through a procedural, algorithmic, process (Barrouillet et al., 2004). Conversely, we have also shown that mildly retarded adolescents presenting learning difficulties often transcode DU forms using algorithmic processes. This exemplifies how the ability to associate different forms of information is important for cognitive development. We already described in Chapter 3 the study by Barrouillet and Lépine (2005) who gathered evidence that this ability is dependent on working memory. Recall that when solving small single-digit additions (e.g. $4+2$), 9-year-old children with high working memory capacity relied on the direct retrieval of the answer from long-term memory to solve addition problems more often than did children with low working memory capacities. Following Geary (1990), Barrouillet and Lépine explained this phenomenon by assuming that children with high working memory capacity are faster in computing the answer of additions through algorithmic processes, this faster processing increasing the probability that the memory traces of the operands are still active in working memory when the answer is reached, thus facilitating their association in long-term memory. This hypothesis was buttressed by the fact that the difference between high- and low-working memory span children in the probability to solve additions by direct retrieval increased with the size of the operands. Large operands involve algorithmic processes that take longer and increase the probability of their forgetting before the answer is reached, thus compromising the operand-answer association on which direct retrieval is based. Low-span children who are slower in implementing algorithmic processes have less chances to form operand-answer associations as the size of the operands increases.

These studies in number transcoding and additions solving illustrate how working memory is important in the learning of declarative knowledge. We have also mentioned several times how important is the speed at which the algorithmic or procedural process is performed to permit such acquisition. A theoretical framework like the TBRS model is particularly adequate to understand the role played by temporal and speed constraints on cognitive development, as we explained in the first section of the present chapter, because the amount of information that can be maintained in an active state depends directly on the speed at which concurrent activities are performed.

Finally, a prerequisite to the acquisition of declarative knowledge is the construction of a working memory representation. In the TBRS model, these representations are stored in the episodic buffer and maintained in the short term through the attentional refreshing mechanism. This implies that maintenance that does not rely on attention, such as the exclusive maintenance of verbal information within the phonological loop, could not give rise to any long-term storage of information. Accordingly, it has been shown in adults that maintaining information in the short term by verbal rehearsal does not promote long-term memory traces, and increasing the duration of rehearsal has no impact on delayed recall task assessing long-term memory (Greene, 1987). On the contrary, maintenance through attentional refreshing creates memory traces in long-term memory that are strengthened by an increasing use of refreshing (Camos & Portrat, 2015; Loaiza & McCabe, 2012). Further exploration of this question remains to be performed in children.

Concluding comments

In this last chapter, we provided an overview of how the TBRS model, its architecture and functioning, can offer a theoretical framework for understanding some

168 Development in the TBRS model

of the developmental changes occurring during childhood. Besides the major working memory phenomena this model is aiming to explain (e.g. the central interference between processing and storage, the sources of forgetting, the domain-specificity of some storage system), the TBRS model can be an adequate tool to describe key processes of human cognitive functioning and hence shed light on their development. In this line, we have shown that the ADAPT model constitutes a first attempt to apply general principles of the TBRS architecture and functioning to the development of a particular cognitive activity, and supportive evidence has been gathered from both behavioural and computational approaches. Moreover, both the acquisition of long-term knowledge through associative processes and the creation of new procedural rules can be easily accounted for by the TBRS model. However, it should be acknowledged that these latter basic processes are not peculiar to this model, but shared with many others (e.g. Anderson, 1983; Cowan, 1988, 1995).

Nonetheless, we have also shown that more specific characteristics of the TBRS model, such as the importance of temporal constraints, can help to understand developmental findings. We previously described how the loss of information during protracted processing explains why children with low working memory capacites are delayed in the developmental shift from algorithmic resolution to direct retrieval of the answer in simple addition problem solving. It remains to examine whether the dynamics of a TBRS working memory can similarly shed light on other developmental changes.

Notes

1 It has been shown that the simplest retrievals from long-term memory, such as identifying a digit, depend on working memory capacity (Barrouillet, Lépine, & Camos, 2008).
2 In the ADAPT model, the transcoding of a number like *two hundred and thirty-six* involves an intermediary step corresponding to the construction of a number chain of the form 2 _ _ in which the two place holders that constitute a two-slot frame are created by a rule triggered by the word *hundred*. This frame is, in a further step, filled by the Arabic form of the number *thirty-six*. The rules triggered by *thousand* create a three-slot frame.
3 In the transcoding literature, lexical primitives are the units (0 to 9), the irregular teens that exist in some languages (e.g. in English, *eleven* and *twelve*; in French, from *onze* to *seize*), the decades, and the separators *hundred* and *thousand*.

EPILOGUE

Searching for working memory in cognitive development

At the end of this journey on working memory in development, does Brainerd's claim that 'cognitive development can, in fact, be reduced to memory development' hold after all, or should we imagine other ways to understand how infants' and children's minds develop? Almost one century ago, Piaget started investigating children development in order to understand what are the origins of human knowledge. He came to the conclusion that, from an initial state of syncretism and absolute confusion between the self and the world, children adapt to their environment by constructing themselves as a set of structured mental operations at the same time as they rationally organize their surrounding world as a set of definite and stable attributes. The advent of the information processing views and the renewal of nativist approaches (e.g. Gelman, 1978, 2015; Mehler & Bever, 1967) totally changed the way psychologists envision children's thinking and how this thinking develops. Early in life, infants would be able to identify relevant aspects, and to construct adequate representations, of their environment. The most natural way of theorizing development within this perspective was to imagine that changes mainly occur in the capacity to process information conceived as a 'given', and not as something to be constructed as in Piaget's theory. Representations would become more and more reliable and functional as they integrate more information, and thinking would become more powerful as more representations can be maintained and efficiently coordinated and manipulated. Through this book, we have tried to show that constructing and maintaining more complex and numerous representations on which a growing repertoire of processes operate more and more smoothly and efficiently with age require a working memory of increasing capacity. Even conceptual changes that at first glance seem to occur independently from working memory development have been assumed to be under the dependence of the development of executive functions (Carey, 2015) that cannot be dissociated from working memory. We have also reported studies demonstrating that learning relies

170 Development in the TBRS model

on working memory, which is also involved in the acquisition of a number of processes that have become autonomous through practice and are part of what is known as Type 1 or System 1 processes. Although we did not address questions related to individual differences and instruction, it has been for a long time established that working memory capacity is among the best predictors of fluid intelligence and academic achievement (Engle, Tuholski et al., 1999; Pickering, 2006). Of course, important aspects of development that are crucial for cognition such as sensorimotor development in infancy might be difficult to account for by some increase in working memory capacity. However, when considering working memory in its broadest, but exact, sense, that is a system devoted to the simultaneous maintenance and processing of information as suggested by Baddeley and Hitch (1974), in other words the centre of human cognition, Brainerd's claim is not far from being true.

It is worth noting that this claim is understandable only if working memory is conceived as something more than a short-term buffer, as is the case in animal and infant studies, but also in a host of contemporary studies in which adults are tested for their memory of visuospatial displays, most often through recognition paradigms, after sometimes extremely short empty delays of retention. Although it is of undeniable interest to know more about human visuospatial short-term memory, it seems to us that reducing working memory to its role of short-term buffer constitutes an impoverishment of the concept. In the same way, conceiving working memory as an executive function among others that would operate at the same level as specific mechanisms such as inhibition and shifting, as is often the case in certain traditions of developmental psychology, constitutes another impoverishment of a central concept for cognitive psychology. We have suggested that working memory might be seen as a representational medium, an operation centre, a learning device, and more generally the seat of thought and intelligence, but it could also be understood and described as a system for controlling attention as in Engle's approach, or the adaptive interface between the self, conceived as the sum of its declarative and procedural knowledge, and its environment. Conceived in this way, working memory is also the medium that allows us to connect our present with our past experience, to interpret, understand, and think about the former in the light of the latter, and to form representations of possible or desired futures that can constitute goals for our plans and actions. Such a working memory plays necessarily *a*, if not *the*, major role in cognitive development.

This developmental role is best exemplified by the extensively documented impact that working memory has on learning and academic achievement. Although we evoked the role of working memory in transcoding numbers and addition problem solving, we chose to not address these important aspects that are also related to individual difference through the study of learning disabilities and that would deserve a complete volume. In the same way, the pivotal role that working memory plays in development probably explains the recent and widespread enthusiasm that working memory training elicited in developmental psychologists. Can working memory capacity be improved through training in such a way that learning would be facilitated and development hastened? Due to its highly contro-versial nature (see Melby-Lervåg & Hulme, 2013; Melby-Lervåg, Redick, & Hulme, 2016; Redick et al., 2013, for recent contributions to the debate), we refrained ourselves to address this issue in this book, but we note that with the hope of obtaining positive transfers to fluid intelligence, attempts to increase working memory capacity through training testify for the central role attributed by psy-chologists to this structure in the cognitive architecture. Finally, another aspect that we did not systematically address in this book concerns the neural structures that underpin working memory components and functions. Although developmental studies are still rare on this area, advances in our knowledge of the development of brain structures associated with working memory might help us in understanding what are the factors of working memory development.

To summarize, we hope that this book has contributed to clarify the role and functions of working memory in cognitive development, explaining the roots of the emergence of this concept in developmental psychology, how working memory develops in infancy and childhood, and why we believe that it is of paramount importance for human cognition and its development. The best we can expect is that this book will stimulate future research on the relationships between the devel-oping working memory and cognitive development.

REFERENCES

Ahmed, A., & Ruffman, T. (1998). Why do infants make a not b errors in a search task, yet show memory for the location of hidden objects in a nonsearch task? *Developmental Psychology, 34*(3), 441–453.

Al-Namlah, A. S., Fernyhough, C., & Meins, E. (2006). Sociocultural influences on the development of verbal mediation: Private speech and phonological recoding in Saudi Arabian and British samples. *Developmental Psychology, 42*, 117–131.

Allik, J. P., & Siegel, A. W. (1976). The use of the cumulative rehearsal strategy: A developmental study. *Journal of Experimental Child Psychology, 21*, 316–327.

Alloway, T. P., & Alloway, R. G. (2010). Investigating the predictive roles of working memory and IQ in academic attainment. *Journal of Experimental Child Psychology, 106*, 20–29.

Alloway, T. P., Gathercole, S. E., & Pickering, S. J. (2006). Verbal and visuospatial short-term memory and working memory in children: Are they separable? *Child Development, 77*, 1698–1716.

Alloway, T. P., Gathercole, S. E., Willis, C., & Adams, A. M. (2004). A structural analysis of working memory and related cognitive skills in young children. *Journal of Experimental Child Psychology, 87*, 85–106.

Anderson, J. R. (1983). *The architecture of cognition*. Cambridge, MA: Harvard University Press.

Anderson, J. R. (1993). *Rules of the mind*. Hillsdale, NJ: Lawrence Erlbaum Associates.

Anderson, J. R. (2007). *How can the human mind occur in the physical universe?* New York, NY: Oxford University Press.

Anderson, J. R., & Lebière, C. (1998). *The atomic components of thought*. Mawhaw, NJ: Lawrence Erlbaum Associates.

Anderson, J. R., Bothell, D., Byrne, M. D., Douglass, S., Lebière, C., & Qin, Y. (2004). An integrated theory of mind. *Psychological Review, 111*, 1036–1060.

Anderson, P. (2002). Assessment and development of executive function during childhood. *Child Neuropsychology, 8*, 71–82.

Andrews, G., & Halford, G. S. (1998). Children's ability to make transitive inferences: The importance of premise integration and structural complexity. *Cognitive Development, 13*, 479–513.

Andrews, G., & Halford, G. S. (2002). A cognitive complexity metric applied to cognitive development. *Cognitive Psychology, 45*, 153–219.

Andrews, G., & Halford, G. S. (2011). Recent advances in relational complexity theory and its application to cognitive development. In P. Barrouillet & V. Gaillard (Eds.), *Cognitive development and working memory* (pp. 47–68). Hove, UK: Psychology Press.

Andrews, G., Birney, D., & Halford, G. S. (2006). Relational processing and working memory capacity in comprehension of relative clause sentences. *Memory and Cognition, 34*, 1325–1340.

Andrews, G., Halford, G. S., Bunch, K. M., Bowden, D., & Jones, T. (2003). Theory of Mind and Relational Complexity. *Child Development, 74*, 1476–1499.

Anderson, J. R., Reder, L. M., & Lebière, C. (1996). Working memory: Activation limitations on retrieval. *Cognitive Psychology, 30*, 221–256.

Anisfeld, M. (1991). Neonatal imitation. *Developmental Review, 11*(1), 60–97.

Arsalidou, M., Pascual-Leone, J. A., & Johnson, J. (2010). Misleading cues improve developmental assessment of working memory capacity: The colour matching tasks. *Cognitive Development, 25*, 262–277.

Ashcraft, M. H. (1992). Cognitive arithmetic: A review of data and theory. *Cognition, 44*, 75–106.

Ashcraft, M. H., & Battaglia, J. (1978). Cognitive arithmetic: Evidence for retrieval and decision processes in mental addition. *Journal of Experimental Psychology: Human Learning and Memory, 4*, 527–538.

Ashcraft, M. H., & Stazyk, E. H. (1981). Mental addition: A test of three verification models. *Memory and Cognition, 9*, 185–196.

Atkinson, R. C., & Shiffrin, R. M. (1968). Human memory: A proposed system and its control processes. In K. W. Spence & J. T. Spence (Eds.), *The Psychology of Learning and Motivation: Advances in Research and Theory* (Vol. 2, pp. 89–195). New York: Academic Press.

Baddeley, A. D. (1966). Short-term memory for word sequences as a function of acoustic, semantic and formal similarity. *Quarterly Journal of Experimental Psychology, 18*(4), 362–365.

Baddeley, A. D. (1986). *Working memory*. Oxford: Clarendon Press.

Baddeley, A. D. (1996). Exploring the central executive. *Quarterly Journal of Experimental Psychology, 49*, 5–28.

Baddeley, A. D. (1998). Recent developments in working memory. *Current Opinion in Neurobiology, 8*, 234–238.

Baddeley, A. D. (2000). The episodic buffer: A new component of working memory? *Trends in Cognitive Sciences, 4*, 417–423.

Baddeley, A. D. (2007). *Working memory, thought, and action*. Oxford: Oxford University Press.

Baddeley, A. D., & Hitch, G. J. (1974). Working memory. In G. A. Bower (Ed.), *Recent advances in learning and motivation* (Vol. 8, pp. 647–667). New York: Academic Press.

Baddeley, A. D., & Logie, R. H. (1999). Working memory: The multiple-component model. In A. Miyake & P. Shah (Eds.), *Models of working memory: Mechanisms of active maintenance and executive control* (pp. 28–61). Cambridge: Cambridge University Press.

Baddeley, A. D., Allen, R. J., & Hitch, G. J. (2010). Investigating the episodic buffer. *Psychologica Belgica, 50*, 223–243.

Baddeley, A. D., Allen, R. J., & Hitch, G. J. (2011). Binding in visual working memory: The role of the episodic buffer. *Neuropsychologia, 49*, 1393–1400.

Baddeley, A. D., Eysenck, M. W., & Anderson, M. C. (2015). *Memory*. Hove, UK: Psychology Press.

174 References

Baddeley, A. D., Gathercole, S. E., & Papagno, C. (1998). The phonological loop as a language learning device. *Psychological Review, 105*, 158–173.

Baddeley, A. D., Thomson, N., & Buchanan, M. (1975). Word length and the structure of short term memory. *Journal of Verbal Learning and Verbal Behavior, 14*, 575–589.

Baillargeon, R. (1986). Representing the existence and the location of hidden objects: Object permanence in 6- and 8-month-old infants. *Cognition, 23*, 21–41.

Baillargeon, R. (1987). Object permanence in 3½- and 4½-month-old infants. *Developmental Psychology, 23*, 655–664.

Baillargeon, R. (1995). A model of physical reasoning in infancy. In C. Rovee-Collier & L. P. Lipsitt (Eds.), *Advances in infancy research* (Vol. 9, pp. 305–371). Norwood, NJ: Ablex.

Baillargeon, R., & Graber, M. (1988). Evidence of location memory in 8-month-old infants in a non-search A-not-B task. *Developmental Psychology, 24*, 502–511.

Baillargeon, R., DeVos, J., & Graber, M. (1989). Location memory in 8-month-old infants in a non-search A-not-B task: Further evidence. *Cognitive Development, 4*, 345–367.

Bardikoff, N., & Sabbagh, M. (2017). The differentiation of executive functioning across development: Insights from developmental neuroscience. In N. Budwig, E. Turiel, & P. D. Zelazo (Eds.) *New perspectives on human development* (pp. 27–46). Cambridge, UK: Cambridge University Press.

Barkley, R. A. (1996). Attention-deficit/hyperactivity disorder. In E. J. Mash & R. A. Barkley (Eds.), *Child Psychopathology* (pp. 63–112). New York: Guilford Press.

Barkley, R. A. (2012). *Executive functions: What they are, how they work, and why they evolved.* New York: The Guildford Press.

Baroody, A. J., & Ginsburg, H. P. (1986). The relationship between initial meaningful and mechanical knowledge of arithmetic. In J. Hiebert (Ed.), *Conceptual and procedural knowledge: The case of mathematics* (pp. 75–112). Hillsdale, NJ: Lawrence Erlbaum Associates.

Barrouillet, P. (1996). Transitive inferences from set inclusion relations and working memory. *Journal of Experimental Psychology: Learning, Memory and Cognition, 22*, 1408–1422.

Barrouillet, P. (2011a). Dual-process theories and cognitive development: Advances and challenges. *Developmental Review, 31*, 151–179.

Barrouillet, P. (2011b). Dual-process theories of reasoning: The test of development. *Developmental Review, 31*, 78–85.

Barrouillet, P. (2015). Theories of development: From Piaget to today. *Developmental Review, 38*, 1–12.

Barrouillet, P., & Camos, V. (2001). Developmental increase in Working Memory Span: Resource sharing or temporal decay? *Journal of Memory and Language, 45*, 1–20.

Barrouillet, P., & Camos, V. (2007). The time-based resource sharing model of working memory. In N. Osaka, R. Logie, & M. D'Esposito (Eds.), *The cognitive neuroscience of working memory* (pp. 59–80). Oxford: Oxford University Press.

Barrouillet, P., & Camos, V. (2009). Interference: Unique source of forgetting in working memory? *Trends in Cognitive Sciences, 13*, 145–146.

Barrouillet, P., & Camos, V. (2010). Working memory and executive function: The TBRS approach. *Psychological Belgica, 50*, 353–382.

Barrouillet, P., & Camos, V. (2012). As time goes by: Temporal constraints in working memory. *Current Directions in Psychological Science, 21*, 413–419.

Barrouillet, P., & Camos, V. (2015). *Working memory: Loss and reconstruction.* Hove, UK: Psychology Press.

Barrouillet, P., & Camos, V. (2017). An European perspective on Bob Siegler's contribution. In P. Lemaire (Ed.), *Cognitive development from a strategy perspective: A festschrift for Robert Siegler* (pp. in press). Hove, UK: Psychology Press.

Barrouillet, P., & Gaillard, V. (2011). Introduction: From neo-Piagetian theories to working memory development studies. In P. Barrouillet & V. Gaillard (Eds.), *Cognitive development and working memory* (pp. 1–10). Hove, UK: Psychology Press.

Barrouillet, P., & Gauffroy, C. (2015). Probability in reasoning: A developmental test on conditionals. *Cognition, 137*, 22–39.

Barrouillet, P., & Lecas, J. F. (1998). How can mental models theory account for content effects in conditional reasoning? A developmental perspective. *Cognition, 67*, 209–253.

Barrouillet, P., & Lecas, J. F. (1999). Mental models in conditional reasoning and working memory. *Thinking and Reasoning, 5*, 289–302.

Barrouillet, P., & Lecas, J. F. (2002). Content and context effects in children's and adults' conditional reasoning. *Quarterly Journal of Experimental Psychology, 55*, 839–854.

Barrouillet, P., & Lépine, R. (2005). Working memory and children's use of retrieval to solve addition problems. *Journal of Experimental Child Psychology, 91*, 183–204.

Barrouillet, P., & Poirier, L. (1997). Comparing and transforming: An application of Piaget's morphisms theory to the development of class inclusion and arithmetic problem solving. *Human Development, 40*, 216–234.

Barrouillet, P., Bernardin, S., & Camos, V. (2004). Time constraints and resource sharing in adults' working memory spans. *Journal of Experimental Psychology: General, 133*, 83–100.

Barrouillet, P., Bernardin, S., Portrat, S., Vergauwe, E., & Camos, V. (2007). Time and cognitive load in working memory. *Journal of Experimental Psychology: Learning, Memory and Cognition, 33(3)*, 570–585.

Barrouillet, P., Camos, V., Perruchet, P., & Seron, X. (2004). A Developmental Asemantic Procedural Transcoding (ADAPT) model: From verbal to Arabic numerals. *Psychological Review, 111*, 368–394.

Barrouillet, P., Dagry, I., & Gauffroy, C. (2017). On the sources of working memory development: Manipulating temporal factors (almost) abolishes developmental differences. Submitted manuscript.

Barrouillet, P. Gavens, N., Vergauwe, E., Gaillard, V., & Camos, V. (2009). Working memory span development: A Time-Based Resource-Sharing model account. *Developmental Psychology, 45*, 477–490.

Barrouillet, P., Fayol, M., & Lathulière, E. (1997). Selecting between competitors in multiplication tasks: An explanation of the errors produced by adolescents with learning difficulties. *International Journal of Behavioral Development, 21*, 253–275.

Barrouillet, P., Gauffroy, C., & Lecas, J. F. (2008). Postscript: A good psychological theory of reasoning must predict behavior and explain the data. *Psychological Review, 115*, 771–772.

Barrouillet, P., Grosset, N., & Lecas, J. F. (2000). Conditional reasoning by mental models: Chronometric and developmental evidence. *Cognition, 75*, 237–266.

Barrouillet, P., Lépine, R., & Camos, V. (2008). Is the influence of working memory capacity on high-level cognition mediated by complexity or resource-dependent elementary processes? *Psychonomic Bulletin and Review, 15*, 528–534.

Barrouillet, P., Markovits, H, & Quinn, S. (2001). Developmental and content effects in reasoning with causal conditionals. *Journal of Experimental Child Psychology, 81*, 235–248.

Barrouillet, P., Portrat, S., & Camos, V. (2011). On the law relating processing to storage in working memory. *Psychological Review, 118(2)*, 175–192.

Barsalou, L. W. (1983). Ad hoc categories. *Memory and Cognition, 11*, 211–227.

Bauer, P. J. (2002). Long-term recall memory: Behavioral and neuro-developmental changes in the first 2 years of life. *Current Directions in Psychological Science, 11*, 137–141.

Bayliss, D. M., Jarrold, C., Baddeley, A. D., & Gunn, D. M. (2005a). The relationship between short-term memory and working memory: Complex span made simple? *Memory, 13*, 414–421.

Bayliss, D. M., Jarrold, C., Baddeley, A. D., Gunn, D. M., & Leigh, E. (2005b). Mapping the developmental constraints on working memory span performance. *Developmental Psychology, 41*, 579–597.

Bayliss, D. M., Jarrold, C., Gunn, M. D., & Baddeley, A. D. (2003). The complexities of complex span: Explaining individual differences in working memory in children and adults. *Journal of Experimental Psychology: General, 32*, 71–92.

Bays, P. M., & Husain, M. (2008). Dynamic shifts of limited working memory resources in human vision. *Science, 321*(5890), 851–854.

Beaman, C. P., Neath, I., & Surprenant, A. M. (2008). Modeling distributions of immediate memory effects: No strategies needed? *Journal of Experimental Psychology: Learning, Memory, and Cognition, 34*, 219–229.

Bebko, J. M., McMorris, C. A., Metcalfe, A., Ricciuti, C., & Goldstein, G. (2014). Language proficiency and metacognition as predictors of spontaneous rehearsal in children. *Canadian Journal of Experimental Psychology, 68*(1), 46–58.

Bell, M., & Fox, N. A. (1992). The relation between frontal brain electrical activity and cognitive development during infancy. *Child Development, 63*, 1142–1163.

Bell, S. M. (1970). The development of the concept of the object as related to infant-mother attachment. *Child Development, 41*, 291–311.

Belmont, J. M., & Butterfield, E. C. (1969). The relation of short-term memory to development and intelligence. In L. P. Lippsitt & H. W. Reese (Eds.), *Advances in child development and behavior* (Vol. 4). New York: Academic Press.

Belmont, J. M., & Butterfield, E. C. (1971). What the development of short-term memory is. *Human Development, 14*, 236–248.

Benson, J. E., Sabbagh, M. A., Carlson, S. M., & Zelazo, P. D. (2013). Individual differences in executive functioning predict preschoolers' improvement from theory-of-mind training. *Developmental Psychology, 49*(9), 1615–1627.

Bertrand, R., & Camos, V. (2015). The role of attention in preschoolers' working memory. *Cognitive Development, 33*, 14–27.

Best, J. R., Miller, P. H., & Jones, L. L. (2009). Executive functions after age 5: Changes and correlates. *Developmental Review, 29*, 180–200.

Birney, D. P., Halford, G. S., & Andrews, G. (2006). Measuring the influence of complexity on relational reasoning: The development of the Latin Square Task. *Educational and Psychological Measurement, 66*, 146–171.

Bjorklund, D. F., & Harnishfeger, K. K. (1990). The resources construct in cognitive development: Diverse sources of evidence and a theory of inefficient inhibition. *Developmental Review, 10*, 48–71.

Bohlmann, N. L., & Fenson, L. (2005). The effects of feedback on preservative errors in preschool aged children. *Journal of Cognition and Development, 6*, 119–131.

Bowey, J. A. (1996). Phonological sensitivity as a proximal contributor to phonological receding skills in children's reading. *Australian Journal of Psychology, 48*, 113–118.

Braine, M. D. S. (1990). The natural approach to reasoning. In W. F. Overton (Ed.), *Reasoning, Necessity, and Logic: Developmental Perspectives* (pp. 135–158). Hillsdale, NJ: Lawrence Erlbaum.

Braine, M. D. S., & O'Brien, D. P. (1991). A theory of If: A lexical entry, reasoning program, and pragmatic principles. *Psychological Review, 98*, 182–203.

Brainerd, C. J. (1978). The stage question in cognitive-developmental theory. *Behavioral and Brain Sciences, 2*, 173–213.

Brainerd, C. J. (1981). Working memory and the developmental analysis of probability judgment. *Psychological Review, 88*, 463–502.

Brainerd, C. J. (1983). Working memory systems and cognitive development. In C. J. Brainerd (Ed.), *Recent advances in cognitive-developmental theory: Progress in cognitive development research* (pp. 167–236). New York: Springer-Verlag.

Brainerd, C. J., & Kingma, J. (1984). Do children have to remember to reason? A fuzzy-trace theory of transitivity development. *Developmental Review, 4,* 311–377.

Brainerd, C. J., & Kingma, J. (1985). On the independence of short-term memory and working memory in cognitive development. *Cognitive Psychology, 24,* 324–334.

Brainerd, C. J., & Reyna, V. F. (1990). Gist is the grist: Fuzzy-trace theory and the new intuitionism. *Developmental Review, 10,* 3–47.

Brainerd, C. J., & Reyna, V. F. (1992). Explaining 'memory free' reasoning. *Psychological Science, 3,* 332–339.

Brainerd, C. J., & Reyna, V. F. (1993). Memory independence and memory interference in cognitive development. *Psychological Review, 100,* 42–67.

Brainerd, C. J., & Reyna, V. F. (2004). Fuzzy-trace theory and memory development. *Developmental Review, 24,* 396–439.

Brainerd, C. J., & Reyna, V. F. (2015). Fuzzy-trace theory and lifespan cognitive development. *Developmental Review, 38,* 89–121.

Brandimonte, M. A., Hitch, G. J., & Bishop, D. V. M. (1992). Verbal recoding of visual-stimuli impairs mental image transformations. *Memory and Cognition, 20*(4), 449–455.

Broadbent, D. E. (1958). *Perception and communication.* London: Pergamon Press.

Brockmole, J. R., & Logie, R. H. (2013). Age-related change in visual working memory: A study of 55,753 participants aged 8–75. *Frontiers in Psychology, 4,* 12.

Brown, J. (1958). Some tests of the decay theory of immediate memory. *Quarterly Journal of Experimental Psychology, 10,* 12–21.

Brown, R. (1977). An examination of visual and verbal coding processes in preschool children. *Child Development, 48,* 38–45.

Bryant, P. E., & Trabasso, T. (1971). Transitive inferences and memory in young children. *Nature, 232,* 456–458.

Bull, G., Thompson, A., Searson, M., Garofalo, J., Park, J., Young, C., & Lee, J. (2008). Connecting informal and formal learning: Experiences in the age of participatory media. *Contemporary Issues in Technology and Teacher Education, 8,* 100–107.

Bull, R., & Scerif, G. (2001). Executive functioning as a predictor of children's mathematics ability: Inhibition, switching, and working memory. *Developmental Neuropsychology, 19,* 273–293.

Bunch, K. M., Andrews, G., & Halford, G. S. (2007). Complexity effects on the children's gambling task. *Cognitive Development, 22,* 376–383.

Bunge, S. A., & Zelazo, P. D. (2006). A brain-based account of the development of rule use in childhood. *Current Directions in Psychological Science, 15,* 118–121.

Burnett Heyes, S., Zokaei, N., & Husain, M. (2016). Longitudinal development of visual working memory precision in childhood and early adolescence. *Cognitive Development, 39,* 36–44.

Burnett Heyes, S., Zokaei, N., van der Staaij, I., Bays, P. M., & Husain, M. (2012). Development of visual working memory precision in childhood. *Developmental Science, 15*(4), 528–539.

Cain, K., Oakhill, J., & Bryant, P. (2004). Children's reading comprehension ability: Concurrent prediction by working memory, verbal ability and component skills. *Journal of Educational Psychology, 96,* 31–42.

Camos, V. (2008). Low working memory capacity impedes both efficiency and learning of number transcoding in children. *Journal of Experimental Child Psychology, 99,* 37–57.

Camos, V. (2015). Storing verbal information in working memory. *Current Directions in Psychological Science, 24,* 440–445.

178 References

Camos, V. (2017). Domain-specific vs. domain-general maintenance in working memory: Reconciliation within the time-based resource sharing model. In B. Ross (Ed.), *The psychology of learning and motivation* (Vol. 67, pp. 135–171). Cambridge, MA: Academic Press.

Camos, V., & Barrouillet, P. (2011a). Factors of working memory development: The Time-Based Resource-Sharing approach. In P. Barrouillet & V. Gaillard (Eds.), *Cognitive development and working memory: From neo-Piagetian to cognitive approaches* (pp. 151–176). Hove, UK: Psychology Press.

Camos, V., & Barrouillet, P. (2011b). Developmental change in working memory strategies: From passive maintenance to active refreshing. *Developmental Psychology, 47*, 898–904.

Camos, V., & Bertrand, R. (2017a). Temporal decay in young children's working memory. Unpublished manuscript.

Camos, V., & Bertrand, R. (2017b). The rate of forgetting over time in working memory during early childhood. Unpublished manuscript.

Camos, V., Lagner, P., & Barrouillet, P. (2009). Two maintenance mechanisms of verbal information in working memory. *Journal of Memory and Language, 61*, 457–469.

Camos, V., Mora, G., & Barrouillet, P. (2013). Phonological similarity effect in complex span task. *Quarterly Journal of Experimental Psychology, 66*, 1927–1950.

Camos, V., Mora, G., & Oberauer, K. (2011). Adaptive choice between articulatory rehearsal and attentional refreshing in verbal working memory. *Memory and Cognition, 39*, 231–244.

Camos, V., & Portrat, S. (2015). The impact of cognitive load on delayed recall. *Psychonomic Bulletin and Review, 22*, 1029–1034.

Campos, I. S., Almeida, L. S., Ferreira, A. I., & Martinez, L. F. (2013). Working memory as separable subsystems: A study with Portuguese primary school children. *Spanish Journal of Psychology, 16*, 1–10.

Caplan, D., & Waters, G. S. (1999). Verbal working memory and sentence comprehension. *Brain and Behavioral Sciences, 22*, 77–126.

Carey, S. (1985). *Conceptual Change in Childhood*. Cambridge, MA: Bradford Books/MIT Press.

Carey, S., & Bartlett, E. J. (1978). Acquiring a single new word. *Papers and Reports on Child Language Development, 15*, 17–29.

Carey, S., Zaitchik, D., & Bascandziev, I. (2015). Theories of development: In dialog with Jean Piaget. *Developmental Review, 38*, 36–54.

Carlson, S. M. (2005). Developmentally sensitive measures of executive function in preschool children. *Developmental Neuropsychology, 28*, 595–616.

Carlson, S. M., & Moses, L. J. (2001). Individual differences in inhibitory control and children's theory of mind. *Child Development, 72*, 1032–1053.

Carlson, S. M., Moses, L. J., & Hix, H. R. (1998). The role of inhibitory processes in young children's difficulties with deception and false belief. *Child Development, 69*, 672–691.

Case, R. (1972). Validation of a neo-Piagetian capacity construct. *Journal of Experimental Child Psychology, 14*, 287–302.

Case, R. (1974). Mental strategies, mental capacity, and instruction: A neo-Piagetian investigation. *Journal of Experimental Child Psychology, 18*, 382–397.

Case, R. (1978). Intellectual development from birth to adulthood: A neo-Piagetian investigation. In R. S. Siegler (Ed.), *Children thinking: What develops?* (pp. 109–150). Hillsdale, NJ: Lawrence Erlbaum Associates.

Case, R. (1985). *Intellectual development: Birth to adulthood*. New York: Academic Press.

Case, R. (1987). The structure and process of intellectual development. *International Journal of Psychology, 22*, 571–607.

Case, R. (1992). *The mind's staircase: Exploring the conceptual underpinnings of children's thought and knowledge*. Hillsdale, NJ: Lawrence Erlbaum Associates.

Case, R., & Globerson, T. (1974). Field independence and central computing space. *Child Development, 45*, 772–778.

Case, R., & Okamoto, Y. (1996). The role of central conceptual structures in the development of children's thought. *Monographs of the Society for Research in Child Development, 61*(1/2), 1–295.

Castle, K., & Needham, J. (2007). First graders' understanding of measurement. *Early Childhood Education Journal, 35*, 215–221.

Case, R., Kurland, D. M., & Goldberg, J. (1982). Operational efficiency and the growth of short-term memory span. *Journal of Experimental Child Psychology, 33*, 386–404.

Cattell, R. B. (1950). *Handbook for the individual of group Culture Fair Intelligence Test. Scale I*. Champaign, IL: IPAT.

Cepeda, N. J., & Munakata, Y. (2007). Why do children perseverate when they seem to know better: Graded working memory, or directed inhibition? *Psychonomic Bulletin and Review, 14*, 1058–1065.

Chapman, M. (1987). Piaget, attentional capacity and the functional implications of formal structure. In H. W. Reese (Ed.), *Advances in child development and behavior* (Vol. 20, pp. 289–334). Orlando, FL: Academic Press.

Chatham, C. H., Frank, M. J., & Munakata, Y. (2009). Pupillometric and behavioral markers of a developmental shift in the temporal dynamics of cognitive control. *Proceedings of the National Academy of Sciences, 106*, 5529–5533.

Chatham, C. H., Yerys, B. E., & Munakata, Y. (2012). Why won't you do what I want? The informative failures of children and models. *Cognitive Development, 27*(4), 349–366.

Chen, Z., & Cowan, N. (2005). Chunk limits and length limits in immediate recall: A reconciliation. *Journal of Experimental Psychology: Learning, Memory, and Cognition, 31*, 1235–1249.

Chen, Z., & Cowan, N. (2009). How verbal memory loads consume attention. *Memory and Cognition, 37*, 829–836.

Chevalier, N., & Blaye, A. (2008). Cognitive flexibility in preschoolers: The role of representation activation and maintenance. *Developmental Science, 11*, 339–353.

Chevalier, N., & Blaye, A. (2009). Setting goals to switch between tasks: Effect of cue transparency on children's cognitive flexibility. *Developmental Psychology, 45*, 782–797.

Chevalier, A., & Chevalier, N. (2009). Influence of proficiency level and constraints on viewpoint switching: A study in web design. *Applied Cognitive Psychology, 23*, 126–137.

Chevalier, N., Blaye, A., & Maintenant, C. (2014). La représentation du but dans le contrôle exécutif chez l'enfant. *Psychologie Française, 59*, 5–20.

Chevalier, N., Dauvier, B., & Blaye, A. (2009). Preschoolers' use of feedback for flexible behavior: Insights from a computational model. *Journal of Experimental Child Psychology, 103*, 251–267.

Chi, M. T. H. (1976). Short-term memory limitations in children: Capacity or processing deficits? *Memory and Cognition, 4*, 559–572.

Chi, M. T. H. (1978). Knowledge structures and memory development. In R. S. Siegler (Ed.), *Children's thinking: What develops?* (pp. 73–96). Hillsdale, NJ: Lawrence Erlbaum Associates.

Chi, M. T. H., & Klahr, D. (1975). Span and rate of apprehension in children and adults. *Journal of Experimental Child Psychology, 19*, 434–439.

Chuah, Y. M. L., & Maybery, M. T. (1999). Verbal and spatial short-term memory: Common sources of developmental changes. *Journal of Experimental Child Psychology, 73*, 7–44.

180 References

Chuderski, A. (2013). When are fluid intelligence and working memory isomorphic and when are they not? *Intelligence, 41*, 244–262.

Clark, E. V. (1997). Conceptual perspective and lexical choice in acquisition. *Cognition, 64*, 1–37.

Clarkson-Smith, L., & Hartley, A. A. (1990). The game of bridge as an exercise in working memory and reasoning. *Journal of Gerontology, 45*, 233–238.

Cohen, R. L., & Heath, M. (1990). The development of serial short-term memory and the articulatory loop hypothesis. *Intelligence, 14*(2), 151–171.

Conrad, R. (1971). The chronology of the development of inner speech. *Developmental Psychology, 5*, 398–405.

Conrad, R., & Hull, A. J. (1964). Information, acoustic confusion and memory span. *British Journal of Psychology, 55*(4), 429–432.

Conti-Ramsden, G. (2003). *Processing and linguistic markers in young children with specific language impairment (SLI). Journal of Speech, Language and Hearing Research, 46*, 1029–1037.

Conway, R. A., Cowan, N., & Bunting, M. F. (2001). The cocktail party phenomenon revisited: The importance of working memory capacity. *Psychonomic Bulletin and Review, 8*, 331–335.

Corbin, L., Moissenet, A., & Camos, V. (2012). Le fonctionnement de la mémoire de travail chez des enfants présentants des difficultés scolaires. *Développements, 11*, 5–12.

Corsi, P. M. (1972). *Human memory and the medial temporal region of the brain.* Unpublished doctoral dissertation. McGill University, Montreal.

Cottini, M., Pieroni, L., Spataro, P., Devescovi, A., Longobardi, E., & Rossi-Arnaud, C. (2015). Feature binding and the processing of global–local shapes in bilingual and monolingual children. *Memory and Cognition, 43*, 441–452.

Couvillon, P. A., & Bitterman, M. E. (1986). A conventional conditioning analysis of 'transitive inference' in pigeons. *Journal of Experimental Psychology: Animal Behavior Processes, 18*, 308–310.

Cowan, N. (1988). Evolving conceptions of memory storage, selective attention, and their natural constraints within the human information processing system. *Psychological Bulletin, 104*, 163–191.

Cowan, N. (1992). Verbal memory span and the timing of spoken recall. *Journal of Memory and Language, 31*, 668–684.

Cowan, N. (1995). *Attention and memory: An integrated framework.* New York: Oxford University Press.

Cowan, N. (1997). The development of working memory. In N. Cowan (Ed.), *The development of memory in childhood* (pp. 163–199). Hove, UK: Psychology Press.

Cowan, N. (1999). An embedded-process model of working memory. In A. Miyake & P. Shah (Eds.), *Models of working memory: Mechanisms of active maintenance and executive control* (pp. 62–101). Cambridge: Cambridge University Press.

Cowan, N. (2001). The magical number 4 in short-term memory: A reconsideration of mental storage capacity. *Behavioral and Brain Sciences, 24*, 87–185.

Cowan, N. (2005). *Working memory capacity.* Hove, UK: Psychology Press.

Cowan, N. (2007). What can infants tell us about working memory development? In L. M. Oakes & P. J. Bauer (Eds.), *Short- and long-term memory in infancy and early childhood: Taking the first steps toward remembering* (pp. 126–150). New York: Oxford University Press.

Cowan, N. (2014). Working memory underpins cognitive development, learning, and education. *Educational Psychology Review, 26*(2), 197–223.

Cowan, N. (2015). Sensational memorability: Working memory for things we see, hear, feel, or somehow sense. In C. LeFebvre, P. Jolicoeur, & J. Martinez-Trujillo (Eds.), *Mechanisms of sensory working memory* (pp. 5–22). San Diego, CA: Elsevier Science Publishing Co.

Cowan, N. (2016). Working memory maturation: Can we get at the essence of cognitive growth? *Perspectives on Psychological Science, 11*, 239–264.

Cowan, N. (2017a). Mental objects in working memory: Development of basic capacity or of cognitive completion? *Advances in Child Development and Behavior, 52*, 81–104.

Cowan, N. (2017b). The many faces of working memory and short-term storage. *Psychonomic Bulletin and Review, 24*, 1158–1170.

Cowan, N., & Alloway, T. (2009). Development of working memory in childhood. In M. L. Courage & N. Cowan (eds.), *The development of memory in infancy and childhood* (pp. 303–342). Hove: Psychology Press.

Cowan, N., AuBuchon, A. M., Gilchrist, A. L., Ricker, T. J., & Saults, J. S. (2011). Age differences in visual working memory capacity: Not based on encoding limitations. *Developmental Science, 14*, 1066–1074.

Cowan, N., Blume, C. L., & Saults, J. S. (2013). Attention to attributes and objects in working memory. *Journal of Experimental Psychology: Learning, Memory, and Cognition, 39*, 731–747.

Cowan, N., Day, L., Saults, J. S., Keller, T. A., Johnson, T., & Flores, L. (1992). The role of verbal output time in the effects of word length on immediate memory. *Journal of Memory and Language, 31*, 1–17.

Cowan, N., Elliott, E. M., Saults, J. S., Morey, C. C., Mattox, S., Hismjatullina, A., et al. (2005). On the capacity of attention: Its estimation and its role in working memory and cognitive aptitudes. *Cognitive Psychology, 51*, 42–100.

Cowan, N., Elliott, E. M., Saults, J. S., Nugent, L. D., Bomb, P., & Hismjatullina, A. (2006). Rethinking speed theories of cognitive development: Increasing the rate of recall without affecting accuracy. *Psychological Science, 17*(1), 67–73.

Cowan, N., Fristoe, N. M., Elliott, E. M., Brunner, R. P., & Saults, J. S. (2006). Scope of attention, control of attention, and intelligence in children and adults. *Memory and Cognition, 34*, 1754–1768.

Cowan, N., Keller, T., Hulme, C., Roodenrys, S., McDougall, S., & Rack, J. (1994). Verbal memory span in children: Speech timing clues to the mechanisms underlying age and word length effects. *Journal of Memory and Language, 33*, 234–250.

Cowan, N., Morey, C. C., AuBuchon, A. M., Zwilling, C. E., & Gilchrist, A. L. (2010). Seven-year-olds allocate attention like adults unless working memory is overloaded. *Developmental Science, 13*(1), 120–133.

Cowan, N., Naveh-Benjamin, M., Kilb, A., & Saults, J. S. (2006). Life-span development of visual working memory: When is feature binding important? *Developmental Psychology, 42*, 1089–1102.

Cowan, N., Nugent, L. D., Elliott, E. M., Ponomarev, I., & Saults, J. S. (2000). The role of attention in the development of short-term memory: Age differences in the verbal span of apprehension. *Child Development, 70*(5), 1082–1097.

Cowan, N., Nugent, L. D., Elliott, E. M., & Saults, J. S. (2000). Persistence of memory for ignored lists of digits: Areas of developmental constancy and change. *Journal of Experimental Child Psychology, 76*, 151–172.

Cowan, N., Ricker, T. J., Clark, K. M., Hinrichs, G. A., & Glass, B. A. (2015). Knowledge cannot explain the developmental growth of working memory capacity. *Developmental Science, 18*, 132–145.

Cowan, N., Saults, J. S., & Morey, C. C. (2006). Development of working memory for verbal-spatial associations. *Journal of Memory and Language, 55*, 274–289.

Cowan, N., Saults, J. S., Winterowd, C., & Sherk, M. (1991). Enhancement of 4-year-old children's memory span for phonologically similar and dissimilar word lists. *Journal of Experimental Child Psychology, 51*, 30–52.

182 References

Cowan, N., Towse, J. N., Hamilton, Z., Saults, J. S., Elliott, E. M., Lacey, J. F., Moreno, M. V., & Hitch, G. J. (2003). Children's working-memory processes: A response-timing analysis. *Journal of Experimental Psychology: General, 132*, 113–132.

Cowan, N., Wood, N. L., Wood, P. K., Keller, T. A., Nugent, L. D., & Keller, C. V. (1998). Two separate verbal processing rates contributing to short-term memory span. *Journal of Experimental Psychology: General, 127*, 141–160.

Cragg, L., & Nation, K. (2007). Self-ordered pointing as a test of working memory in typically developing children. *Memory, 15*, 526–535.

Crowder, R. G. (1993). Short-term memory: Where do we stand? *Memory & Cognition, 21*, 142–145.

Cunningham, W. A., & Zelazo, P. D. (2007). Attitudes and evaluations: A social cognitive neuroscience perspective. *Trends in Cognitive Sciences, 11*, 97–104.

Daisley, J. N., Mascalzoni, E., Rosa-Salva, O., Rugani, R., & Regolin, L. (2009). Lateralization of social cognition in the domestic chicken (*Gallus gallus*). *Philosophical Transactions of the Royal Society B, 364*, 965–981.

Daneman, M., & Carpenter, P. A. (1980). Individual differences in comprehending and producing words in context. *Journal of Memory and Language, 19*, 450–466.

Daneman, M., & Green, I. (1986). Individual differences in comprehending and producing words in context. *Journal of Memory and Language, 25*, 1–18.

Daneman, M., & Merikle, P. M. (1996). Working memory and language comprehension: A meta-analysis. *Psychonomic Bulletin and Review, 3*, 422–433.

Darki, F., & Klingberg, T. (2015). The role of fronto-parietal and fronto-striatal networks in the development of working memory: A longitudinal study. *Cerebral Cortex, 25*, 1587–1595.

Darling, S., & Havelka, J. (2010). Visuospatial bootstrapping: Evidence for binding of verbal and spatial information in working memory. *Quarterly Journal of Experimental Psychology, 63*, 239–245.

Darling, S., Allen, R. J., Havelka, J., Campbell, A., & Rattray, E. (2012). Visuospatial bootstrapping: Long-term memory representations are necessary for implicit binding of verbal and visuospatial working memory. *Psychonomic Bulletin and Review, 19*, 258–263.

Darling, S., Parker, M-J., Goodall, K. E., Havelka, J., & Allen, R. J. (2014). Visuospatial bootstrapping: Implicit binding of verbal working memory to visuospatial representations in children and adults. *Journal of Experimental Child Psychology, 119*, 112–119.

Davidson, M. C., Amso, D., Cruess Anderson, L., & Diamond, A. (2006). Development of cognitive control and executive functions from 4 to 13 years: Evidence from manipulations of memory, inhibition, and task switching. *Neuropsychologia, 44*, 2037–2078.

de Boysson-Bardies, B., & O'Regan, K. (1973). What children do in spite of adults' hypotheses. *Nature, 246*, 531–534.

de Neys, W., & Vanderputte, K. (2011). When less is not always more: Stereotype knowledge and reasoning development. *Developmental Psychology, 47*, 431–441.

de Renzi, E., & Nichelli, P. (1975). Verbal and nonverbal memory impairment following hemispheric damage. *Cortex, 11*, 341–354.

de Saint Victor, C., Smith, P. H., & Loboschefski, T. (1997). Ten-month-old infants' retrieval of familiar information from short-term memory. *Infant Behavior and Development, 20*, 111–122.

Deak, G. O. (2003). The development of cognitive flexibility and language abilities. In R. Kail (Ed.), *Advances in child development and behavior* (Vol. 31, pp. 271–327). San Diego, CA: Academic Press.

Della Sala, S., Gray, C., Baddeley, A., Allamano, N., & Wilson, L. (1999). Pattern span: A tool for unwelding visuo-spatial memory. *Neuropsychologia, 37*, 1189–1199.

Demetriou, A., & Mouyi, A. (2011). Processing efficiency, representational capacity, and reasoning: Modeling their dynamic interactions. In P. Barrouillet & V. Gaillard (Eds.), *Cognitive development and working memory* (pp. 69–104). Hove, UK: Psychology Press.

Demetriou, A., & Raftopoulos, A. (1999). Modeling the developing mind: From structure to change. *Developmental Review, 19*, 319–368.

Demetriou, A., Christou, C., Spanoudis, G., & Platsidou, M. (2002). *The development of mental processing: Efficiency, working memory, and thinking.* Monographs of the Society for Research in Child Development, 67. Wiley.

Demetriou, A., Efklides, A., Papadaki, M., Papantoniou, G., & Economou, A. (1993). Structure and development of causal-experimental thought: From early adolescence to youth. *Developmental Psychology, 29*, 480–497.

Demetriou, A., Efklides, A., and Platsidou, M. (1993). *The architecture and dynamics of developing mind: Experiential structuralism as a frame for unifying cognitive developmental theories.* Monographs of the Society for Research in Child Development, 58. Wiley.

Dempster, F. N. (1981). Memory span: Sources of individual and developmental differences. *Psychological Bulletin, 89*(1), 63–100.

Dempster, F. N. (1985). Short-term memory development in childhood and adolescence. In C. J. Brainerd and M. Pressley (Eds.), *Basic processes in memory development* (pp. 209–248). New York: Springer-Verlag.

Dempster, F. N. (1992). The rise and fall of the inhibitory mechanism: Toward a unified theory of cognitive development and aging. *Developmental Review, 12*, 45–75.

Dempster, F. N. (1993). Resistance to interference: Developmental changes in a basic processing mechanism. In M. L. Howe & R. Pasnak (Eds.), *Emerging themes in cognitive development* (Vol. 1, pp. 3–27). New York: Springer-Verlag.

Dempster, F. N. (1995). Interference and inhibition in cognition: An historical perspective. In F. N. Dempster & C. J. Brainerd (Eds.), *Interference and inhibition in cognition* (pp. 3–26). San Diego: Academic Press.

Denckla, M. B. (1996). A theory and model of executive function: A neuropsychological perspective. In G. R. Lyon & N. A. Krasnegor (Eds.), *Attention, memory, and executive function* (pp. 263–278). Baltimore, MD: Brookes.

Denckla, M. B., & Reiss, A. L. (1997). Prefrontal-subcortical circuits in developmental disorders. In N. A. Krasnegor, G. R. Lyon, & P. S. Goldman-Rakic (Eds.), *Development of the prefrontal cortex: Evolution, neurobiology, and behaviour* (pp. 283–294). Baltimore: Brookes Publishing Co.

Diamond, A. (1985). Development of the ability to use recall to guide action, as indicated by infants' performance on AB. *Child Development, 56*, 868–883.

Diamond, A. (1990). The development and neural bases of memory functions as indexed by the AB and delayed response tasks in human infants and infant monkeys. *Annals of the New York Academy of Sciences, 608*, 267–317.

Diamond, A. (2001). Looking closely at infants' performance and experimental procedures in the A-not-B task. *Behavioral and Brain Sciences, 24*(1), 38.

Diamond, A. (2006). The early development of executive functions. In E. Bialystok & F. I. M. Craik (Eds.), *Lifespan cognition mechanisms of change* (pp. 70–95). Oxford, UK: Oxford University Press.

Diamond, A. (2012). Activities and programs that improve children's executive functions. *Current Directions in Psychological Science, 21*, 335–341.

Diamond, A. (2014). Want to optimize executive functions and academic outcomes? In P. D. Zelazo & M. D. Sera (Eds.), *Minnesota Symposia on Child Psychology Developing Cognitive Control Processes: Mechanisms, Implications, and Interventions* (Vol. 37, pp. 205–230). Hoboken, NJ: John Wiley & Sons.

184 References

Diamond, A., & Doar, B. (1989). The performance of human infants on a measure of frontal-cortex function, the delayed-response task. *Developmental Psychobiology, 22*(3), 271–294.

Diamond, A., & Gilbert, J. (1989). Development as progressive inhibitory control of action: Retrieval of a contiguous object. *Cognitive Development, 4*, 223–249.

Diamond, A., Kirkham, N. Z., & Amso, D. (2002). Conditions under which young children can hold two rules in mind and inhibit a prepotent response. *Developmental Psychology, 38*, 352–362.

Doherty, M., & Perner, J. (1998). Metalinguistic awareness and theory of mind: Just two words for the same thing? *Cognitive Development, 13*, 279–305.

Dosher, B. A., & Ma, J. J. (1998). Output loss or rehearsal loop? Output-time versus pronunciation-time limits in immediate recall for forgetting-matched materials. *Journal of Experimental Psychology: Learning, Memory and Cognition, 24*(2), 316–335.

Duff, S. C., & Logie, R. H. (1999). Processing and storage in visuo-spatial working memory. *Scandinavian Journal of Psychology, 40*, 251–259.

Duff, S. C., & Logie, R. H. (2001). Processing and storage in working memory span. *Quarterly Journal of Experimental Psychology, 54*, 31–48.

Dulany, D. E. (1991). Conscious representation and thought systems. In R. S. Wyer & T. K. Srull (Eds.), *Advances in social cognition* (Vol. 4, pp. 97–120). Hillsdale, NJ: Lawrence Erlbaum Associates.

Dulany, D. E. (1997). Consciousness in the explicit (deliberative) and implicit (evocative). In J. Cohen & J. Schooler (Eds.), *Scientific approaches to consciousness* (pp. 179–211). Mahwah, NJ: Lawrence Erlbaum Associates.

Einstein, G. O., McDaniel, M. A., Thomas, R., Mayfield, S., Shank, H., Morrisette, N., & Breneiser, J. (2005). Multiple processes in prospective memory retrieval: Factors determining monitoring versus spontaneous retrieval. *Journal of Experimental Psychology: General, 134*, 327–342.

Ellis, N. C., & Hennelly, R. A. (1980). A bilingual word-length effect: Implications for intelligence testing and the relative ease of mental calculation in Welsh and English. *British Journal of Psychology, 71*, 43–52.

Emerson, M. J., & Miyake, A. (2003). The role of inner speech in task switching: A dual-task investigation. *Journal of Memory and Language, 48*, 148–168.

Engle, R. W. (2002). Working memory capacity as executive attention. *Current Directions in Psychological Science, 11*, 19–23.

Engle, R. W., & Kane, M. J. (2004). Executive attention, working memory capacity, and a two-factor theory of cognitive control. In B. Ross (Ed.), *The Psychology of learning and motivation* (Vol. 44, pp. 145–199). New York: Elsevier.

Engle, R. W., Carullo, J. J., & Collins, K. W. (1991). Individual differences in working memory for comprehension and following directions. *Journal of Educational Research, 84*, 253–262.

Engle, R. W., Kane, M. J., & Tuholski, S. W. (1999). Individual differences in working memory capacity and what they tell us about controlled attention, general fluid intelligence and functions of the prefrontal cortex. In A. Miyake & P. Shah (Eds.), *Models of working memory: Mechanisms of active maintenance and executive control* (pp. 102–134). Cambridge: Cambridge University Press.

Engle, R. W., Tuholski, S. W., Laughlin, J. E., & Conway, A. R. A. (1999). Working memory, short-term memory, and general fluid intelligence: A latent-variable approach. *Journal of Experimental Psychology: General, 128*, 309–331.

Enns, J. T., & Girgus, J. S. (1985). Developmental changes in selective and integrative visual attention. *Journal of Experimental Child Psychology, 40*, 319–337.

Ericsson, K. A., & Kintsch, W. (1995). Long-term working memory. *Psychological Review, 102*, 211–245.

Ericsson, K. A., & Simon, H. A. (1980). Verbal reports as data. *Psychological Review, 87*, 215–251.

Ernst, J. O., Lian, A., & Karlsen, P. J. (2007). Reasons for the growth of traditional memory span across age. *European Journal of Cognitive Psychology, 19*(2), 233–270.

Evans, J. St. B. T. (2007). *Hypothetical thinking: Dual processes in reasoning and judgement.* Hove, UK: Psychology Press.

Evans, J. St. B. T. (2011). Dual-process theories of reasoning: Contemporary issues and developmental applications. *Developmental Review, 31*, 86–102.

Evans, J. St. B. T. (2012). Dual-process theories of reasoning: Facts and fallacies. In K. Holyoak & R. G. Morrison (Eds.), *The Oxford handbook of thinking and reasoning* (pp. 115–133). New York: Oxford University Press.

Evans, J. St. B. T., & Over, D. E. (2004). *If.* Oxford: Oxford University Press.

Evans, J. St. B. T., & Stanovich, K. E. (2013). Dual-process theories of higher cognition: Advancing the debate. *Perspectives on Psychological Science, 8*, 223–241.

Fantz, R. L. (1956). A method for studying early visual development. *Perceptual and Motor Skills, 6*(1), 13–16.

Favrel, J., & Barrouillet, P. (2000). On the relation between representations constructed from text comprehension and transitive inference production. *Journal of Experimental Psychology: Learning, Memory, and Cognition, 26*, 187–203.

Feigenson, L. (2007). Continuity of format and computation in short-term memory development. In L. M. Oakes & P. L. Bauer (Eds.), *Short- and long-term memory in infancy: Taking the first step toward remembering* (pp. 51–74). New York: University Press.

Feigenson, L., & Carey, S. (2003). Tracking individuals via object files: Evidence from infants' manual search. *Developmental Science, 6*, 568–584.

Feigenson, L., & Carey, S. (2005). On the limits of infants' quantification of small object arrays. *Cognition, 97*(3), 295–313.

Feigenson, L., Carey, S., & Hauser, M. (2002). The representations underlying infants' choice of more: Object files versus analog magnitudes. *Psychological Science, 13*, 150–156.

Feldman Barrett, L., Tugade, M. M., & Engle, R. W. (2004). Individual differences in working memory and dual-process theories of the mind. *Psychological Bulletin, 130*, 553–573.

Ferguson, A. N., & Bowey, J. A. (2005). Global processing speed as a mediator of developmental changes in children's auditory memory span. *Journal of Experimental Child Psychology, 91*, 89–112.

Ferguson, A. N., Bowey, J. A., & Tilley, A. (2002). The association between auditory memory span and speech rate in children from kindergarten to sixth grade. *Journal of Experimental Child Psychology, 81*, 141–156.

Fischer, K. W. (1980). A theory of cognitive development: The control and construction of hierarchies of skills. *Psychological Review, 87*, 477–531.

Flavell, J. H. (1971). First discussant's comments: What is memory development the development of? *Human Development, 14*, 272–278.

Flavell, J. H. (1988). The development of children's knowledge about the mind: From cognitive connections to mental representations. In J. W. Astington, P. L. Harris, and D. R. Olson (Eds.), *Developing theories of mind* (pp. 244–267). Cambridge, UK: Cambridge University Press.

Flavell, J. H., Beach, D. R., & Chinsky, J. M. (1966). Spontaneous verbal rehearsal in a memory task as a function of age. *Child Development, 37*, 283–299.

Flavell, J. H., Flavell, E. R., & Green, F. L. (1983). Development of the appearance-reality distinction. *Cognitive Psychology, 15*, 95–120.

Fodor, J. (1982). *The modularity of mind.* Cambridge, MA: MIT Press.

186 References

Ford, S., & Silber, K. P. (1994). Working memory in children: A developmental approach to the phonological coding of pictorial material. *British Journal of Developmental Psychology, 12*, 165–175.

Frick, R. W. (1988a). Issues of representation and limited capacity in the auditory short-term store. *British Journal of Psychology, 79*(2), 213–240.

Frick, R. W. (1988b). Issues of representation and limited capacity in the visuospatial sketchpad. *British Journal of Psychology, 79*(3), 289–308.

Friedman, N. P., Miyake, A., Robinson, J. L., & Hewitt, J. K. (2011). Developmental trajectories in toddlers' self-restraint predict individual differences in executive functions 14 years later: A behavioral genetic analysis. *Developmental Psychology, 47*, 1410–1430.

Friedman, N. P., Miyake, A., Young, S. E., DeFries, J. C., Corley, R. P., & Hewitt, J. K. (2008). Individual differences in executive functions are almost entirely genetic in origin. *Journal of Experimental Psychology: General, 137*, 201–225.

Frye, D., Zelazo, P. D., & Burack, J. A. (1998). I. Cognitive complexity and control: Implications for theory of mind in typical and atypical development. *Current Directions in Psychological Science, 7*, 116–121.

Frye, D., Zelazo, P. D., & Palfai, T. (1995). Theory of mind and rule-based reasoning. *Cognitive Development, 10*, 483–527.

Fuson, K. (1982). An analysis of the counting-on procedure. In T. Carpenter, J. Moser & T. Romberg (Eds.), *Addition and subtraction: A cognitive perspective* (pp. 67–81). Hillsdale, NJ: Lawrence Erlbaum Associates.

Fuster, J. M. (1989). *The prefrontal cortex* (2nd ed.). New York: Raven Press.

Fuster, J. M. (1997). *The prefrontal cortex: Anatomy, physiology, and neuropsychology of the frontal lobe*. New York: Lippincott-Raven.

Gaillard, V., Barrouillet, P., Jarrold, C., & Camos, V. (2011). Developmental differences in working memory: Where do they come from? *Journal of Experimental Child Psychology, 110*, 469–479.

Garavan, H. (1998). Serial attention within working memory. *Memory and Cognition, 26*, 263–276.

Garon, N., Bryson, S. E., & Smith, I. M. (2008). Executive functions in preschoolers: A review using an integrative framework. *Psychological Bulletin, 134*, 31–60.

Gathercole, S. E. (1995). Is nonword repetition a test of phonological memory or long-term knowledge? It all depends on the nonwords. *Memory and Cognition, 23*, 83–94.

Gathercole, S. E. (1998). The development of memory. *Journal of Child Psychology and Psychiatry, 39*, 3–27.

Gathercole, S. E. (1999). Cognitive approaches to the development of short-term memory. *Trends in Cognitive Sciences, 3*, 410–419.

Gathercole, S. E. (2006). Complexities and constraints in nonword repetition and word learning. *Applied Psychology, 27*, 599–613.

Gathercole, S. E., & Adams, A-M. (1993). Phonological working memory in very young children. *Developmental Psychology, 29*, 770–778.

Gathercole, S. E., & Baddeley, A. D. (1990). Phonological memory deficits in language-disordered children: Is there a causal connection? *Journal of Memory and Language, 29*, 336–360.

Gathercole, S. E., & Baddeley, A. D. (1993). *Working memory and language*. Hove, UK: Erlbaum.

Gathercole, S. E., & Pickering, S. J. (2000). Working memory deficits in children with low achievements in the national curriculum at 7 years of age. *British Journal of Educational Psychology, 70*, 177–194.

Gathercole, S. E., Adams, A-M., & Hitch, G. J. (1994). Do young children rehearse? An individual differences analysis. *Memory and Cognition, 22*, 201–207.

Gathercole, S. E., Frankish, C. R., Pickering, S. J., & Peaker, S. (1999). Phonotactic influences on short-term memory. *Journal of Experimental Psychology: Learning, Memory and Cognition, 25*, 84–95.

Gathercole, S. E., Pickering, S. J., Ambridge, B., & Wearing, H. (2004). The structure of working memory from 4 to 15 years of age. *Developmental Psychology, 40*(2), 177–190.

Gathercole, S. E., Pickering, S. J., Hall, M., & Peaker, S. M. (2001). Dissociable lexical and phonological influences on serial recognition and serial recall. *Quarterly Journal of Experimental Psychology, 54*, 1–30.

Gathercole, S. E., Pickering, S. J., Knight, C., & Stegmann, Z. (2004). Working memory skills and educational attainment: Evidence from National Curriculum assessments at 7 and 14 years. *Applied Psychology, 18*, 1–16.

Gauffroy, C., & Barrouillet, P. (2009). Heuristic and analytic processes in mental models for conditional: An integrative developmental theory. *Developmental Review, 29*, 249–282.

Gauffroy, C., & Barrouillet, P. (2011). The primacy of thinking about possibilities in the development of reasoning. *Developmental Psychology, 47*, 1000–1011.

Gauffroy, C., & Barrouillet, P. (2014). Conditional reasoning in context: A developmental dual process account. *Thinking and Reasoning, 20*, 372–384.

Gavens, N., & Barrouillet, P. (2004). Delays of retention, processing efficiency, and attentional resources in working memory span development. *Journal of Memory and Language, 51*, 644–657.

Gawronski, B., & Creighton, L. A. (2013). Dual process theories. In *The Oxford Handbook of Social Cognition* (pp. 282–312). Oxford: Oxford University Press.

Geary, D. C. (1990). A componential analysis of an early learning deficit in mathematics. *Journal of Experimental Child Psychology, 49*, 363–383.

Geary, D. C. (1995). Reflections on evolution and culture in children's cognition: Implications for mathematical development and instruction. *American Psychologist, 50*, 24–37.

Geary, D. C. (2011). Cognitive predictors of achievement growth in mathematics: A 5-year longitudinal study. *Developmental Psychology, 47*, 1539–1552.

Geary, D. C. (2013). Early foundations for mathematics learning and their relations to learning disabilities. *Current Directions in Psychological Science, 22*(1), 23–27.

Geary, D. C., & Burlingham-Dubree, M. (1989). External validation of the strategy choice model for addition. *Journal of Experimental Child Psychology, 47*, 175–192.

Geary, D. C., Hoard, M. K., Byrd-Craven, J., & DeSoto, C. (2004). Strategy choices in simple and complex addition: Contributions of working memory and counting knowledge for children with mathematical disability. *Journal of Experimental Child Psychology, 88*, 121–151.

Geary, D. C., Hoard, M. K., & Hamson, C. O. (1999). Numerical and arithmetical cognition: Patterns of functions and deficits in children at risk for a mathematical disability. *Journal of Experimental Child Psychology, 74*, 213–239.

Gelman, R. (1978). Cognitive development. *Annual Review of Psychology, 29*, 297–332.

Gelman, R. (1990). Structuralist contraints on cognitive development: Introduction to a special issue. *Cognitive Science, 14*, 3–9.

Gelman, R. (2015). Learning in core and non-core number domains. *Developmental Review, 38*, 185–200.

Gentner, D., & Stevens, A. L. (Eds.). (1983). *Mental models*. Hillsdale, NJ: Lawrence Erlbaum Associates.

Gerstadt, C. L., Hong, Y. J., & Diamond, A. (1994). The relationship between cognition and action: Performance of children 3½–7 years old on a Stroop-like day-night test. *Cognition, 53*, 129–153.

Gilchrist, A. L., Cowan, N., & Naveh-Benjamin, M. (2009). Investigating the childhood development of working memory using sentences: New evidence for the growth of chunk capacity. *Journal of Experimental Child Psychology, 104*, 252–265.

188 References

Giofre, D., Mammarella, I., & Cornoldi, C. (2013). The structure of working memory and how it relates to intelligence in children. *Intelligence, 41*, 396–406.

Gioia, G. A., Isquith, P. K., & Guy, S. C. (2001). Assessment of executive functions in children with neurological impairment. In R. J. Simeonsson & S. L. Rosenthal (Eds.), *Psychological and developmental assessment: Children with disabilities and chronic conditions* (pp. 317–356). New York: Guilford Press.

Girotto, V. (2014). Probabilistic reasoning: Rational expectations in young children and infants. In W. De Neys & M. Osman (Eds.), *New approaches in reasoning research* (pp. 187–201). Hove, UK: Psychology Press.

Girotto, V., & Gonzalez, M. (2008). Children's understanding of posterior probability. *Cognition, 106*, 325–344.

Glanzer, M., & Clark, W. H. (1963). The verbal loop hypothesis: Binary-numbers. *Journal of Verbal Learning and Verbal Behavior, 2*(4), 301–309.

Globerson, T. (1983a). Mental capacity, mental effort and cognitive style. *Developmental Review, 3*, 292–302.

Globerson, T. (1983b). Mental capacity and cognitive functioning: Developmental and social class differences. *Developmental Psychology, 2*, 225–230.

Globerson, T. (1985). Field dependence/independence and mental capacity: A developmental approach. *Developmental Review, 5*, 261–273.

Goel, V., Makale, M., & Grafman, J. (2004). The hippocampal system mediates logical reasoning about familiar spatial environments. *Journal of Cognitive Neuroscience, 16*, 654–662.

Goldman-Rakic, P. S. (1987). Circuitry of primate prefrontal cortex and regulation of behavior by representational memory. In F. Plum & V. Mountcastle (Eds.), *Handbook of physiology* (Vol. 5, pp. 373–417). Bethesda, MD: American Physiological Society.

Goldman-Rakic, P. S. (1992). Working memory and the mind. *Scientific American, 267*, 110–117.

Gomes, C. F. A., & Brainerd, C. J. (2013). Dual processes in the development of reasoning: The memory side of the story. In P. Barrouillet & C. Gauffroy (Eds.), *The development of thinking and reasoning* (pp. 221–242). Hove, UK: Psychology Press.

Gopnik, A., Glymour, C., Sobel, D., Schulz, L., Kushnir, T., & Danks, D. (2004). A theory of causal learning in children: Causal maps and Bayes nets. *Psychological Review, 111*, 1–30.

Gordon, A. C. L., & Olson, D. (1998). The relation between acquisition of a theory of mind and information processing capacity. *Journal of Experimental Child Psychology, 68*, 70–83.

Grant, A. D., & Berg, E. A. (1948). A behavioral analysis of reinforcement and ease of shifting to new responses in a Weigl-type card sorting. *Journal of Experimental Psychology, 38*, 404–411.

Gray, S., Green, S., Alt, M., Hogan, T., Kuo, T., Brinkley, S., & Cowan, N. (2017). The structure of working memory in young children and its relation to intelligence. *Journal of Memory and Language, 92*, 183–201.

Greene, A. J., Spellman, B., Dusek, J. A., Eichenbaum, H. B., & Levy, W. B. (2001). Relational learning with and without awareness: Transitive inference using nonverbal stimuli in humans. *Memory and Cognition, 29*, 893–902.

Greene, R. L. (1987). Effects of maintenance rehearsal on human memory. *Psychological Bulletin, 102*, 403–413.

Groen, G. J., & Parkman, J. M. (1972). A chronometric analysis of simple addition. *Psychological Review, 79*, 329–343.

Gruber, O. (2001). Effects of domain-specific interference on brain activation associated with verbal working memory task performance. *Cerebral Cortex, 11*, 1047–1055.

Guttentag, R. E. (1984). The mental effort requirement of cumulative rehearsal: A developmental study. *Journal of Experimental Child Psychology, 37*, 92–106.

Haberlandt, K. (1997). *Cognitive psychology* (2nd ed.). Boston: Allyn & Bacon.

Halford, G. S. (1978). Cognitive Developmental Stages emerging from levels of learning. *International Journal of Behavioral Development, 1*, 341–354.

Halford, G. S. (1982). *The development of thought.* Hillsdale, NJ: Lawrence Erlbaum Associates.

Halford, G. S. (1993). *Children's understanding: The development of mental models.* Hillsdale, NJ: Lawrence Erlbaum Associates.

Halford, G. S., & Andrews, G. (2004). The development of deductive reasoning: How important is complexity? *Thinking and Reasoning, 10*, 123–145.

Halford, G. S., & Galloway, W. (1977). Children who fail to make transitive inferences can remember comparisons. *Australian Journal of Psychology, 29*, 1–5.

Halford, G. S., & Wilson, W. H. (1980). A category theory approach to cognitive development. *Cognitive Psychology, 12*, 356–411.

Halford, G. S., Andrews, G., Dalton., C. Boag, C., & Zielinski, T. (2002). Young children's performance on the balance scale: The influence of relational complexity. *Journal of Experimental Child Psychology, 81*, 417–445.

Halford, G. S., Andrews, G., Phillips, S., & Wilson, W. H. (2013). The role of working memory in the subsymbolic-symbolic transition. *Current Directions in Psychological Science, 22*, 210–216.

Halford, G. S., Bain, G. S., & Maybery, M. T. (1984). Working memory and representational processes: Implications for cognitive development. *Attention and Performance, 10*, 459–470.

Halford, G. S., Baker, R., McCredden, J. E., & Bain, J. D. (2005). How many variables can humans process? *Psychological Science, 16*, 70–76.

Halford, G. S., Cowan, N., & Andrews, G. (2007). Separating cognitive capacity from knowledge: A new hypothesis. *Trends in Cognitive Sciences, 11*, 236–242.

Halford, G. S., Maybery, M. T., O'Hare, A. W., & Grant, P. (1994). The development of memory and processing capacity. *Child Development, 65*, 1338–1356.

Halford, G. S., Wilson, W. H., Andrews, G., & Phillips, S. (2014). *Categorizing cognition: Toward conceptual coherence in the foundations of psychology.* Cambridge: MIT Press.

Halford, G. S., Wilson, W. H., & Phillips, S. (1998). Processing capacity defined by relational complexity: Implications for comparative, developmental, and cognitive psychology. *Behavioral and Brain Sciences, 21*, 803–864.

Halford, G. S., Wilson, W. H., & Phillips, S. (2010). Relational knowledge: The foundation of higher cognition. *Trends in Cognitive Sciences, 14*, 497–505.

Halliday, M. S., Hitch, G. J., Lennon, B., & Pettipher, C. (1990). Verbal short-term memory in children: The role of the articulatory loop. *European Journal of Cognitive Psychology, 2*, 23–38.

Hamilton, C., Coates, R., & Heffernan, T. (2003). What develops in visuo-spatial working memory development? *European Journal of Cognitive Psychology, 15*(1), 43–69.

Hanlon, F. M., Houck, J. M., Pyeatt, C. J., Lundy, S. L., Euler, M. J., Weisend, M. P., et al. (2011). Bilateral hippocampal dysfunction in schizophrenia. *NeuroImage, 58*, 1158–1168.

Happaney, K., & Zelazo, P. D. (2003). Inhibition as a problem in the psychology of behavior. *Developmental Science, 6*, 468–470.

Hardman, K., & Cowan, N. (2015). Remembering complex objects in visual working memory: Do capacity limits restrict objects or features? *Journal of Experimental Psychology: Learning, Memory, and Cognition, 41*, 325–347.

Harnishfeger, K. K., & Bjorklund, D. F. (1993). The ontogeny of inhibition mechanisms: A renewed approach to cognitive development. In M. L. Howe & R. Pasnak (Eds.), *Emerging themes in cognitive development: Foundations* (Vol. 1, pp. 28–49). New York: Springer-Verlag.

190 References

Harris, P., & Nuñez, M. (1996). Understanding of permission rules by preschool children. *Child Development, 67*, 1572–1591.

Hasher, L., & Zacks, R. T. (1979). Automatic and effortful processes in memory. *Journal of Experimental Psychology: General, 108*(3), 356–388.

Hasselhorn, M., & Grube, D. (2003). The phonological similarity effect on memory span in children: Does it depend on age, speech rate, and articulatory suppression? *International Journal of Behavioral Development, 27*(2), 145–152.

Hebb, D. O. (1949). *The organization of behaviour.* New York: Wiley.

Heitz, R. P., & Engle, R. W. (2007). Focusing the spotlight: Individual differences in visual attention control. *Journal of Experimental Psychology: General, 136*, 217–240.

Henry, L. A. (1991). The effect of word-length and phonemic similarity in young children's short-term memory. *Quarterly Journal of Experimental Psychology, 43A*, 35–52.

Henry, L. A. (1994). The relationship between speech rate and memory span in children. *International Journal of Behavioral Development, 17*, 37–56.

Henry, L. A. (2012). *The development of working memory in children.* London: Sage.

Henry, L. A., & Millar, S. (1991). Memory span increase with age: A test of two hypotheses. *Journal of Experimental Child Psychology, 51*, 459–484.

Henry, L. A., & Millar, S. (1993). Why does memory span increase with age? A review of the evidence of two current hypotheses. *European Journal of Cognitive Psychology, 5*, 241–287.

Henry, L. A., Messer, D., Luger-Klein, S., & Crane, L. (2012). Phonological, visual, and semantic coding strategies and children's short term picture memory span. *Quarterly Journal of Experimental Psychology, 65*, 2033–2053.

Henry, L. A., Turner, J. E., Smith, P. T., & Leather, C. (2000). Modality effects and the development of the word length effect in children. *Memory, 8*, 1–17.

Hitch, G. J. (1990). Developmental fractionation of working memory. In G. Vallar and T. Shallice (Eds.), *Neuropsychological impairment of short-term memory* (pp. 221–246). Cambridge: Cambridge University Press.

Hitch, G. J., Halliday, M. S., Dodd, A., & Littler, J. E. (1989). Development of rehearsal in short-term memory: Differences between pictorial and spoken stimuli. *British Journal of Developmental Psychology, 7*, 347–362.

Hitch, G. J., Halliday, M. S., & Littler, J. E. (1989). Item identification time and rehearsal rate as predictors of memory span in children. *Quarterly Journal of Experimental Psychology, 41A*, 321–337.

Hitch, G. J., Halliday, M. S., & Littler, J. E. (1993). Development of memory span for spoken words: The role of rehearsal and item identification processes. *British Journal of Developmental Psychology, 11*, 159–170.

Hitch, G. J., Halliday, M. S., Schaafstal, A. M., & Heffernan, T. M. (1991). Speech, 'inner speech', and the development of short-term memory: Effects of picture labelling on recall. *Journal of Experimental Child Psychology, 51*, 220–234.

Hitch, G. J., Halliday, M. S., Schaafstal, A. M., & Schraagen, J. M. C. (1988). Visual working memory in children. *Memory and Cognition, 16*, 120–132.

Hitch, G., Towse, J. N., & Hutton, U. (2001). What limits children's working memory span? Theoretical accounts and applications for scholastic development. *Journal of Experimental Psychology: General, 130*, 184–198.

Hitch, G. J., Woodin, M. E., & Baker, S. (1989). Visual and phonological components of working memory in children. *Memory and Cognition, 17*, 175–185.

Hofstadter, M., & Reznick, J. S. (1996). Response modality affects human infant delayed response performance. *Child Development, 67*, 646–658.

Hongwanishkul, D., Happaney, K. R., Lee, W. S. C., & Zelazo, P. D. (2005). Assessment of hot and cool executive function in young children: Age-related changes and individual differences. *Developmental Neuropsychology, 28*, 617–644.

Hornung, C., Brunner, M., Reuter, R. A. P., & Martin, R. (2011). Children's working memory: Its structure and relationship to fluid intelligence. *Intelligence, 39*, 210–221.

Hughes, C. (1998). Executive function in preschoolers: Links with theory of mind and verbal ability. *British Journal of Developmental Psychology, 16*, 233–253.

Huizinga, M., Dolan, C. V., & van der Molen, M. (2006). Age-related change in executive function: Developmental trends and a latent variable analysis. *Neuropsychologia, 44*, 2017–2036.

Hulme, C. (1987). The effects of acoustic similarity on memory in children: A comparison between visual and auditory presentation. *Applied Cognitive Psychology, 1*(1), 45–51.

Hulme, C., & Muir, C. (1985). Developmental changes in speech rate and memory span: A causal relationship? *British Journal of Developmental Psychology, 3*, 175–181.

Hulme, C., & Tordoff, V. (1989). Working memory development: The effects of speech rate, word length, and acoustic similarity on serial recall. *Journal of Experimental Child Psychology, 47*, 72–87.

Hulme, C., Roodenrys, S., Schweickert, R., Brown, G. D., Martin, S., & Stuart, G. (1997). Word-frequency effects on short-term memory tasks: Evidence for a redintegration process in immediate serial recall. *Journal of Experimental Psychology: Learning, Memory, and Cognition, 23*, 1217–1232.

Hulme, C., Stuart, G., Surprenant, A. M., Neath, I., Shostak, L., & Brown, G. (2006). The distinctiveness of the word-length effect. *Journal of Experimental Psychology: Learning, Memory, and Cognition, 32*, 586–594.

Hulme, C., Thomson, N., Muir, C., & Lawrence, A. (1984). Speech rate and the development of short-term memory span. *Journal of Experimental Child Psychology, 38*, 241–253.

Hunter, W. S. (1913). *Delayed reaction in animals and children*. New York, NY: Holt.

Huttenlocher, J., Newcombe, N., & Sandberg, E. H. (1994). The coding of spatial location in young-children. *Cognitive Psychology, 27*(2), 115–147.

Inhelder, B., & Cellerier, G. (1992). *Le cheminement des découvertes de l'enfant (recherche sur les microgenèses cognitives)*. Neuchâtel: Delachaux & Niestlé.

Inhelder, B., & Piaget., J. (1958). *The growth of logical thinking from childhood to adolescence*. New York: Basic Books.

Inhelder, B., & Piaget, J. (1964). *The early growth of logic in the child: Classification and seriation*. (E. A. Lunzer & D. Papert, Trans.). New York: Harper & Row.

Isaacs, E., & Vargha-Khadem, F. (1989). Differential course of the development of spatial and verbal memory span: A normative study. *British Journal of Developmental Psychology, 7*, 377–380.

Jacobs, J. E., & Potenza, M. (1991). The use of judgment heuristics to make social and object decisions: A developmental perspective. *Child Development, 62*, 166–178.

James, W. (1890). *The principles of psychology*. New York: Henry Holt.

Janveau-Brennan, G., & Markovits, H. (1999). The development of reasoning with causal conditionals. *Developmental Psychology, 35*, 904–911.

Jarrold, C. (2016). Working out how working memory works: Evidence from typical and atypical development. *Quarterly Journal of Experimental Psychology, 70*, 1747–1767.

Jarrold, C., & Citroën, R. (2013). Reevaluating key evidence for the development of rehearsal: Phonological similarity effects in children are subject to proportional scaling artefacts. *Developmental Psychology, 49*, 837–847.

Jarrold, C., Danielsson, H., & Wang, X. (2015). Absolute and proportional measures of potential markers of rehearsal, and their implications for accounts of its development. *Frontiers in Psychology, 6*, 299.

192 References

Jarrold, C., Hewes, A. K., & Baddeley, A. D. (2000). Two separate speech measures constrain verbal short-term memory in children. *Journal of Experimental Psychology: Learning, Memory, and Cognition, 26*, 1626–1637.

Johnson-Laird, P. N. (1983). *Mental models: Towards a cognitive science of language, inference, and consciousness.* Cambridge, MA: Harvard University Press.

Johnson-Laird, P. N. (2002). Peirce, logic diagrams, and the elementary operations of reasoning. *Thinking and Reasoning, 8*, 69–95.

Johnson-Laird, P. N., & Byrne, R. M. J. (1991). *Deduction.* Hillsdale, NJ: Lawrence Erlbaum.

Johnson-Laird, P. N., & Byrne, R. M. J. (2002). Conditionals: A theory of meaning, pragmatics, and inference. *Psychological Review, 96*, 658–673.

Johnson-Laird, P. N., Byrne, R. M. J., & Schaeken, W. (1992). Propositional reasoning by model. *Psychological Review, 3*, 418–439.

Jones, G., Gobet, F., & Pine, J. M. (2007). Linking working memory and long-term memory: A computational model of the learning of new words. *Developmental Science, 10*, 853–873.

Jones, G., Gobet, F., & Pine, J. M. (2008). Computer simulations of developmental change: The contributions of working memory capacity and long-term knowledge. *Cognitive Science, 32*, 1148–1176.

Jordan, N. C., Hanich, L. B., & Kaplan, D. (2003). A longitudinal study of mathematical competencies in children with specific mathematics difficulties versus children with comorbid mathematics and reading difficulties. *Child Development, 74*, 834–850.

Kagan, J. (1981). *The second year.* Cambridge, MA: Harvard University Press.

Kahneman, D. (1973). *Attention and effort.* Englewood Cliffs, NJ: Prentice-Hall.

Kahneman, D. (2013). *Thinking fast and slow.* New York: Farrar, Straus and Giroux.

Kahneman, D., & Frederick, S. (2002). Representativeness revisited: Attribute substitution in intuitive judgement. In T. Gilovich, D. Griffin, & D. Kahneman (Eds.), *Heuristics and biases: The psychology of intuitive judgment* (pp. 49–81). Cambridge: Cambridge University Press.

Kahneman, D., Treisman, A., & Gibbs, B. J. (1992). The reviewing of object files: Object-specific integration of information. *Cognitive Psychology, 24*, 175–219.

Kail, R. (1991). Developmental change in speed of processing during childhood and adolescence. *Psychological Bulletin, 109*, 490–501.

Kail, R. (1992). Processing speed, speech rate, and memory. *Developmental Psychology, 28*, 899–904.

Kail, R. (1997). Processing time, imagery, and spatial memory. *Journal of Experimental Child Psychology, 64*, 67–78.

Kail, R. (2000). Speed of information processing: Developmental change and links to intelligence. *Journal of School Psychology, 38*, 51–61.

Kail, R., & Park, Y. (1994). Processing time, articulation time, and memory span. *Journal of Experimental Child Psychology, 57*, 281–291.

Kail, R., & Salthouse, T. A. (1994). Processing speed as a mental capacity. *Acta Psychologica, 86*, 199–225.

Kane, M. J., & Engle, R. W. (1998). Full frontal fluidity: Working memory capacity, controlled attention, intelligence, and the prefrontal cortex. Unpublished manuscript.

Kane, M. J., & Engle, R. W. (2000). Working-memory capacity, proactive interference, and divided attention: Limits on long-term memory retrieval. *Journal of Experimental Psychology: Learning, Memory, and Cognition, 26*, 336–358.

Kane, M. J., & Engle, R. W. (2002). The role of prefrontal cortex in working-memory capacity, executive attention, and general fluid intelligence: An individual-differences perspective. *Psychonomic Bulletin and Review, 9*, 637–671.

Kane, M. J., & Engle, R. W. (2003). Working-memory capacity and the control of attention: The contributions of goal neglect, response competition, and task set to Stroop interference. *Journal of Experimental Psychology: General, 132*, 47–70.

Kane, M. J., Bleckley, M. K., Conway, A. R. A., & Engle, R. W. (2001). A controlled-attention view of working memory capacity. *Journal of Experimental Psychology: General, 130*, 169–183.

Kane, M. J., Hambrick, D. Z., Tuholski, S. W., Wilhelm, O., Payne, T., & Engle, R. W. (2004). The generality of working memory capacity: A latent-variable approach to verbal and visuospatial memory span and reasoning. *Journal of Experimental Psychology: General, 133*, 189–217.

Karbach, J., & Kray, J. (2007). Developmental changes in switching between mental task sets: The influence of verbal labelling in childhood. *Journal of Cognition and Development, 8*, 1–32.

Karmiloff-Smith, A. (1979). *A functional approach to child language*. Cambridge, UK: Cambridge University Press.

Karmiloff-Smith, A. (1992). *Beyond modularity*. Cambridge, MA: MIT Press.

Karmiloff-Smith, A. (1995). *Beyond modularity: A developmental perspective on cognitive science*. Cambridge, MA: MIT Press.

Keller, T. A., & Cowan, N. (1994). Developmental increase in the duration of memory for tone pitch. *Developmental Psychology, 30*, 855–863.

Kemps, E., De Rammelaere, S., & Desmet, T. (2000). The development of working memory: Exploring the complementarity of two models. *Journal of Experimental Child Psychology, 77*, 89–109.

Keppel, G., & Underwood, B. J. (1962). Proactive inhibition in short-term retention of single items. *Journal of Verbal Learning and Verbal Behavior, 1*, 153–161.

Kibbe, M. M. (2015). Varieties of visual working memory representation in infancy and beyond. *Current Directions in Psychological Science, 24*(6), 433–439.

Kibbe, M. M., & Leslie, A. M. (2013). What's the object of object working memory in infancy? Unravelling 'what' and 'how many'. *Cognitive Psychology, 66*, 380–404.

Kintsch, W. (1988). The role of knowledge in discourse comprehension: A construction-integration model. *Psychological Review, 95*, 163–182.

Kirkham, N. Z., & Diamond, A. (2003). Sorting between theories of perseveration: Performance in conflict tasks requires memory, attention and inhibition. *Developmental Science, 6*, 474–476.

Kirkham, N. Z., Cruess, L., & Diamond, A. (2003). Helping children apply their knowledge to their behavior on a dimension-switching task. *Developmental Science, 6*, 449–467.

Klahr, D., & Wallace, J. G. (1976). *Cognitive development: An information processing view*. Hillsdale, NJ: Lawrence Erlbaum Associates.

Klapp, S. T., Marshburn, E. A., & Lester, P. T. (1983). Short-term memory does not involve the 'working memory' of information processing: The demise of a common assumption. *Journal of Experimental Psychology: General, 112*, 240–264.

Kloo, D., & Perner, J. (2003). Training transfer between card sorting and false belief understanding: Helping children apply conflicting descriptions. *Child Development, 74*, 1823–1839.

Korkman, M., Kirk, U., & Kemp, S. L. (1998). *NEPSY: A developmental neuropsychological assessment*. San Antonio, TX: Psychological Corporation.

Kray, J., Eber, J., & Karbach, J. (2008). Verbal self-instructions in task switching: A compensatory tool for action-control in childhood and old age. *Developmental Science, 11*, 223–236.

Kuhn, D., Amsel, E., & O'Loughlin, M. (1988). *The development of scientific thinking skills*. Orlando, FL: Academic.

194 References

Kushnir, T., & A. Gopnik (2007). Conditional probability versus spatial contiguity in causal learning: Preschoolers use new contingency evidence to overcome prior spatial assumptions. *Developmental Psychology, 43*, 186–196.

Kyllonen, P. C., & Christal, R. E. (1990). Reasoning ability is (little more than) working memory capacity? *Intelligence, 14*, 389–433.

LaPointe, L. B., & Engle, R. W. (1990). Simple and complex word spans as measures of working memory capacity. *Journal of Experimental Psychology: Learning, Memory, and Cognition, 16*, 1118–1133.

Lebel, C., & Beaulieu, C. (2011). Longitudinal development of human brain wiring continues from childhood into adulthood. *Journal of Neuroscience, 31*, 10937–10947.

Lecas, J. F., & Barrouillet, P. (1999). Understanding conditional rules in childhood and adolescence: A mental models approach. *Current Psychology of Cognition, 18*, 363–396.

Lehmann, M., & Hasselhorn, M. (2007). Variable memory strategy use in children's adaptive intra-task learning behavior: Developmental changes and working memory influences in free recall. *Child Development, 78*, 1068–1082.

Lehto, J. E., Juujärvi, P., Kooistra, L., & Pulkkinen, L. (2003). Dimensions of executive functioning: Evidence from children. *British Journal of Developmental Psychology, 21*, 59–80.

Lépine, R., Bernardin, S., & Barrouillet, P. (2005). Attention switching and working memory spans. *European Journal of Cognitive Psychology, 17*, 329–346.

Levin, H. S., Culhane, K. A., Hartmann, J., Evankovich, K., Mattson, A. J., Harward, H., et al. (1991). Developmental changes in performance on tests of purported frontal lobe functioning. *Developmental Neuropsychology, 7*, 377–395.

Lewandowsky, S., Oberauer, K., & Brown, G. D. A. (2009). No temporal decay in verbal short-term memory. *Trends in Cognitive Sciences, 13*, 120–126.

Li, D., Cowan, N., & Saults, J. S. (2013). Estimating working memory capacity for lists of nonverbal sounds. *Attention, Perception, and Psychophysics, 75*, 145–160.

Liben, L. S., & Bowman, C. R. (2014). The development of memory from a Piagetian perspective. In P. J. Bauer & R. Fivush (Eds.), *The Wiley handbook on the development of children's memory* (pp. 65–86). Malden, MA: Wiley-Blackwell.

Liberman, I. Y, Mann, V. A, Shankweiler, D., & Werfelman, M. (1982). Children's memory for recurring linguistic and non-linguistic material in relation to reading ability. *Cortex, 18*, 367–375.

Light, P., Blaye, A., Gilly, M., & Girotto, V. (1989). Pragmatic schemas and logical reasoning in 6 to 8 year old children. *Cognitive Development, 4*, 49–64.

Loaiza, V. M., & McCabe, D. P. (2012). Temporal-contextual processing in working memory: Evidence from delayed cued recall and delayed free recall tests. *Memory and Cognition, 40*, 193–203.

Logie, R. H. (1995). *Visuo-spatial working memory*. Hove, UK: Psychology Press.

Logie, R. H., & Pearson, D. G. (1997). The inner eye and the inner scribe of the visuo-spatial working memory: Evidence from developmental fractionation. *European Journal of Cognitive Psychology, 9*(3), 241–257.

Logie, R. H., Della Sala, S., Laiacona, M., Chambers, P., & Wynn, V. (1996). Group aggregates and individual reliability: The case of verbal short-term memory. *Memory and Cognition, 24*, 305–321.

Logie, R. H., Della Sala, S., Wynn, V., & Baddeley, A. D. (2000). Visual similarity effects in immediate verbal serial recall. *Quarterly Journal of Experimental Psychology, 53A*, 626–646.

Longoni, A. M., & Scalisi, T. G. (1994). Developmental aspects of phonemic and visual similarity effects: Further evidence in Italian children. *International Journal of Behavioural Development, 17*, 57–71.

Luck, S. J., & Vogel, E. K. (1997). The capacity of visual working memory for features and conjunctions. *Nature, 390*, 279–281.

Luria, A. R. (1959). The directive function of speech in development and dissolution. Part I: Development of the directive function of speech in early childhood. *Word, 15*, 341–352.

Luria, A. R. (1961). *The role of speech in the regulation of normal and abnormal behavior.* Oxford: Liveright.

Luria, A. R. (1966). *Higher cortical functions in man.* New York: Basic Books.

Luria, A. R. (1973). *The working brain: An introduction to neuropsychology.* New York: Basic Books.

Lutkus, A., & Trabasso, T. (1974). Transitive inferences by preoperational retarded adolescents. *American Journal of Mental Deficiency, 78*, 599–606.

Maccoby, E. E., & Hagen, J. H. (1965). Effects of distraction upon central versus incidental recall: Developmental trends. *Journal of Experimental Child Psychology, 2*, 280–289.

Manis, F. R., Keating, D. P., & Morrison, F. J. (1980). Developmental differences in the allocation of processing capacity. *Journal of Experimental Child Psychology, 29*, 156–169.

Mansfield, P. (1977). Multi-planar image formation using NMR spin echoes. *Journal of Physics C: Solid State Physics, 10*, L55–L58.

Marcovitch, S., & Zelazo, P. D. (2009). A hierarchical competing systems model of the emergence and early development of executive function. *Developmental Science, 12*, 1–18.

Marcovitch, S., Boseovski, J. J., & Knapp, R. J. (2007). Use it or lose it: Examining preschoolers' difficulty in maintaining and executing a goal. *Developmental Science, 10*, 559–564.

Markman, E. M. (1979). Realizing that you don't understand: Elementary school children's awareness of inconsistencies. *Child Development, 50*, 643–655.

Markman, E. M., & Wachtel, G. F. (1988). Children's use of mutual exclusivity to constrain the meanings of words. *Cognitive Psychology, 20*, 121–157.

Markovits, H. (2000). A mental model analysis of young children's conditional reasoning with meaningful premises. *Thinking and Reasoning, 6*, 335–347.

Markovits, H. (2013). The development of abstract conditional reasoning. In P. Barrouillet & C. Gauffroy (Eds.), *The development of thinking and reasoning* (pp. 71–92). New York: Psychology Press.

Markovits, H., & Barrouillet, P. (2002). The development of conditional reasoning: A mental model account. *Developmental Review, 22*, 5–36.

Markovits, H., & Dumas, C. (1992). Can pigeons really make transitive inference? *Journal of Experimental Psychology, Animal Behaviour Processes, 18*, 311–312.

Markovits, H., & Dumas, C. (1999). Developmental patterns in the understanding of social and physical transitivity. *Journal of Experimental Child Psychology, 73*, 95–114.

Markovits, H., & Lortie-Forgues, H. (2011). Conditional reasoning with false premises facilitates the transition between familiar and abstract reasoning. *Child Development, 82*, 646–660.

Markovits, H., & Thompson, V. (2008). Different developmental patterns of simple deductive and probabilistic inferential reasoning. *Memory and Cognition, 36*, 1066–1078.

Markovits, H., Dumas, C., & Malfait, N. (1995). Understanding transitivity of a spatial relationship: A developmental analysis. *Journal of Experimental Child Psychology, 59*, 124–141.

Markovits, H., Venet, M., Janveau-Brennan, G., Malfait, N., Pion, N., & Vadeboncoeur, I. (1996). Reasoning in young children: Fantasy and information retrieval. *Child Development, 67*, 2857–2872.

Masterson, J., Laxon, V., Carnegie, E., Wright, S., & Horslen, J. (2005). Nonword recall and phonemic discrimination in four- to six-year-old children. *Journal of Research in Reading, 28*, 183–201.

Mate, J., Allen, R. J., & Baqués, J. (2012). What you say matters: Exploring visual–verbal interactions in visual working memory. *Quarterly Journal of Experimental Psychology, 65*, 395–400.

McCulloch, W. S. (1949). The brain as a computing machine. *Electrical Engineering, 6*, 492–497.

McCulloch, W. S., & Pitts, W. (1943). A logical calculus of the ideas immanent in nervous activity. *Bulletin of Mathematical Biophysics, 5*, 115–133.

McElree, B. (1998). Attended and nonattended states in working memory: Accessing categorized structures. *Journal of Memory and Language, 38*, 225–252.

McElree, B. (2001). Working memory and focal attention. *Journal of Experimental Psychology: Learning, Memory and Cognition, 27*, 817–835.

McGilly, K., & Siegler, R. S. (1989). How children choose among serial recall strategies. *Child Development, 60*, 172–182.

McGilly, K., & Siegler, R. S. (1990). The influence of encoding and strategic knowledge on children's choices among serial recall strategies. *Developmental Psychology, 26*, 931–941.

McGonigle, B. O., & Chalmers, M. (1992). Monkeys are rational. *Quarterly Journal of Experimental Psychology, 45B*, 189–228.

McLaughlin, G. H. (1963). Psycho-logic: A possible alternative to Piaget's formulation. *British Journal of Educational Psychology, 33*, 61–67.

McLean, J. F., & Hitch, G. J. (1999). Working memory impairments in children with specific arithmetic learning difficulties. *Journal of Experimental Child Psychology, 74*, 240–260.

Mehler, J., & Bever, T. G. (1967). Cognitive capacity of very young children. *Science, 158*, 141–142.

Melby-Lervåg, M., & Hulme, C. (2013). Is working memory training effective? A meta-analytic review. *Developmental Psychology, 49*(2), 270–291.

Melby-Lervåg, M., Redick, T., & Hulme, C. (2016). Working memory training does not improve performance on measures of intelligence or other measures of 'far transfer': Evidence from a meta-analytic review. *Perspectives on Psychological Science, 11*(4), 512–534.

Meltzoff, A. N. (1985). Immediate and deferred imitation in fourteen and twenty-four-month-old infants. *Child Development, 56*, 62–72.

Meltzoff, A. N., & Moore, M. K. (1983). Newborn infants imitate adult facial gestures. *Child Development, 54*(3), 702–709.

Michalczyk, K., Malstadt, N., Worgt, M., Konen, T., & Hasselhorn, M. (2013). Age differences and measurement invariance of working memory in 5- to 12-year-old children. *European Journal of Psychological Assessment, 29*, 220–229.

Michas, I. C., & Henry, L. A (1994). The link between phonological memory and vocabulary acquisition. *British Journal of Developmental Psychology, 12*, 147–164.

Miles, C., Morgan, M. J., Milne, A. B., & Morris, E. D. M. (1996). Developmental and individual differences in visual memory span. *Current Psychology, 15*(1), 53–67.

Miller, G. A. (1956). The magical number seven, plus or minus two: Some limits on our capacity for processing information. *Psychological Review, 63*, 81–97.

Miller, G. A., Galanter, E., & Pribam, K. H. (1960). *Plans and the structure of behavior.* New York: Holt, Rinehart and Winston.

Milner, B. (1971). Interhemispheric differences in the location of psychological processes in man. *British Medical Bulletin, 27*, 272–277.

Miyake, A., Friedman, N. P., Emerson, M. J., Witzki, A. H., Howerter, A., & Wager, T. D. (2000). The unity and diversity of executive functions and their contributions to complex 'frontal lobe' tasks: A latent variable analysis. *Cognitive Psychology, 41*, 49–100.

Moore, M. K., & Meltzoff, A. N. (2004). Object permanence after a 24-hr delay and leaving the locale of disappearance: The role of memory, space, and identity. *Developmental Psychology, 40*, 606–620.

Mora, G., & Camos, V. (2013). Two systems of maintenance in verbal working memory: Evidence from the word length effect. *PLoS One, 8*(7), e70026.

Mora, G., & Camos, V. (2015). Dissociating rehearsal and refreshing in the maintenance of verbal information in 8-year-old children. *Frontiers in Psychology: Developmental Psychology, 6*, 11.

Morey, C. C., & Bieler, M. (2013). Visual short-term memory always requires general attention. *Psychonomic Bulletin and Review, 20*, 163–170.

Morey, C. C., & Cowan, N. (2004). When visual and verbal memories compete: Evidence of cross-domain limits in working memory. *Psychonomic Bulletin and Review, 11*, 296–301.

Morey, C. C., & Cowan, N. (2005). When do visual and verbal memories conflict? The importance of working-memory load and retrieval. *Journal of Experimental Psychology: Learning Memory and Cognition, 31*, 703–713.

Morey, C. C., Morey, R. D., van der Reijden, M., & Holweg, M. (2013). Asymmetric cross-domain interference between two working memory tasks: Implications for models of working memory. *Journal of Memory and Language, 69*, 324–348.

Morra, S. (1994). Issues in working memory measurement: Testing for M capacity. *International Journal of Behavioural Development, 17*, 143–159.

Morra, S., Gobbo, C., Marini, Z., & Sheese, R. (2008). *Cognitive development: Neo-Piagetian perspectives*. New York: Erlbaum.

Morsanyi, K., & Handley, S. J. (2008). How smart do you need to be to get it wrong? The role of cognitive capacity in the development of heuristic-based judgment. *Journal of Experimental Child Psychology, 99*, 18–36.

Morton, J. B., & Munakata, Y. (2002a). Active versus latent representations: A neural network model of perseveration, dissociation, and decalage. *Developmental Psychobiology, 40*, 255–265.

Morton, J. B., & Munakata, Y. (2002b). Are you listening? Exploring a knowledge action dissociation in a speech interpretation task. *Developmental Science, 5*, 435–440.

Mosse, E. K., & Jarrold, C. (2008). Hebb learning, verbal short-term memory, and the acquisition of phonological forms in children. *The Quarterly Journal of Experimental Psychology, 61*, 505–514.

Mosse, E. K., & Jarrold, C. (2010). Searching for the Hebb effect in Down syndrome: Evidence for a dissociation between verbal short-term memory and domain-general learning of serial order. *Journal of Intellectual Disability Research, 54*, 295–307.

Müller, U., Dick, A. S., Gela, K., Overton, W. F., & Zelazo, P. D. (2006). The role of negative priming in preschoolers' flexible rule use on the Dimensional Change Card Sort task. *Child Development, 77*, 395–412.

Munakata, Y. (2001). Graded representations in behavioral dissociations. *Trends in Cognitive Sciences, 5*, 309–315.

Munakata, Y., & Yerys, B. E. (2001). When dissociations between knowledge and action disappear. *Psychological Science, 12*, 335–337.

Munakata, Y., McClelland, J. L., Johnson, M. H., & Siegler, R. (1997). Rethinking infant knowledge: Toward an adaptive process account of successes and failures in object permanence tasks. *Psychological Review, 104*, 686–713.

198 References

Munakata, Y., Morton, J. B., & Yerys, B. E. (2003). Children's perseveration: Attentional inertia and alternative accounts. *Developmental Science, 6,* 471–473.

Munakata, Y., Snyder, H. R., & Chatham, C. H. (2012). Developing cognitive control. *Current Directions in Psychological Science, 21,* 71–77.

Nadler, R. T., & Archibald, L. M. D. (2014). The assessment of verbal and visuospatial working memory with school age Canadian children. *Canadian Journal of Speech-Language Pathology and Audiology, 38,* 262–279.

Nagy, Z., Westerberg, H., & Klingberg, T. (2004). Maturation of white matter is associated with the development of cognitive functions during childhood. *Journal of Cognitive Neuroscience, 16,* 1227–1233.

Naus, M. J., Ornstein, P. A., Aivano, S. (1977). Developmental changes in memory: The effects of processing time and rehearsal instructions. *Journal of Experimental Child Psychology, 23,* 237–251.

Navon, D. (1984). Resources: A theoretical soup stone? *Psychological Review, 91,* 216–234.

Nelson, K. E., & Kosslyn, S. M. (1975). Semantic retrieval in children and adults. *Developmental Psychology, 11,* 807–813.

Newcombe, N., Huttenlocher, J., & Learmonth, A. (1999). Infants' coding of location in continuous space. *Infant Behavior and Development, 22*(4), 483–510.

Newell, A., Shaw, J. C., & Simon, H. A. (1958). Chess-playing programs and the problem of complexity. *IBM Journal of Research and Development, 2,* 320–335.

Nicolson, R. (1981). The relationship between memory span and processing speed. In M. Friedman, J. P. Das, and N. O'Connor (Eds.), *Intelligence and learning* (pp. 179–184). New York: Plenum Press.

Nigg, J. T., & Casey, B. J. (2005). An integrative theory of attention-deficit/hyperactivity disorder based on the cognitive and affective neurosciences. *Development and Psychopathology, 17,* 785–806.

Norman, D. A., & Shallice, T. (1986). Attention to action: Willed and automatic control of behavior. In R. J. Davidson, G. E. Schwartz, & D. Shapiro (Eds.), *Consciousness and self-regulation.* New York: Plenum Press.

Oakes, L. M., & Luck, S. J. (2014). Short-term memory in infancy. In P. J. Bauer & R. Fivush (Eds.), *The Wiley handbook on the development of children's memory* (pp. 157–180). Malden, MA: John Wiley & Sons.

Oakes, L. M., Ross-Sheehy, S., & Luck, S. J. (2006). Rapid development of feature binding in visual short-term memory. *Psychological Science, 17*(9), 781–787.

Oberauer, K. (2002). Access to information in working memory: Exploring the focus of attention. *Journal of Experimental Psychology: Learning, Memory, and Cognition, 28,* 411–421.

Oberauer, K. (2009). Design for a working memory. *Psychology of Learning and Motivation, 51,* 45–100.

Oberauer, K., & Bialkova, S. (2009). Accessing information in working memory: Can the focus of attention grasp two elements at the same time? *Journal of Experimental Psychology: General, 138,* 64–87.

Oberauer, K., & Bialkova, S. (2011). Serial and parallel processes in working memory after practice. *Journal of Experimental Psychology: Human Perception and Performance, 37,* 606–614.

Oberauer, K., & Eichenberger, S. (2013). Visual working memory declines when more features must be remembered for each object. *Memory and Cognition, 41,* 1212–1227.

Oftinger, A.-L., & Camos, V. (2016). Maintenance mechanisms in children's verbal working memory. *Journal of Educational and Developmental Psychology, 6,* 16–28.

Oftinger, A.-L., & Camos, V. (2017). Developmental improvement in strategies to maintain verbal information in children's working memory. *International Journal of Behavioral Development,* in press.

Olson, D. R. (1993). The development of representations: The origins of mental life. *Canadian Psychology, 34*, 293–304.

Ornstein, P. A., & Naus, M. J. (1978). Rehearsal processes in children's memory. In P. A. Ornstein (Ed.), *Memory development in children* (pp. 69–99). Hillsdale, NJ: Lawrence Erlbaum Associates.

Ornstein, P. A., Naus, M. J., & Liberty, C. (1975). Rehearsal and organizational processes in children's memory. *Child Development, 46*, 818–830.

Orsini, A. (1994). Corsi's block-tapping test: Standardisation and concurrent validity with WISC-R for children aged 11 to 16. *Perceptual and Motor Skills, 79*, 1547–1554.

Orsini, A., Grossi, D., Capitabi, E., Laiacona, M., Papagno, C., & Vallar, G. (1987). Verbal and spatial immediate memory span: Normative data from 1355 adults and 1112 children. *Italian Journal of Neurological Science, 8*, 539–548.

Ottem, E. J., Lian, A., & Karlsen, P. J. (2007) Reasons for the growth of traditional memory span across age. *European Journal of Cognitive Psychology, 19*(2), 233–270.

Page, M. P. A., & Norris, D. (1998). The primacy model: A new model of immediate serial recall. *Psychological Review, 105*, 761–781.

Palmer, S. (2000a). Working memory: A developmental study of phonological recoding. *Memory, 8*, 179–193.

Palmer, S. (2000b). Development of phonological recoding and literacy acquisition: A four-year cross-sequential study. *British Journal of Developmental Psychology, 18*, 533–555.

Parkin, A. J. (1998). The central executive does not exist. *Journal of the International Neuropsychological Society, 4*, 518–522.

Pascual-Leone, J. A. (1970). A mathematical model for the transition rule in Piaget's developmental stage. *Acta Psychologica, 32*, 301–345.

Pascual-Leone, J. A. (1978). Compounds, confounds, and models in developmental information processing: A reply to critics. *Journal of Experimental Child Psychology, 26*, 18–40.

Pascual-Leone, J. A. (1988). Organismic processes for Neo-Piagetian theories: A dialectical causal account of cognitive development. In A. Demetriou (Ed.), *The neo-Piagetian theories of cognitive development: Toward an integration* (pp. 25–64). Amsterdam: Elsevier.

Pascual-Leone, J. A. (1995). Learning and development as dialectical factors in cognitive growth. *Human Development, 38*, 338–348.

Pascual-Leone, J. A. (1996). Vygotsky, Piaget, and the problems of Plato. *Swiss Journal of Psychology, 55*, 84–92.

Pascual-Leone, J. A., & Baillargeon, R. (1994). Developmental measurement of mental attention. *International Journal of Behavioral Development, 17*, 161–200.

Pascual-Leone, J. A., & Goodman, D. (1979). Intelligence and experience. *Instructional Science, 8*, 301–367.

Pascual-Leone, J. A., & Johnson, J. (1999). A dialectical constructivist view of representation: Role of mental attention, executives, and symbols. In I. E. Sigel (Ed.), *Development of mental representation: Theories and applications* (pp. 169–200). Mahwah, NJ: Lawrence Erlbaum.

Pascual-Leone, J. A., & Johnson, J. (2011). A developmental theory of mental attention: Its applications to measurement and task analysis. In P. Barrouillet & V. Gaillard (Eds.), *Cognitive development and working memory* (pp. 47–68). Hove, UK: Psychology Press.

Pashler, H. E. (1998). *The psychology of attention*. Cambridge, MA: MIT Press.

Pears, R., & Bryant, P. E. (1990). Transitive inference by young children about spatial position. *British Journal of Psychology, 81*, 497–510.

Pelphrey, K. A., & Reznick, J. S. (2003). Working memory in infancy. In R. Kail (Ed.), *Advances in child development and behavior* (Vol. 31, pp. 173–227). New York: Academic Press.

200 References

Peng, P., Namkung, J., Barnes, M., & Sun, C. (2016). A meta-analysis of mathematics and working memory: Moderating effects of working memory domain, type of mathematics skill, and sample characteristics. *Journal of Educational Psychology, 108*(4), 455–473.

Pennings, A. H., & Hessels, M. G. P. (1996). The measurement of mental attentional capacity: A neo-piagetian developmental study. *Intelligence, 23*, 59–78.

Pennington, B. F. (1997). Dimensions of executive functions in normal and abnormal development. In N. Krasnegor, R. Lyon, & P. Goldman-Rakic (Eds.), *Development of the prefrontal cortex: Evolution, neurobiology, and behavior* (pp. 265–281). Baltimore: Brookes.

Pennington, B. F., & Ozonoff, S. (1996). Executive functions and developmental psychopathology. *Journal of Child Psychology and Psychiatry, 37*, 51–87.

Perner, J. (1991). *Understanding the representational mind.* Cambridge, MA: MIT Press.

Perner, J. (1998). The meta-intentional nature of executive functions and theory of mind. In P. Carruthers & J. Boucher (Eds.), *Language and thought: Interdisciplinary themes* (pp. 270–283). Cambridge, UK: Cambridge University Press.

Perner, J., & Lang, B. (2002). What causes 3-year-olds' difficulty on the dimensional change card sorting task? *Infant and Child Development, 11*, 93–105.

Perner, J., Stummer, S., & Lang, B. (1999). Executive functions and theory of mind: Cognitive complexity or functional dependence? In P. D. Zelazo, J. W. Astington, & D. R. Olson (Eds.), *Developing theories of intention: Social understanding and self-control* (pp. 133–152). Mahwah, NJ: Erlbaum.

Perner, J., Stummer, S., Sprung, M., & Doherty, M. (2002). Theory of mind finds its Piagetian perspective: Why alternative naming comes with understanding belief. *Cognitive Development, 17*, 1451–1472.

Perruchet, P., & Vinter, A. (2002). The self-organizing consciousness. *Behavioral and Brain Sciences, 25*, 297–388.

Petrides, M., & Milner, B. (1982). Deficits on subject ordered tasks after frontal- and temporal-lobe lesions in man. *Neuropsychologia, 20*, 249–262.

Piaget, J. (1921). Essai sur quelques aspects du développement de la notion de partie chez l'enfant. *Journal de Psychologie, 18*, 449–480.

Piaget, J. (1923). *Le langage et la pensée chez l'enfant.* Neuchâtel: Delachaux et Niestlé.

Piaget, J. (1924/1959). *Le jugement et le raisonnement chez l'enfant.* Neuchâtel: Delachaux et Niestlé.

Piaget, J. (1937/1954). *The construction of reality in the child.* New York, NY: Basic.

Piaget, J. (1941). Le mécanisme du développement mental et les lois du groupement des opérations: esquisse d'une théorie opératoire de l'intelligence. *Archives de psychologie, 28*(112), 215–285.

Piaget, J. (1945/1962). *Play dreams and imitation in childhood.* New York: Norton.

Piaget, J. (1950). *The psychology of intelligence.* London: Routledge.

Piaget, J. (1956). Les stades du développement intellectual de l'enfant et de l'adolescent. In P. Osterrieth, J. Piaget, R. Saussure, J. Tanner, H. Wallon, R. Zazzo et al. (Eds.), *Le problème des stades en psychologie de l'enfant* (pp. 33–42). Paris: Presses Universitaires de France.

Piaget, J. (1966). *La psychologie de l'enfant.* Paris: Presses Universitaires de France.

Piaget, J. (1969). *The psychology of the child* (translated by H. Weaver). New York: Basic Books.

Piaget, J. (1971). *The language and thought of the child* (translated by M. and R. Gabain). London: Routledge & Kegan Paul.

Piaget, J. (1973). *Memory and intelligence* (translated by A. J. Pomeranz). New York: Basic Books.

Piaget, J. (1975). *L'équilibration des structures cognitives: Problème central du développement.* Paris: Presses Universitaires de France.

Piaget, J. (1985). *The equilibration of cognitive structures: The central problem of intellectual development* (translated by T. Brown and K. J. Thampy). Chicago: University of Chicago Press.

Piaget, J., & Inhelder, B. (1951). *La genèse de l'idée de hasard chez l'enfant.* Paris: Presses Universitaires de France.

Piaget, J., & Inhelder, B. (1959). *La genèse des structures logiques élémentaires: Classifications et sériations.* Neuchâtel: Delachaux et Niestlé.

Piaget, J., & Inhelder, B. (1964). *The early growth of logic in the child: Classification and seriation* (translated by E. A. Lunzer and D. Papert). London: Routledge & Kegan Paul.

Piaget, J., & Inhelder, B. (1966). *La psychologie de l'enfant.* Paris: Presses Universitaires de France.

Piaget, J., & Inhelder, B. (1968). *Mémoire et intelligence.* Paris: Presses Universitaires de France.

Pickering, S. J. (2006). *Working memory and education.* Oxford: Academic Press.

Pickering, S. J., Gathercole, S. E., & Peaker, S. M. (1998). Verbal and visuospatial short-term memory in children: Evidence for common and distinct mechanisms. *Memory and Cognition, 26,* 1117–1130.

Pire, G. (1958). Notion du hazard et développement intellectuel. *Enfance, 2,* 131–143.

Popper, K. R. (1968). Conjecture and refutations: The growth of scientific knowledge. New York: Harper.

Portrat, S., Camos, V., & Barrouillet, P. (2009). Working memory in children: A time-related functioning similar to adults. *Journal of Experimental Child Psychology, 102,* 368–374.

Pribram, K. H. (1973). The primate frontal cortex-executive of the brain. In K. H. Pribram & A. R. Luria (Eds.), *Psychophysiology of the frontal lobes* (pp. 293–314). New York: Academic Press.

Pribram, K. H. (1976). Executive functions of the frontal lobes. In T. Desiraju (Ed.), *Mechanisms in transmission of signals for conscious behaviour* (pp. 303–320). Amsterdam: Elsevier.

Rabinowicz, T. (1980). The differentiate maturation of the human cerebral cortex. In F. Falkner & J. M. Tanner (Eds.), *Human Growth, Vol. 3: Neurobiology and Nutrition* (pp. 97–123). New York: Plenum Press.

Raghubar, K. P., Barnes, M. A., & Hecht, S. A. (2010). Working memory and mathematics: A review of developmental, individual difference, and cognitive approaches. *Learning and Individual Differences, 20,* 110–122.

Raven, J. C., Court, J. H., & Raven, J. (1977). *Standard progressive matrices.* London: H. K. Lewis & Co.

Redick, T. S., Shipstead, Z., Harrison, T. L., Hicks, K. L., Fried, D. E., Hambrick, D. Z., et al. (2013). No evidence of intelligence improvement after working memory training: A randomized, placebo-controlled study. *Journal of Experimental Psychology: General, 142,* 359–379.

Repovs, G., & Baddeley, A. D. (2006). The multi-component model of working memory: Explorations in experimental cognitive psychology. *Neuroscience, 139,* 5–21.

Reyna, V. F., & Brainerd, C. J. (1994). The origins of probability judgment: A review of data and theories. In G. Wright & P. Ayton (Eds.), *Subjective probability* (pp. 239–272). New York: Wiley.

Reyna, V. F., & Brainerd, C. J. (1995). Fuzzy-trace theory: An interim synthesis. *Learning and Individual Differences, 7,* 1–75.

Reyna, V. F., & Brainerd, C. J. (2011). Dual processes in decision making and developmental neuroscience: A fuzzy-trace model. *Developmental Review, 31,* 180–206.

Reyna, V. F., & Farley, F. (2006). Risk and rationality in adolescent decision making: Implications for theory, practice, and public policy. *Psychological Science in the Public Interest, 7,* 1–44.

Reyna, V. F., Estrada, S. M., DeMarinis, J. A., Myers, R. M., Stanisz, J. M., & Mills, B. A. (2011). Neurobiological and memory models of risky decision making in adolescents versus young adults. *Journal of Experimental Psychology: Learning, Memory, and Cognition, 37*, 1125–1142.

Reznick, J. S. (2007). Working memory in infants and toddlers. In L. M. Oakes & P. J. Bauer (Eds.), *Short- and long-term memory in infancy and early childhood: Taking the first step toward remembering* (pp. 3–26). Oxford, UK: Oxford University Press.

Reznick, J. S. (2014). Methodological challenges in the study of short-term working memory in infants. In P. J. Bauer & R. Fivush (Eds.), *The Wiley handbook on the development of children's memory* (Vol. 1, pp. 181–201). Malden, MA: John Wiley & Sons.

Reznick, J. S., Corley, R., & Robinson, J. (1997). *A longitudinal twin study of intelligence in the second year*. Monographs of the Society for Research in Child Development, 62 (1, Serial No. 249).

Reznick, J. S., Morrow, J. D., Goldman, B. D., & Snyder, J. (2004). The onset of working memory in infants. *Infancy, 6*, 145–154.

Riggs, K. J., McTaggart, J., Simpson, A., & Freeman, R. P. J. (2006). Changes in the capacity of visual working memory in 5- to 10-year-olds. *Journal of Experimental Child Psychology, 95*, 18–26.

Riggs, K. J., Simpson, A., & Potts, T. (2011). The development of visual short-term memory for multifeature items during middle childhood. *Journal of Experimental Child Psychology, 108*, 802–809.

Riley, C. A., & Trabasso, T. R. (1974). Comparatives, logical structures and encoding in a transitive inference task. *Journal of Experimental Child Psychology, 17*, 187–203.

Rips, L. J. (1994). *The psychology of proof*. Cambridge, MA: MIT Press.

Robin, N., & Holyoak, K. J. (1995). Relational complexity and the functions of prefrontal cortex. In M. Gazzaniga (Ed.), *The cognitive neurosciences* (pp. 987–997). Cambridge, MA: MIT Press.

Rochat, P. (2015). Layers of awareness in development. *Developmental Review, 38*, 122–145.

Romani, C., McAlpine, S., Olson, A., Tsouknida, E., & Martin, R. (2005). Length, lexicality, and articulatory suppression in immediate recall: Evidence against the articulatory loop. *Journal of Memory and Language, 52*, 398–415.

Roodenrys, S., Hulme, C., & Brown, G. (1993). The development of short-term memory: Separable effects of speech rate and long-term memory. *Journal of Experimental Child Psychology, 56*, 431–442.

Rose, S. A., Feldman, J. F., & Jankowski, J. J. (2003). Visual short-term memory in the first year of life: Capacity and recency effects. *Developmental Psychology, 37*, 539–549.

Rose, S. A., Feldman, J. F., Jankowski, J. J, & Van Rossem, R. (2011). The structure of memory in infants and toddlers: A SEM study with full-terms and preterms. *Developmental Science, 14*(1), 83–91.

Rosen, V. M., & Engle, R. W. (1997). The role of working memory capacity in retrieval. *Journal of Experimental Psychology: General, 126*, 211–227.

Ross-Sheehy, S., Oakes, L. M., & Luck, S. J. (2003). The development of visual short-term memory capacity in infants. *Child Development, 74*, 1807–1822.

Ross-Sheehy, S., Oakes, L. M., & Luck, S. J. (2011). Exogenous attention influences visual short-term memory in infants. *Developmental Science, 14*(3), 490–501.

Rouder, J. N., Morey, R. D., Cowan, N., Zwilling, C. E., Morey, C. C., & Pratte, M. S. (2008). An assessment of fixed-capacity models of visual working memory. *Proceedings of the National Academy of Sciences USA (PNAS), 105*, 5975–5979.

Roy, P., & Chiat, S. (2004). A prosodically controlled word and non-word repetition task for 2- to 4-year-olds: Evidence from typically developing children. *Journal of Speech, Language and Hearing Research, 47*, 223–234.

Russell, J. (1981). Children's memory for premises in a transitive measurement task assessed by elicited and spontaneous justifications. *Journal of Experimental Child Psychology, 31*, 300–309.

Russell, J., Mauthner, N., Sharpe, S., & Tidswell, T. (1991). The 'windows task' as a measure of strategic deception in preschoolers and autistic subjects. *British Journal of Developmental Psychology, 9*, 331–349.

Sabbagh, M. A., Xu, F., Carlson, S. M., Moses, L. J., & Lee, K. (2006). The development of executive functioning and theory of mind: A comparison of Chinese and US pre-schoolers. *Psychological Science, 17*, 74–81.

Salthouse, T. A. (1996). The processing speed theory of adult age differences in cognition. *Psychological Review, 103*, 403–428.

Sarigiannidis, I., Crickmore, G., Astle, D. E. (2016). Developmental and individual differences in the precision of visuospatial memory. *Cognitive Development, 39*, 1–12.

Saults, J. S., & Cowan, N. (1996). The development of memory for ignored speech. *Journal of Experimental Child Psychology, 63*, 239–261.

Saults, J. S., & Cowan, N. (2007). A central capacity limit to the simultaneous storage of visual and auditory arrays in working memory. *Journal of Experimental Psychology: General, 136*, 663–684.

Schneider, W. (1985). Developmental trends in the metamemory–memory relationship: An integrative review. In D. L. Forrest-Pressley, G. E. MacKinnon, and T. G. Waller (Eds.), *Metacognition, cognition, and human performance* (Vol. 1, pp. 57–109). New York: Academic Press.

Schneider, W., & Pressley, M. (1997). *Memory development between two and twenty* (2nd ed.). Mahwah, NJ: Erlbaum.

Schneider, W., Gruber, H., Gold, A., & Opwis, K. (1993). Chess expertise and memory for chess positions in children and adults. *Journal of Experimental Child Psychology, 56*, 328–349.

Schneider, W., Kron, V., Hünnerkopf, M., & Krajewski, K. (2004). The development of young children's memory strategies: First findings from the Würzburg Longitudinal Memory Study. *Journal of Experimental Child Psychology, 88*, 193–209.

Schwartz, B. B., & Reznick, J. S. (1999). Measuring infant spatial working memory with a windows and curtains delayed-response procedure. *Memory, 7*, 1–17.

Senn, T. E., Espy, K. A., & Kaufmann, P. M. (2004). Using path analysis to understand executive function organization in preschool children. *Developmental Neuropsychology, 26*, 445–464.

Shah, P., & Miyake, A. (1999). *Models of working memory*. New York: Cambridge University Press.

Shallice, T. (1988). *From neuropsychology to mental structure*. New York: Cambridge University Press.

Shipstead, Z., Harrison, T. L., & Engle, R. W. (2016). Working memory capacity and fluid intelligence: Maintenance and disengagement. *Psychological Science, 11*, 771–799.

Shipstead, Z., Lindsey, D. R. B., Marshall, R. L., & Engle, R. W. (2014). The mechanisms of working memory capacity: Primary memory, secondary memory, and attention control. *Journal of Memory and Language, 72*, 116–141.

Shipstead, Z., Redick, T. S., & Engle, R. W. (2012). Is working memory training effective? *Psychological Bulletin, 138*, 628–654.

Shipstead, Z., Redick, T. S., Hicks, K. L., & Engle, R. W. (2012). The scope and control of attention as separate aspects of working memory. *Memory, 20*, 608–628.

204 References

Shore, D. I., Burack, J. A., Miller, D., Joseph, S., & Enns, J. T. (2006). The development of change detection. *Developmental Science, 9*, 490–497.

Shrager, J., & Siegler, R. S. (1998). SCADS: A model of children's strategy choices and strategy discoveries. *Psychological Science, 9*, 405–410.

Siegel, L. S. (1994). Working memory and reading: A life-span perspective. *International Journal of Behavioral Development, 17*, 109–124.

Siegler, R. S. (1976). Three aspects of cognitive development. *Cognitive Psychology, 8*, 481–520.

Siegler, R. S. (1978). *Children's thinking: What develops?* Hillsdale, NJ: Erlbaum.

Siegler, R. S. (1996). *Emerging minds: The process of change in children's thinking.* Oxford, UK: Oxford University Press.

Siegler, R. S., & Robinson, M. (1982). The development of numerical understandings. In H. W. Reese & L. P. Lipsitt (Eds.), *Advances in child development and behaviour* (Vol. 16, pp. 241–312). New York: Academic Press.

Siegler, R. S., & Shrager, J. (1984). Strategy choices in addition and subtraction: How do children know what to do? In C. Sophian (Ed.), *Origins of cognitive skills* (pp. 229–293). Hillsdale, NJ: Lawrence Erlbaum Associates.

Simmering, V. R. (2012). The development of visual working memory capacity in early childhood. *Journal of Experimental Child Psychology, 111*, 695–707.

Simmering, V. R. (2016). Working memory capacity in context: Modeling dynamic processes of behavior, memory, and development. *Monographs of the Society for Research in Child Development, 81*, 7–148.

Simmering, V. R., & Patterson, R. (2012). Models provide specificity: Testing a proposed mechanism of visual working memory capacity development. *Cognitive Development, 27*, 419–439.

Simon, H. A. (1962). An information processing theory of intellectual development. In W. Kessen & C. Kuhlman (Eds.), *Thought in the young child* (pp. 150–161). Yellow Springs, OH: The Antioch Press.

Simon, H. A. (1969). *The sciences of artificial.* Cambridge, MA: MIT Press.

Smith, L. B., Thelen, E., Titzer, R., & McLin, D. (1999). Knowing in the context of acting: The task dynamics of the a-not-b error. *Psychological Review, 106*, 235–260.

Snowling, M., Chiat, S., & Hulme, C. (1991). Words, nonwords and phonological process: Some comments on Gathercole, Willis, Emslie and Baddeley. *Applied Psycholinguistics, 12*, 369–373.

Snyder, H. R., & Munakata, Y. (2010). Becoming self-directed: Abstract representations support endogenous flexibility in children. *Cognition, 116*, 155–167.

Somsen, R. J. M. (2007). The development of attention regulation in the Wisconsin Card Sorting Task. *Developmental Science, 10*, 664–680.

Spelke, E. S. (1988). Where perceiving ends and thinking begins: The apprehension of objects in infancy. In A. Yonas (Ed.), *Perceptual development in infancy: The Minnesota symposia in child psychology* (pp. 197–234). Hillsdale, NJ: Lawrence Erlbaum Associates.

Sperling, G. (1960). The information available in brief visual presentations. *Psychological Monographs, 74*(11, No. 498), 1–29.

St Clair-Thompson, H., Stevens, R., Hunt, A., & Bolder, E. (2010). Improving children's working memory and classroom performance. *Educational Psychology, 30*, 203–219.

Standing, L., & Curtis, L. (1989). Subvocalization rate versus other predictors of the memory span. *Psychological Reports, 65*, 487–495.

Stanovich, K. E. (1999). *Who is rational? Studies of individual differences in reasoning.* Mahway, NJ: Lawrence Elrbaum Associates.

Stanovich, K. E. (2010). *Rationality and the reflective mind.* New York: Oxford University Press.

Stanovich, K. E., West, R. F., & Toplak, M. E. (2011). The complexity of developmental predictions from dual process models. *Developmental Review, 31*, 103–118.

Stern, W. (1924). *Psychology of early childhood up to the sixth year of age.* New York: Holt.

Sternberg, R. J. (2008). Increasing fluid intelligence is possible after all. *Proceedings of the National Academy of Sciences of the United States of America (PNAS), 105*, 6791–6792.

Sternberg, S. (1966). High-speed scanning in human memory. *Science, 153*, 652–654.

Stuss, D. T., & Benson, D. F. (1986). *The frontal lobes.* New York: Raven Press.

Stuss, D. T., Alexander, M., Floden, D., Binns, M., Levine, B., McIntosh, A., et al. (2002). Fractionation and localization of distinct frontal lobe processes: Evidence from focal lesions in humans. In D. Stuss & R. Knight (Eds.), *Principles of frontal lobe function* (pp. 392–407). New York: Oxford University Press.

Swanson, H. L. (2011). Intellectual growth in children as a function of domain specific and domain general working memory subgroups. *Intelligence, 39*, 481–492.

Swanson, H. L. (2017). Verbal and visual-spatial working memory: What develops over a life span? *Developmental Psychology, 53*, 971–995.

Szmalec, A., Brysbaert, M., & Duyck, W. (2011). Working memory and (second) language processing. In J. Altarriba & L. Isurin (Eds.), *Memory, language, and bilingualism: Theoretical and applied approaches* (pp. 74–94). New York: Cambridge University Press.

Tam, H., Jarrold, C., Baddeley, A. D., & Sabatos-DeVito, M. (2010). The development of memory maintenance: Children's use of phonological rehearsal and attentional refreshment in working memory tasks. *Journal of Experimental Child Psychology, 107*, 306–324.

Thevenot, C., Barrouillet, P., & Fayol, M. (2001). Algorithmic solution of arithmetic problems and operands–answer associations in long-term memory. *Quarterly Journal of Experimental Psychology, 54*, 599–611.

Thompson, P. M., Giedd, J. N., Woods, R. P., MacDonald, D., Evans, A. C., & Toga, A. W. (2000). Growth patterns in the developing brain detected by using continuum mechanical tensor maps. *Nature, 404*, 190–193.

Thomson, J. M., Richardson, U., & Goswami, U. (2005). Phonological similarity neighborhoods and children's short-term memory: Typical development and dyslexia. *Memory and Cognition, 33*, 1210–1219.

Tipper, S. P., Bourque, T. A., Anderson, S. H., & Brehaut, J. C. (1989). Mechanisms of attention: A developmental study. *Journal of Experimental Child Psychology, 48*, 353–378.

Towse, J. N., & Hitch, G. J. (1995). Is there a relationship between task demand and storage space in tests of working memory capacity? *Quarterly Journal of Experimental Psychology, 48*, 108–124.

Towse, J. N., & Houston-Price, C. M. T. (2001). Reflections on the concept of central executive. In J. Andrade (Ed.), *Working memory in perspective* (pp. 240–260). Philadelphia, PA: Psychology Press.

Towse, J. N., Hitch, G. J., & Hutton, U. (1998). A reevaluation of working memory capacity in children. *Journal of Memory and Language, 39*, 195–217.

Towse, J. N., Hitch, G. J., & Hutton, U. (2000). On the interpretation of working memory spans in adults. *Memory and Cognition, 28*, 341–348.

Towse, J. N., Hitch, G. J., & Hutton, U. (2002). On the nature of the relationship between processing activity and item retention in children. *Journal of Experimental Child Psychology, 82*, 156–184.

Towse, J. N., Hitch, G. J., & Skeates, S. (1999). Developmental sensitivity to temporal grouping effects in short-term memory. *International Journal of Behavioral Development, 23*, 391–411.

Towse, J. N., Lewis, C., & Knowles, M. (2007). When knowledge is not enough: The phenomenon of goal neglect in preschool children. *Journal of Experimental Child Psychology, 96*, 320–332.

Towse, J. N., Redbond, J., Houston-Price, C. M. T., & Cook, S. (2000). Understanding the dimensional change card sort: Perspectives from task success and failure. *Cognitive Development, 15*, 347–365.

Trabasso, T. (1975a). Representation, memory and reasoning: How do we make transitive inferences? In A. D. Pick (Ed.), *Minnesota symposia on child psychology* (Vol. 9, pp. 135–172). Minneapolis: University of Minnesota Press.

Trabasso, T. (1975b). The role of memory as a system in making transitive inferences. In R. V. Kail, Jr. & J. W. Hagen (Eds.), *Perpectives on the development of memory and cognition* (pp. 333–366). Hillsdale, NJ: Lawrence Erlbaum.

Trabasso, T. (1977). The role of memory as a system in making transitive inferences. In R. V. Kail & J. W. Hagen (Eds.), *Perspectives on the development of memory and cognition* (pp. 333–366). Hillsdale, NJ: Lawrence Erlbaum.

Trabasso, T. (1978). On the estimation of parameters and evaluation of a mathematical model: A reply to Pascual-Leone. *Journal of Experimental Child Psychology, 26*, 41–45.

Trabasso, T., & Foellinger, D. B. (1978). Information processing capacity in children: A test of Pascual-Leone's model. *Journal of Experimental Child Psychology, 26*, 1–17.

Trabasso, T., Riley, C., & Wilson, E. (1975). The representation of linear and spatial strategies in reasoning: A developmental study. In R. J. Falmagne (Ed.), *Reasoning: Representation and process in children and adults* (pp. 201–229). Hillsdale, NJ: Lawrence Erlbaum.

Trost, S., & Gruber, O. (2012). Evidence for a double dissociation of articulatory rehearsal and non-articulatory maintenance of phonological information in human verbal working memory. *Neuropsychobiology, 65*, 133–140.

Turing, A. M. (1950). Computing machinery and intelligence. *Mind, 59*, 433–460.

Turner, J. E., Henry, L. A., Brown, P., & Smith, P. T. (2004). Redintegration and lexicality effects in children: Do they depend upon the demands of the memory task? *Memory and Cognition, 32*, 501–510.

Turner, J. E., Henry, L. A., & Smith, P. T. (2000). The development of the use of long-term knowledge to assist short-term recall. *Quarterly Journal of Experimental Psychology, 53A*, 457–478.

Turner, M. L., & Engle, R. W. (1989). Is working memory capacity task dependent? *Journal of Memory and Language, 28*, 127–154.

Van Leijenhorst, L., Crone, E. A., & van der Molen, M. W. (2007). Developmental trajectories for object and spatial working memory: A psychophysiological analysis. *Child Development, 78*, 987–1000.

Vergauwe, E., Barrouillet, P., & Camos, V. (2009). Visual and spatial working memory are not that dissociated after all: A Time-Based Resource-Sharing account. *Journal of Experimental Psychology: Learning, Memory, and Cognition, 35*, 1012–1028.

Vergauwe, E., Barrouillet, P., & Camos, V. (2010). Verbal and visuo-spatial working memory: A case for domain-general Time-Based Resource Sharing. *Psychological Science, 21*, 384–390.

Vergauwe, E., Camos, V., & Barrouillet, P. (2014). The impact of storage on processing: Implications for structure and functioning of working memory. *Journal of Experimental Psychology: Learning, Memory, and Cognition, 40*(4), 1072–1095.

Visu-Petra, L., Cheie, L., & Benga, O. (2008). Short-term memory performance and metamemory judgments in preschool and early school-age children: A quantitative and qualitative analysis. *Cognition, Brain, Behavior, 12*, 71–101.

Vogel, E. K., & Awh, E. (2008). How to exploit diversity for scientific gain: Using individual differences to constrain cognitive theory. *Current Directions in Psychological Science, 17,* 171–176.

von Fersen, L., Wynne, C. D. L., Delius, J. D., & Staddon, J. E. R. (1991). Transitive inference formation in pigeons. *Journal of Experimental Psychology: Animal Behavior Processes, 17,* 334–341.

Vygotsky, L. S. (1934/1962). *Thought and language.* Cambridge, MA: MIT Press.

Walker, P., Hitch, G. J., Doyle, A., & Porter, T. (1994). The development of short-term visual memory in young children. *International Journal of Behavioural Development, 17,* 73–89.

Wallon, H. (1945). *Les origines de la pensée chez l'enfant.* Paris: PUF.

Wang, X., Logie, R. H., & Jarrold, C. (2016). Interpreting potential markers of storage and rehearsal: Implications for studies of verbal short-term memory and neuropsychological cases. *Memory and Cognition, 44,* 910–921.

Ward, H., Shum, D., McKinlay, L., Baker-Tweney, H., & Wallace, G. (2005). Development of prospective memory: Tasks based on the prefrontal-lobe model. *Child Neuropsychology, 11,* 527–549.

Waugh, N. C., & Norman, D. A. (1965). Primary memory. *Journal of Experimental Psychology, 72,* 89–104.

White, S. H. (1965). Evidence for a hierarchical arrangement of learning processes. In L. P. Lipsitt & C. C. Spiker (Eds.), *Advances in child development and behaviour* (Vol. 2, pp. 59–96). New York: Academic Press.

Wilcox, T., Nadel, L., & Rosser, R. (1996). Location memory in healthy preterm and full-term infants. *Infant Behavior and Development, 19,* 309–323.

Wilson, J. T. L., Scott, J. H., & Power, K. G. (1987). Developmental differences in the span of visual memory for pattern. *British Journal of Developmental Psychology, 5,* 249–255.

Wimmer, H., and Perner, J. (1983). Beliefs about beliefs: Representation and constraining function of wrong beliefs in young children's understanding of deception. *Cognition, 13,* 103–128.

Winsler, A., & Naglieri, J. (2003). Overt and covert verbal problem-solving strategies: Developmental trends in use, awareness, and relations with task performance in children aged 5 to 17. *Child Development, 74*(3), 659–678.

Witkin, H. A., Dyk, R., B., Faterson, H. F, Goodenough, D. R., & Karp, S. A. (1962). *Psychological differentiation.* New York: Wiley.

Wright, B. C. (2001). Reconceptualizing the transitive inference ability: A framework for existing and future research. *Developmental Review, 21,* 375–422.

Wright, B. C. (2006). On the emergence of the discriminative mode for transitive-inference. *European Journal of Cognitive Psychology, 18,* 776–800.

Wright, B. C. (2012). The case for a dual-process theory of transitive reasoning. *Developmental Review, 32,* 89–124.

Wright, B. C., & Dowker, A. D. (2002). The role of cues to differential absolute size in children's transitive inferences. *Journal of Experimental Child Psychology, 81,* 249–275.

Wright, B. C., Robertson, S., & Hadfield, S. L. (2011). Transitivity for height versus speed: To what extent do the under-7s really have a transitive capacity? *Thinking and Reasoning, 17,* 57–81.

Yuzawa, M. (2001). Effects of word length on young children's memory performance. *Memory and Cognition, 29*(4), 557–564.

Zacks, R. T., & Hasher, L. (1994). Directed ignoring: Inhibitory regulation of working memory. In D. Dagenbach & T. H. Carr (Eds.), *Inhibitory mechanisms in attention, memory, and language* (pp. 241–264). San Diego, CA: Academic Press.

208 References

Zelazo, P. D. (2004). The development of conscious control in childhood. *Trends in Cognitive Sciences, 8*, 12–17.

Zelazo, P. D. (2006). The Dimensional Change Card Sort (DCCS): A method of assessing executive function in children. *Nature Protocols, 1*, 297–301.

Zelazo, P. D. (2015). Executive function: Reflection, iterative reprocessing, complexity, and the developing brain. *Developmental Review, 38*, 55–68.

Zelazo, P. D., & Frye, D. (1998). Cognitive complexity and control: II. The development of executive function in childhood. *Current Directions in Psychological Science, 7*, 121–126.

Zelazo, P. D., & Müller, U. (2002). Executive function in typical and atypical development. In U. Goswami (Ed.), *Handbook of childhood cognitive development* (pp. 445–469). Oxford, UK: Blackwell.

Zelazo, P. D., Carter, A., Resnick, J. S., & Frye, D. (1997). Early development of executive function: A problem-solving framework. *Review of General Psychology, 1*, 1–29.

Zelazo, P. D., Müller, U., Frye, D., & Marcovitch, S. (2003). *The development of executive function in early childhood.* Monographs of the Society for Research in Child Development, 68, 1–137.

Zelazo, P. D., Qu, L., & Müller, U. (2004). Hot and cool aspects of executive function: Relations in early development. In W. Schneider, R. Schumann-Hensteler, & B. Sodian (Eds.), *Young children's cognitive development: Interrelationships among executive function, working memory, verbal ability, and theory of mind* (pp. 71–93). Mahwah, NJ: Erlbaum.

Zelazo, P. D., Reznick, J. S., & Piñon, D. E. (1995). Response control and the execution of verbal rules. *Developmental Psychology, 31*, 508–517.

Zhang, W., & Luck, S. J. (2008). Discrete fixed-resolution representations in visual working memory. *Nature, 453*(7192), 233–235.

Zosh, J. M., & Feigenson, L. (2015). Array heterogeneity prevents catastrophic forgetting in infants. *Cognition, 136*, 365–380.

INDEX

Page numbers in *italics* denote tables, those in **bold** denote figures.

abstract goal representations 107–8
abstract shape span 92
action span tasks 27
ACT-R model 11, 135, 156, 157, 164
ADAPT model 165, 166–7
Ahmed, A. 78, 79
Alloway, T. P. 76, 91
Al-Namlah, A. S. 87, 88
Anderson, J. R. 69, 135, 164–5
Andrews, G. 35, 36, 38
A-not-B error 35, 78, 100
A-not-B task 77–9, 80–1, 100, 120
anterior prefrontal cortex 133
antisaccade task 73, 74
arithmetic, mental 57–9, **58**
articulation rate 82–6, **84**
articulatory loop 67
articulatory rehearsal 86–7, 88–9, 122,
    123–4, 133, 135, 136, 144, 146–8
Atkinson, R. C. 66
attention: controlled 41, 71–4, 95, 99;
    field of 4, 6–7; focus of 40, 41, 49, 68,
    69–70, 71, 119–21, 134–5, 162–3;
    selective 96, 99
attentional inertia 107, 109–10
attentional refreshing 133, 136, 141–8, **143**

backward digit span task 38
Baddeley, A. D. 15, 35, 37, 38, 41, 59, 63,
    65–7, 70–1, 72, 82, 83, 84, 86–7, 95,
    122, 125, 126, 130, 134

balance beam problem 24–6, **25**
balance scale problems 36
Bardikoff, N. 98
Barkley, R. A. 96, 159
Barrouillet, P. 51–2, 58–9, **58**, 65, 113–14,
    131–2, **132**, **134**, 136–7, 140–1, 142,
    143, 145–6, 147, 152, 166–7
Bayliss, D. M. 76
Bays, P. M. 93
Bertrand, R. 138–9, 146
bifocal coordination **25**, 26
binary relations 35, 36
biologically primary abilities 122
biologically secondary abilities 122
Bjorklund, D. F. 120
Bose-Einstein occupancy model 13
Bowey, J. A. 85
Brainerd, C. J. 22, 43, 44–6, 53–6, 65, 154
Brown-Peterson task 99, 147
Bryant, P. E. 46–9
Burnett Heyes, S. 93
Byrne, R. M. J. 50–1

Camos, V. **132**, 133, **134**, 138–9, 145–8, 165
Caplan, D. 59
Carey, S. 33, 81, 161
Carpenter, P. A. 38, 72
Case, R. 16–17, 19, 20, 22, 23–33, **25**,
    29, **30**, **32**, 34, 38, 40, 41, 63, 65, 95,
    104, 118, 121, 129, 135, 139, 152, 156,
    157, 160

Cattell Culture Fair test 73
CCC *see* Control Complexity and Cognitive (CCC) theory
central computing space *M* 1, 10–21, 23–4, 40–1, 117–18
central conceptual structures (CCSs) 33, 34
central executive 15, 41, 75, 97; controlled attention 41, 71–4, 95, 99; embedded-process model 68, 70; multi-component model 63, 66–7, 95; in TBRS model 150, 155–9; visuospatial storage and 91–2; *see also* executive control
central general-purpose system 39, 41
Cepeda, N. J. 111
change detection tasks 81, 90, 92
Chapman, M. 34
Chatham, C. H. 107
Chen, Z. 69–70
Chi, M. T. H. 124
chunk span and chunk size 162–4
class inclusion 9, 35, 36, 54
cognitive control *see* executive control
cognitive development: central computing space *M* 1, 10–21, 23–4, 40–1, 117–18; creation of new procedures and 164–6; dual-process theories 48–9, 55, 153–4; emergence of information processing approach 7–10; Fuzzy-Trace Theory 55–6, 57, 154; neo-Piagetian theories 1–2, 22–42, **25**, *29*, **30**, **32**, **39**, 117–18, 119–20, 121, 156–7, 160, 163; Piaget's theory ix, 1–2, 3–7, **5**, **6**, 22, 35, 40, 44–5, 156, 157; processing speed and 151–3; TBRS model and 150–68; thinking outside working memory 153–4; *see also* domain-specific developmental theories
cognitive flexibility 96, 98, 100–2, 158
cognitive load, in TBRS model 131–2, **132**, 135–7, 140–1, 142, 145–6, 147
cognitive representations 34–5
cognitive resources 117–19
cognitivism x, 3, 34
cold executive functions 96
colour discrimination task 146, 147
colour matching task (CMT) 17, 19
colour naming task 145–6
colour span task 120
complex response inhibition tasks 100
complex span tasks 72–3, 76, 90, 99, 130, 131, 133, 136–7, 139–41, 142, **143**, 145–8
complexity theories 35–7, 102–6, **103**
compound-stimuli visual information task (CSVI) 12–14, 16, 18, 19, 20

conceptual complexity, Halford's theory 34–6
concrete operational stage 9, 12, 35, 44
conditional reasoning 49–53
conditions-actions rules 11, 135
confirmatory factor analysis (CFA) 98
Conrad, R. 87
consciousness 112, 134, 151, 161
constructive operators, theory of 14–16
constructivism 4–7, 8, 34; *see also* neo-Piagetian theories
continuous operation span task 140
Control Complexity and Cognitive (CCC) theory 102–6, **103**, 107, 111
controlled attention 41, 71–4, 95, 99
Corsi block task 79, 90–1
counting span tasks 27, *29*, 31, **32**, 38, 41–2, 72, 73, 118, 121–2, 125, 129
counting speed tasks 31–3, **32**, 129
Cowan, N. 37, 40, 41, 56–7, 60, 65, 66, 67–71, 81, 86, 92, 116–17, 119, 120, 121, 123–4, 125, 126, 134, 144, 148, 149, 156–7, 162, 163
CSVI *see* compound-stimuli visual information task (CSVI)
CUCUI tasks 27–8

Daneman, M. 38, 72
Day-Night task 100, 109, 110
DCCS *see* Dimensional Change Card Sort (DCCS)
de Saint Victor, C. 79–80
décalage 10, 79, 106–7
decay of memory traces 115–17, 138–9
declarative knowledge 166–7
deductive reasoning 36, 52
delayed-response tasks 77, 80–1
Denckla, M. B. 96–7
Diamond, A. 80–1, 109, 110–11, 113
digit placement task 16–17, 19, 20
digit span tasks 38, 59, 66
Dimensional Change Card Sort (DCCS) 101, 102–4, **103**, 106, 107, 109–10, 112–13
dimensional stage 24–6, **25**, 27–8, *29*, 30–1
dimensionality of concepts 35, 36–7
direction following task (DFT) 17–18
disengagement 74
distraction 130
Doherty, M. 112
domain-specific developmental theories 23, 33, 43–60, **58**; acquisition of arithmetic facts 57–9, **58**; conditional reasoning 49–53; Fuzzy-Trace Theory 55–6, 57, 154; language learning 59–60;

probability judgements 44–6, 53, 54; reasoning-memory independence effect 53–6; transitive inference 46–9, 53–4
dorsolateral prefrontal cortex 80–1, 109
dual-process theories 48–9, 55, 153–4
Duff, S. C. 66–7, 71
Dulany, D. E. 159

egocentrism 4, 44
elaborated coordination **25**, 26
elaborative rehearsal 123, 124
embedded-process model 67–71
Engle, R. W. 41, 71–4, 95, 99
English Nonsense list 31, **32**
episodic buffer 67, 70, 134, **134**, 135, 142, 150, 151, 156, 157, 158–9, 163–4, 166
equilibration of cognitive structures ix, 4–7, **5**, **6**, 22
Ericsson, K. A. 126
Eriksen Flankers task 100
executive control 15, 95–114; of articulatory rehearsal 89; Case's theory 23, 24–7, **25**, 33; cognitive flexibility 96, 98, 100–2, 158; complexity theories 102–6, **103**; controlled attention 41, 71–4, 95, 99; definitions of 96–7; development of 97–102; inhibition 98, 99–100, 101, 120, 158; inhibitory control models 108–11; memory accounts 106–8; models of 102–13, **103**; multi-component model 63, 66–7, 95; representational redescription models 111–13; shifting 96, 98, 100–2, 158; in TBRS model 150, 155–9; theory of mind and 112, 161; unity and diversity of 97–8; updating of working memory 98–9, 107, 158; visuospatial storage and 91–2
executive loop, in TBRS model **134**, 135, 150, 151, 156, 157, 158, 164, 166
executive processing load (EPL) 26–7

false-belief task 112–13, 161
familiarize-recognize procedure 79–80
feature binding in visuospatial maintenance 93
feedbacks 45, 107
Feigenson, L. 81
Ferguson, A. N. 83, 85
field dependence 14, 21
field of attention 4, 6–7
figural intersection task (FIT) 17, 19
figurative schemes 11, 15, 17, 20, 23, 27, 40–1, 156, 157
Find Circular Next (FCN) 8

Find Circular Next with Carry (FCNC) 8
Find Next (FN) 8
Flavell, J. H. 111, 123
fluid intelligence (*gF*) 21, 36, 72–3, 74
focus of attention 40, 41, 49, 68, 69–70, 71, 119–21, 134–5, 163–4
Foellinger, D. B. 18
Foreign Nonsense list 31, **32**
formal operational stage 9, 12, 44
four-dimensional concepts 35, 37
fractionation of working memory 63, 65–7, 71
Fuzzy-Trace Theory 55–6, 57, 154

Gaillard, V. 141, 142, **143**
gambling task 36
Garon, N. 113
Gathercole, S. E. 76
Gavens, N. 136–7, 140
Geary, D. C. 57–8, 122–4, 167
general fluid intelligence (*gF*) 21, 36, 72–3, 74
General Problem Solver 8
Gentner, D. 34
Gerstadt, C. L. 109
Gilchrist, A. L. 118, 162, 163
Girotto, V. 45
gist traces 54–6, 57, 154
Globerson, T. 20, 21
goal representations 107–8
Goldman-Rakic, P. S. 1
Go/no-Go tasks 100
Gonzalez, M. 45
Groen, G. J. 57
Guttentag, R. E. 123

Hagen, J. H. 120
Halford, G. S. 33–9, **39**, 40, 41–2, 49, 57, 63, 102, 104–5, 119–20, 134, 156, 160, 163
Halliday, M. S. 87
Happaney, K. 111
Harnishfeger, K. K. 120
Hasher, L. 93
Hebb, D. O. 68
Hebb repetition effect 59
Henry, L. A. 83, 84–5, 88, 89
hide-find procedure 77–9
Hitch, G. J. 37, 63, 66, 70, 72, 87, 121–2, 129–30, 139
horizontal *décalage* 10, 79
hot cognition 36
hot executive functions 96
Houston-Price, C. M. T. 121, 129
Hughes, C. 98

212 Index

Huizinga, M. 98
Hulme, C. 67, 83
Hunter, W. S. 77
Husain, M. 93

'If ... then' rules 11, 135
immediate memory 8–9, 66
immediate serial recall tasks 59
inferior parietal cortex 133
information processing approach ix–x, 1,
   7–10, 43, 44
Inhelder, B. 8, 24, 44–5, 111
inhibition 98, 99–100, 101, 120, 158;
   models emphasizing inhibitory control
   108–11
inner scribe 67, 70
intelligence, working memory as seat of
   151–5
intentional maintenance 74
intuitions 55–6, 154
IQ tests 82
Iterative Reprocessing (IR) model 105

James, W. 68
Jarrold, C. 59, 86
Johnson, J. 15, 19
Johnson-Laird, P. N. 34, 50–1
Jones, G. 125

Kagan, J. 81
Kahneman, D. 21
Kail, R. 84, 85, 121
Kane, M. J. 72–4
Karmiloff-Smith, A. 52, 112
Keller, T. A. 116
Kingma, J. 53–5, 56
Kintsch, W. 126
Kirkham, N. Z. 107, 109, 110, 111
Klahr, D. 19, 113
Kloo, D. 112–13

Lang, B. 109, 110, 112
language learning 59–60
Latin square task 38, **39**
learning: language learning 59–60; working
   memory as learning device 164–7
Lecas, J. F. 51–2
Lehto, J. E. 98
Lépine, R. 58–9, **58**, 65, 166–7
Levels of Consciousness model 105
Levin, H. S. 97
Liberman, I. Y. 89
lists and list structures in memory 8–9
location judgement task 131, **132**, 136
logical thinking *see* reasoning development

Logie, R. H. 66–7, 71, 91
long-term memory 124–5; arithmetic facts
   57–9, **58**; conditional reasoning and 52;
   declarative knowledge acquisition
   166–7; elaborative rehearsal and 123,
   124; embedded-process model 68–71;
   hide-find tasks 78; verbal memory span
   and 85–6
Luck, S. J. 77, 81, 93, 119, 121
Luria, A. R. 97, 105, 108, 159

M-operator model 1, 10–21, 23–4, 40–1,
   117–18
Maccoby, E. E. 120
McGilly, K. 89
McLaughlin, G. H. 9, 12
magical number four 39–40
maintenance strategies 122–4; articulatory
   rehearsal 86–7, 88–9, 122, 123–4, 133,
   135, 136, 144, 146–8; attentional
   refreshing 133, 136, 141–8, **143**;
   coordinating different 146–8; efficacy of
   use 84–5; elaborative rehearsal 123, 124;
   emergence of 144–6; in TBRS model
   133, 144–8
majoring equilibration 4–7, **5**, **6**
Markovits, H. 48, 52
Meltzoff, A. N. 78
memory scanning tasks 86
memory spans *see* working memory spans
mental arithmetic 57–9, **58**
mental attention memory task (MAM)
   17, 19
mental effort 21
mental logic theories 49–50
mental models 34–5, 50–3, 133–4, **134**
metamemory skills 89
meta-representations 160–1
Michas, I. C. 89
Miles, C. 91
Miller, G. A. x, 1, 9, 10, 12, 37, 39, 40, 63,
   66, 162
Miyake, A. 97–8
modal model 66
Moore, M. K. 78
Mora, G. 147–8
Morey, C. C. 71
Morra, S. 19
Morton, J. B. 106–7
Mosse, E. K. 59
motor inhibition tasks 100
multi-component model 59, 63, 65–7,
   70–1, 82, 95, 125
Munakata, Y. 106–7, 108, 111, 113
myelinization, neuronal 33

neo-Piagetian theories 1–2, 22–42, 117–18, 156–7; Case's theory 23–33, **25**, *29*, **30**, **32**, 34, 38, 40, 41, 121, 156, 157, 160; Halford's theory 33–9, **39**, 40, 41–2, 119–20, 156, 160, 163; Pascual-Leone's theory 1, 10–21, 22, 23–4, 28, **30**, 34, 39, 40–1, 63, 95, 117, 157
NEPSY battery 100
neuronal myelinization 33
Nicolson, R. 83
nonsense syllables 31, **32**
non-word repetition tasks 59–60, 85, 86
non-word span tasks 85, 86, 124, 125
Norman, D. A. 66
Norris, D. 59
number transcoding 165, 166–7

Oakes, L. M. 77
Oberauer, K. 134, 157
object permanence 35
observe-perform procedure 79
Oftinger, A.-L. 146–7
Okamoto, Y. 33
one-dimensional concepts 35
operand-answer associations 57–9, **58**, 65, 167
operating space (OS) decrease model 28–33, **30**, 38, 41
operation centre, working memory as 150, 155–9
operation span tasks 72, 73, 122, 140
operational consolidation 24, **25**
operative schemes 11, 19, 20, 23, 24, 27, 40–1, 156, 157
Ottem, E. J. 162

Page, M. P. A. 59
paired-associate learning tasks 59
Palmer, S. 87–8
parallel gistification 55
parity task 131, **132**
Park, Y. 84, 85
Parkman, J. M. 57
Pascual-Leone, J. A. 1, 10–21, 22, 23–4, 28, **30**, 34, 39, 40–1, 63, 95, 117, 157
Pears, R. 48
Pearson, D. G. 91
Pennington, B. F. 97
Perner, J. 109, 110, 111–13, 160–1
Perruchet, P. 159
perseveration errors 45, 78, 104, 106, 107, 109–11
phonological coding of nonverbal information 86–8, 91

phonological loop 38, 59, 67, 70, 82, 83, 84, 85, 86, 108, 125, **134**, 135
phonological similarity effect 86–7, 88, 89
phonological skills 85
Piaget, J. ix, 1–2, 3–7, **5**, **6**, 8–9, 10, 11, 22, 24, 35, 40, 44–5, 47, 77, 78, 111, 152–3, 156, 157
Pickering, S. J. 89–90
picture span tasks 87, 88
pitch tone memory task 116
Portrat, S. 136
prefrontal cortex 48, 80–1, 96, 105, 106, 107, 108, 109, 133
pre-operational stage 9, 12, 47
prepotent responses, inhibition of 98, 99–100
probability judgements 44–6, 53, 54
processing capacity, Halford's theory 36–9, **39**
processing efficiency 40–1, 121–2, 139, 142, **143**
processing speed 28–30, 83, 85, 118, 121–2, 129–30, 139–41, 151–3
production rules 11, 135, 158, 161

quaternary relations 35, 37

ratio span tasks 28, *29*
Raven, J. C. 73
reading digit span task 131, 136–7, 140–1, 142
reading rate 83
reading span task 38, 41–2, 72, 73, 122
reasoning development: conditional reasoning 49–53; Fuzzy-Trace Theory 55–6, 57, 154; probability judgements 44–6, 53, 54; reasoning-memory independence effect 53–6; transitive inference 9, 35, 36, 37–8, 46–9, 53–4
redescription 111–13
redintegration 85–6
reflection 105–7
refreshing, attentional 133, 136, 141–8, **143**
rehearsal: articulatory 86–7, 88–9, 122, 123–4, 133, 135, 136, 144, 146–8; elaborative 123, 124
Reiss, A. L. 96–7
relational complexity theory 35–7, 102, 104–5
relational processing capacity tasks 38, **39**
relational stage 24, 26, 27, *29*, 30–1
representation coding of nonverbal information 86–8, 91
representational medium, working memory as 150–1, 159–64

representational redescription 111–13
response inhibition tasks 100
Reyna, V. F. 53, 55–6, 154
Reznick, J. S. 77, 78, 80
Riggs, K. J. 92
Riley, C. A. 47–8
Roodenrys, S. 85, 124
Ross-Sheehy, S. 81
rote rehearsal *see* articulatory rehearsal
Ruffman, T. 78, 79
running memory span task 119

Sabbagh, M. 98
Sarigiannidis, I. 93
Saults, J. S. 116–17
selective attention 96, 99
self-ordered pointing task 99
self-organising consciousness theory 159
self-regulatory skills 96
semantic coding of nonverbal information 88
semantic similarity effect 88
Senn, T. E. 98
sensorimotor stage 9, 15, 24, 26, 30
serial reaction time task 147
Shallice, T. 66
Shiffrin, R. M. 66
shifting 96, 98, 100–2, 158
Shipstead, Z. 74
shopping span task 139, 146
short-term memory/storage space 76–94,
   155; articulation rate and 82–6, **84**;
   articulatory rehearsal 86–7, 88–9, 122,
   123–4, 133, 135, 136, 144, 146–8;
   Case's theory 27–33, *29*, **30**, 38, 41;
   controlled attention and 72–3;
   embedded-process model 68–71;
   Halford's theory 36, 37–8, 41; in infancy
   76–82; Miller's theory 1, 39, 40, 63, 66;
   modal model 66; multi-component
   model 63, 65–7, 70–1, 82; phonological
   coding of nonverbal information 86–8,
   91; reasoning-memory independence
   effect 53–6; transitive inference and 49;
   verbal information maintenance 76,
   82–90, **84**; violation-of-expectation
   paradigm 78–9; visuospatial information
   maintenance 76, 89–94
Shrager, J. 114
Siegler, R. S. 24, 26, 43, 89, 114, 148, 157
Simon, H. A. 7–9, 43, 53
simplicity hypothesis 43, 53
Specific Language Impairment (SLI) 59–60
speech rate 82–6, **84**
speech-interpretation task 107

spoken recall tasks 82–6, **84**
Standard Progressive Matrices 73
Stanovich, K. E. 154
statue task 100
Stevens, A. L. 34
story inference 54
Stroop task 73–4, 100, 120
Subject–Object interactions 5–7, **5**, **6**
supervisory attentional system 66, 95, 97, 155
Swanson, H. L. 76

TBRS model *see* Time-Based Resource-
   Sharing (TBRS) model
ternary relations 35, 36, 37
theory of constructive operators (TCO)
   14–16
theory of mind 36, 112, 160–1
thought, working memory as seat of 151–5
three-dimensional concepts 35, 37
Time-Based Resource-Sharing (TBRS)
   model 127, 129–68; attentional refreshing
   efficiency 141–4, **143**; cognitive
   architecture 133–5, **134**; cognitive
   development and 150–68; cognitive load
   and 131–2, **132**, 135–7, 140–1, 142,
   145–6, 147; creation of new procedures
   164–6; decay of memory traces 138–9;
   declarative knowledge acquisition 166–7;
   maintenance strategy use 133, 144–8;
   overview of 130–7; processing speed
   139–41, 151–3; sources of working
   memory development in 138–48; time-
   based resource-sharing mechanism in
   children 135–7; working memory as
   learning device 164–7; working memory
   as operation centre 150, 155–9; working
   memory as representational medium
   150–1, 159–64; working memory as seat
   of thought and intelligence 151–5
Tipper, S. P. 120
total processing space (TPS) increase model
   28–31, **30**, 38, 41
Towse, J. N. 110, 121–2, 129–30, 139
Trabasso, T. 18–19, 20, 46–9
trade-off hypothesis 28–33, **30**, 38, 41, 129
transcoding of numbers 165, 166–7
transitive inference 9, 35, 36, 37–8, 46–9,
   53–4
Turing, A. M. ix–x
Turner, J. E. 85–6
Turner, M. L. 72
two-dimensional concepts 35
Type 1 and Type 2 thinking 153–4

unary relations 35

unattended stimuli memory tasks 116–17, 119

unifocal coordination 24–6, **25**

updating of working memory 98–9, 107, 158

vectorial stage 24, 26, 28, *29*

verbal coding of nonverbal information 86–8, 91

verbal information maintenance 59–60, 67, 70, 76, 82–90; articulation rate and 82–6, **84**; articulatory rehearsal 86–7, 88–9, 122, 123–4, 133, 135, 136, 144, 146–8; attentional refreshing 133, 136, 141–8, **143**; independence from visuospatial memory 89–90; phonological coding of nonverbal information 86–8, 91; in TBRS model 132, 133, **134**, 135, 136, 141–8, **143**

verbal–spatial mapping task 123–4

verbatim traces 54–5, 56, 57, 59, 60

Vergauwe, E. 132, 133, 164

Vinter, A. 159

violation-of-expectation paradigm 78–9

visual array task 81, 118, 119, 121

visual coding of nonverbal information 87–8, 91

visual pattern span task 90–1

visual similarity effect 87, 88

visuospatial bootstrapping 90

visuospatial information maintenance 67, 70, 76, 89–94, 118; in TBRS model 132, 133, **134**, 135

visuospatial sketchpad 67, 70, 92

vocabulary acquisition 59–60

Vogel, E. K. 81, 93, 119, 121

Vygotsky, L. S. 88, 105

Walker, P. 92–3

Wallace, J. G. 113

Wallon, Henri 9

Waters, G. S. 59

Wechsler Intelligence Scale for Children (WISC) 82

White, S. H. 108

Wimmer, H. 161

Wisconsin Card Sorting Test (WCST) 97, 101

Witkin, H. A. 14

word length effect 87, 88, 89

word repetition tasks 30–1, **32**, 82–3

word span tasks 27, *29*, 30–1, **32**, 72, 73, 85–6, 124

working memory x, 1–2; cognitive resources and 117–19; conditional reasoning and 49–53; as controlled attention 41, 71–4, 95, 99; declarative knowledge acquisition and 166–7; in domain-specific theories 43–60, **58**; embedded-process model 67–71; focus of attention size and 119–21, 163–4; fractionation of 63, 65–7, 71; generic definition of 71, 126; language learning and 59–60; as learning device 164–7; long-term memory and 124–5; maintenance strategy use 122–4, 133, 144–8; mental arithmetic and 57–9, **58**; multi-component model 59, 63, 65–7, 70–1, 82, 95, 125; in neo-Piagetian theories 1–2, 22–42, **25**, *29*, **30**, **32**, **39**, 117–18, 119–20, 121, 156–7, 160, 163; as operation centre 150, 155–9; probability judgements and 44–6, 53, 54; processing speed and 118, 121–2, 139–41, 151–3; reasoning-memory independence effect 53–6; as representational medium 150–1, 159–64; as seat of thought and intelligence 151–5; sources of development of 115–26, 138–49; speed of decay 115–17, 138–9; in theory of constructive operators 15–16; thinking outside of 153–4; transitive inference and 46–9, 53–4; updating of 98–9, 107, 158; *see also* executive control; short-term memory/storage space; Time-Based Resource-Sharing (TBRS) model

working memory spans 9, 24, 66, 129–30; articulation rate and 82–6, **84**; attentional refreshing efficiency and 142–3, **143**; Case's theory 27–8, *29*, 30–1, **32**, 118, 129; cognitive load and 131–2, **132**, 135–7, 140–1, 142, 145–6, 147; controlled attention and 72–3; focus of attention size and 119, 120, 121, 163–4; Halford's theory 37–8, 41–2; language learning and 59–60; long-term memory and 85–6, 124–5; maintenance strategy use and 133, 145–8; processing speed and 118, 121–2, 139–41; representation coding and 87–8; speed of decay and 138–9; visuospatial information 90–1, 92

Wright, B. C. 48–9

Zacks, R. T. 93

Zelazo, P. D. 97, 102–6, **103**, 109, 111, 113, 159

Taylor & Francis eBooks

Helping you to choose the right eBooks for your Library

Add Routledge titles to your library's digital collection today. Taylor and Francis ebooks contains over 50,000 titles in the Humanities, Social Sciences, Behavioural Sciences, Built Environment and Law.

Choose from a range of subject packages or create your own!

Benefits for you
- Free MARC records
- COUNTER-compliant usage statistics
- Flexible purchase and pricing options
- All titles DRM-free.

Benefits for your user
- Off-site, anytime access via Athens or referring URL
- Print or copy pages or chapters
- Full content search
- Bookmark, highlight and annotate text
- Access to thousands of pages of quality research at the click of a button.

REQUEST YOUR FREE INSTITUTIONAL TRIAL TODAY

Free Trials Available
We offer free trials to qualifying academic, corporate and government customers.

eCollections – Choose from over 30 subject eCollections, including:

Archaeology	Language Learning
Architecture	Law
Asian Studies	Literature
Business & Management	Media & Communication
Classical Studies	Middle East Studies
Construction	Music
Creative & Media Arts	Philosophy
Criminology & Criminal Justice	Planning
Economics	Politics
Education	Psychology & Mental Health
Energy	Religion
Engineering	Security
English Language & Linguistics	Social Work
Environment & Sustainability	Sociology
Geography	Sport
Health Studies	Theatre & Performance
History	Tourism, Hospitality & Events

For more information, pricing enquiries or to order a free trial, please contact your local sales team:
www.tandfebooks.com/page/sales

 | The home of Routledge books

www.tandfebooks.com